MATTHEW ARNOLD

From the Painting by G. F. Watts, R. A.
MATTHEW ARNOLD—1880

MATTHEW ARNOLD

HOW TO KNOW HIM

By

STUART P. SHERMAN

ARCHON BOOKS
1968

LIBRARY OF CONGRESS CATALOG CARD NUMBER: 68-26927
PRINTED IN THE UNITED STATES OF AMERICA

CONTENTS

CONTENTS—*Continued*

pline—Carlyle's John Bull Unsatisfactory—Inadequacy of the Puritan Ideal of Perfection—Hebraism and Hellenism.

Arnold a Friend to Religion—Adverse Comments—His Reluctance to Enter the Field of Religious Controversy—His Conviction that a Revolution Had Been Accomplished—Signs of the Revolution—His Belief in a National Church —Recasting Religion—A Verifiable Basis for the Bible—His Literary Approach—Rejects the God of Miracles—Rejects the God of Metaphysics—Sets up the God of Experience—Protestant and Catholic Miracles—Christian and Pagan Miracles—Protestant and Catholic Theological Doctrine—The Mass and the Three Lords Shaftesbury—The Law of Man's Being—Arnold's Psychology: the Doctrine of the Two Selves—God Defined—Religion Defined—Conduct Three-Fourths of Life—Illustrations of Morality Touched with Emotion—Value of Old Testament — Desiccation of Judaism — Method and Secret of Jesus—Divinity of Christ—Power of Jesus Founded on Human Nature—Paul and the Theologians—The Worth of a Religious Teacher—Paul a Great Realistic Moralist—His Religion Psychologically Sound—Resurrection Spiritually Interpreted—Immortality.

MATTHEW ARNOLD

ARNOLD

CHAPTER I

CHARACTER AND CAREER

"The aimless and unsettled, but also open and liberal state
of our youth we *must* perhaps all leave and take refuge in our
morality and character; but with most of us it is a melancholy passage from which we emerge shorn of so many beams
that we are almost tempted to quarrel with the law of nature
which imposes it on us."—*Letters,* I, 17.

MATTHEW ARNOLD is a charming but not
an altogether conciliatory writer. If you
disagree with him, he does not encourage you to
believe that you may be in the right. When he was
a middle-aged man, his favorite sister said to him
that he was "becoming as dogmatic as Ruskin." "I
told her," writes Arnold, good-humoredly reporting
the incident to his mother, "the difference was that
Ruskin was 'dogmatic and *wrong.*'" This is in the
true critical temper—gentle but firm and just a little
provocative!

In this temper Arnold worked at the main task
of his life: making aristocratic tastes prevail in a

world which was becoming rapidly democratic. Radical democrats, bent on extolling middle-class virtues, and popular orators who go about persuading the people that the fruits of culture are green grapes sought, and still seek, to thrust him aside as a "high priest of the kid glove persuasion." But he, in his fashion, was as worldly, as positive, as aggressive, and as progressive as his adversaries. He was better rooted in the past than they, and he intended to go with them into the future. He had wit to win attention, and clearness to profit by it. He held and extended his ground by pertinacity and versatility in attack. Where he did not gain assent he ultimately commanded the respect due to a distinguished, sincere, weighty, and thoroughly organized character. In an unsettled epoch of English thought he found a central position, and sharply defined his attitude toward the important movements in literature, education, society, politics and religion. He said something pertinent and stimulating or irritating about everybody's business; so that he remains, for all his air of exclusive refinement, one of the unavoidable writers of the nineteenth century, one of the reconstructive forces in the twentieth.[1] Various as are his themes, his work as a whole is a remarkably harmonious and symmetrical

---

[1] Interesting tribute is paid by H. G. Wells in *Mr. Britling Sees It Through*, N. Y., 1916; see pages 256 and 289, where England's difficulties in the European war are attributed to the fact that "we didn't listen to Matthew Arnold."

expression of "general ideas" which will appeal to what he liked in later life to call "the body of quiet, reasonable people" in every age. Whether in the end one accepts or rejects him, he is a suggestive guide to a man who is trying to discover what he ought to think on most subjects which concern him.

Behind the impeccable front of Arnold's prose works there was a human being with human frailties, who attained his definiteness of outline and finish of surface by processes which are a legitimate subject of our interest. But it is not easy to recover what he discarded when he cut and polished and set his character. Not wishing to amuse posterity with his private affairs, he forbade a formal biography. His published letters, from which too intimate and too piquant matters have been removed, begin in his late twenties when the first ferment of youth was over, and he was already reflecting that we can "only acquire any solidity of shape and power of acting by narrowing and narrowing our sphere, and diminishing the number of affections and interests which continually distract us while young, and hold us unfixed and without energy to mark our place in the world." One of the rare glimpses of his impressionable early manhood he gives us in "The French Play in London": "I remember how in my youth, after a first sight of the divine Rachel at the Edinburgh Theatre, in the part of Hermione, I followed her to Paris, and for two months never missed one of her representations." To the stream of his instinctive and spontaneous feelings, which was frequently of a poignant melancholy, he gave, indeed, some outlet through a portion of his poetry; and there are hints in his letters and note-books of wayward desires, unsocial moods, and unprofitable impulses. After the age of thirty-five, however, he wrote very little poetry, and his critical sense progressively suppressed the melancholy in which the most personal part of it originated. "To make a habitual war on depression and low spirits, which in one's early youth one is apt to indulge and be somewhat interested in," so he writes in his thirty-fourth year, "is one of the things one learns as one gets older. They are noxious alike to body and mind, and already partake of the nature of death." The writer of that passage had very deliberately taken his own nature under criticism and cultivation. As he presents himself through his prose to our later time, he is the most rigorously disciplined of men, the most coherently purposeful of writers.

For his ability to get himself in hand and to get under way without much preliminary storm and stress he was immensely indebted to parental guidance and to the circumstances of his birth and breeding. He had not, like Carlyle, for example, to fight his way up from the peasantry and the provinces, but was born—at Laleham on Christmas Eve, 1822 —near the intellectual center of England, and in the heart of the intellectual upper middle class of which he was to be a conspicuous representative. He was a model son to a mother who followed every step of his career and read every line of his writing with affection and intelligent interest. In Thomas Arnold, the Liberal clergyman, the historian of ancient Rome, the famous Master of Rugby, he had a father by whose reputation he was long proud to be overshadowed, whose achievements kindled his emulation, and whose character, ideas, purposes, and keen sense of duty were a perpetual and gratefully acknowledged source of inspiration to him. Thomas Arnold died in 1842, but his memory is in perennial blossom through the letters of his son, which extend from 1848 to 1888. To his mother he reported with a beautiful filial piety not only his own projects and triumphs but also all the good things that he heard or read or felt about his father. Those who have made the acquaintance of the great schoolmaster through *Tom Brown at Rugby* will think of him, perhaps, as primarily a moral force. His son, though of course fully conscious of this element in his influence, emphasizes rather his intellectual qualities: the energy, breadth and openness of his mind, his European outlook, his sense of the unity of history. "Whatever talent I have in this direction [pamphleteering]," he writes to Miss Arnold, "I certainly inherit from him, for his pamphleteering talent was one of his very strongest and most pronounced literary sides. . . . Even the positive style of statement I inherit." Writing to his mother in 1865, he says: "Papa's greatness consists in his bringing such a torrent of freshness into English religion by placing history and politics in connexion with it." In another letter, also to his mother: "In my notions of the State I am quite papa's son, and his continuator. I often think of this—the more so because in this direction he had so few who felt with him. But I inherit from him a deep sense of what, in the Greek and Roman world, was sound and rational." In considering his patrimony, we must also, from a merely worldly point of view, reckon in the hosts of his father's friends and distinguished pupils who readily connected him with the best society in England.

Arnold does not so obviously spring from any locality as Wordsworth springs from the Cumberland hills or as Hardy springs from "Wessex," yet it is evident that his poetic sensibility was early stimulated and permanently impressed by the mellowed civility and the fresh annual beauty of the ancient towns and gardens of his childhood along the valley of the Thames, and especially by the river itself. As a traveler in Italy he complains that "all the water-courses are dry. This is what breaks my heart in the Apennines; for as Dicky used to say at Viel Salm, 'Papa loves rivers.'" Revisiting his birthplace in 1848, he revives his early associations with it, and recalls in a letter to his mother the affecting notes in the landscape: "It was nearly dark when I left the Weybridge Station, but I could make out the wide sheet of the gray Thames gleaming through the general dusk as I came out on Chertsey Bridge. I never go along that shelving gravelly road up towards Laleham without interest, from Chertsey Lock to the turn where the drunken man lay. Today, after morning church, I went up to Pentonhook, and found the stream with the old volume, width, shine, rapid fulness, 'kempshott,' and swans, unchanged and unequalled, to my partial and remembering eyes at least. On the Hook itself they have been draining and cutting a little; but the old paved part of the barge road on the Laleham side of the Lock-house is all as it was, and the campanulas, they told me, grow as much as ever there in summer. Yesterday I was at Chertsey, the poetical town of our childhood as opposed to the practical, historical Staines: it is *across* the river, reached by no bridges and roads, but by the primitive ferry; the meadow path, the Abbey river with its wooden bridge and the narrow lane by the old wall; and, itself the stillest of country towns, backed by St. Ann's, leads nowhere, but to the heaths and pines of Surrey. . . . I was yesterday at the old house and under the cedars and by the old pink acacia." As this passage perhaps suggests, Arnold was touched less by the "outward shows of sky and earth" than by their human associations, their subtle stirring of the perfume of memory, their symbolical suggestiveness. He called himself a "Wordsworthian," and one of his homes was in the Wordsworth country; but if he had written a *Prelude,* he would have given less credit to nature for the formation of his mind than to books and formal education.

His education was of course admirably conducted. After some years of elementary instruction under his uncle at Laleham, and a year at Winchester under the stiff discipline of Doctor Moberly, later bishop of Salisbury, he entered Rugby School in 1837, where he spent five years under the supervision of his father. He was a good student in the classics and he distinguished himself in 1840 by winning the school prize for poetry with his "Alaric at Rome." In 1841 he went up to Oxford with a classical scholarship at Balliol. In 1841 he won the Newdigate prize with his poem "Cromwell." At the university, the strengthening appeals of poetry, politics, miscellaneous reading, and the delight of exchanging views with his great friend and brother poet, Arthur Hugh Clough, somewhat diverted his attention, one infers, from the routine of study; for he was graduated in 1844 with respectable rather than first-class standing.

Toward Oxford as toward many other ancient and venerated objects, Arnold's feeling remained interestingly duplex. The poet in him responded

instinctively with a strong romantic inclination to
the unworldly charm of the place, its idealism, its
odor of vanishing sanctity, its shadowy traditions,
its old-fashioned undeviating method of molding
English gentlemen. The critic in him asked on the
other hand what Oxford was doing to prepare young
Englishmen to play an effective part in the more
urgent modern society which he perceived was coming into being on the Continent. Visiting the university in 1854, after some acquaintance with educational methods abroad, he says, with the touch of
superiority inevitable in a worldly young alumnus,
"I am much struck with the apathy of the people
here, as they strike me, and their petty pottering
habits compared with the students of Paris, or Germany, or even of London." He himself, however,
emerged from the "educative process" not merely
with a love for the "beauty and sweetness" of the
Oxford tradition but also with alert faculties and
a power of concentrated independent work which
enabled him to continue his self-education indefi-
nitely. He carried with him, too, a critical admiration for the literatures of Greece and Rome which
was to be a decisive factor in his career. His ultimate loyalty to both the method and the matter of
the old classical discipline is half humorously suggested in a letter written at the age of sixty-four:
"I read five pages of Greek anthology every day,
looking out all the words I do not know; this is

what I shall always understand by *education,* and it does me good, and gives me great pleasure."

When Arnold left the university, he undoubtedly desired, above everything else, to be a poet. Why he was less exclusively a poet than Tennyson or Browning, is an engaging question, to which there are many answers. Of these one of the most obvious is that, when he found his dearest ambition in conflict with various other desires, he entered a bread-and-butter profession, upon which the Muses frowned, and postponed full literary activity in the expectation of leisure which he never attained. Between the end of his college course, however, and the beginning of his career as inspector of schools, there is a significant interim of three years, from 1847 to 1851, in which he acted as private secretary to Lord Lansdowne, President of the Council.

The few but important letters of this period reveal a young man seriously absorbed in charging his batteries and meditating his course. In his secretarial capacity he saw a good deal of aristocratic political society, which affected his political sympathies, and quickened his interest in public affairs. One infers that his duties allowed him considerable time for poetical composition and for the thoughtful reading of early manhood. In 1849 he published his first volume, *The Strayed Reveller, and Other Poems.* Already the poet and the critic in him are contending for supremacy. One aspect of the poet-secretary is exhibited in a letter addressed to his sister and dated at Lansdowne House in May, 1848, of which the entire burden is a report that "it is beginning to grow dusk, but it has been a sweet day, with sun and a playing wind and a softly broken sky. The crocuses, which have long starred the lawn in front of the windows, growing like daisies out of the turf, have nearly vanished . . . but the lilacs that border the court are thrusting out their leaves to make amends." One is reminded of the young Milton watching the "dappled dawn" through his vine-screened window at Horton.[2] In the same year, looking beyond the crocuses of Lansdowne House at the rising tide of democracy in England, Arnold says: "I see a wave of more than American vulgarity"—his private references to America are seldom soothing—"moral, intellectual, and social, preparing to break over us." Political democracy he recognizes as inevitable, and he is already casting about for something to render its social consequences supportable: "You must by this time begin to see what people mean by placing France politically in the van of Europe; it is the *intelligence* of their *idea-moved masses* which makes them, politically, as far superior to the *insensible masses* of England as to the Russian serfs, and at

---

[2] "I also heard from Morley yesterday that G. Sand had said to Renan that when she saw me years ago, *'Je lui faisais l'effet d'un Milton jeune et voyageant.'*"—*Letters,* II, 151.

the same time they do not threaten the educated world with the intolerable *laideur* of the well-fed American masses, so deeply anti-pathetic to continental Europe."

From the ugliness of America and the stupidity of England, the fastidious young secretary retreats into his books. In this period he finds something consolatory in the Transcendentalists. He has a pleasant interview with Emerson; and "amidst the hot dizzy trash" of contemporary journalism he finds an article of Carlyle's "deeply restful." "The source of repose in Carlyle's article," he observes, "is that he alone puts aside the din and whirl and brutality which envelop a movement of the masses, to fix his thoughts on its ideal invisible character." A noteworthy passage in a letter of 1849 indicates the sort of distillation and concentration that were taking place in him while he was finding his "line": "I have within this year read through all Homer's works, and all those ascribed to him. But I have done little, though more than most years, though I am getting more of a distinct feeling as to what I want to read; however this, though a great step, is not enough without strong command over oneself to make oneself follow one's rule; conviction, as the Westminster divines say, must precede conversion, but does not imply it." What he wanted to read is revealed in a letter of January, 1851; "I read his [Goethe's] letters, Bacon, Pindar, Sophocles, Th. à

Kempis, and Ecclesiasticus, and retire more and more from the modern world and modern literature, which is all only what has been before and what will be again, and not bracing or edifying in the least."

From his quiet communing with the sages, Arnold was withdrawn by his appointment as inspector of schools in 1851, which one associates with his marriage in the same year to Frances Lucy, daughter of Sir William Wightman, a judge of the Court of Queen's Bench. Of his qualifications as a family man there can be no question. In all his correspondence there is not the faintest symptom of the churlish self-absorption and the peevishness by which sundry poets and men of letters have made a purgatory of their domestic circles. There is abundant evidence, on the contrary, that his attitude toward his wife and his six children was one of delighted and painstaking devotion. In reply to some careless reviewer who said that "Mr. Arnold appeared to have loved his parents, brothers, sisters, and children, but not to have cared so much for his wife," Mr. G. W. E. Russell declares that "to one who knew the beauty of that life-long honeymoon, the criticism is almost too absurd to write down."[3] Better than any second-hand testimony to his admirable domestic temper are passages like this in a letter to his sister written in 1859: "You can't

---

[3] *Matthew Arnold,* London, 1904, p. 8.

think how nicely the two boys go on with Mrs. Querini, their governess. From my little study I can hear all that passes[!] She said to Budge this morning, 'Who do you love best of anybody in the world?' 'Nobody at all,' says Budge. 'Yes,' says Mrs. Querini, 'you love your papa and mamma.' 'Well,' says Budge. 'But,' goes on Mrs. Querini, 'you are to love God more than any one, more even than your papa and mamma.' 'No, I shan't,' says Budge. Jolly little heathen. My love to all.—I am ever your most affectionate   M. A."

Turning from his family to his work, one feels at first perhaps that the Lansdowne secretaryship and the unworldly reading accomplished in that period were not the most practical preparation possible for the busy career upon which he was about to enter, and for the daily contacts with all sorts of commonplace people, which his tasks necessitated. Yet in the earlier years of his labors he seems to have stood in need of all the consolation that Sophocles and Ecclesiasticus afford. With a strong attachment to his home and family life, he found himself obliged to knock around the country like a commercial traveler, with what physical discomfort a few extracts from his letters will suggest. Derby, October 22, 1852: "I write this very late at night, with S., a young Derby banker, *très sport,* completing an orgy in the next room." Battersea, December, 1852: "This certainly has been one of the most uncomfortable weeks I ever spent. Battersea is so far off, the roads so execrable, and the rain so incessant." Cambridge, February 28, 1853: "I have had a long and tiring day, and it certainly will be a relief when I get these Eastern Counties over. The worst of it is that invitations to go and see schools are *rained* upon me; and the managers who have held out till now against the Government plan ask me, on my father's account, to come and inspect them, and to refuse is hard." Sudbury, March 8, 1853: "This is positively the first moment I have had. I am obliged to remain here to-night, having found an immense school and a great number of pupil teachers; however, I shall get on to Ipswich tomorrow morning. . . . I did not arrive here till just two, as the train was late; went to the school, and found there were three of them. About four o'clock I found myself so exhausted, having eaten nothing since breakfast, that I sent out for a bun, and ate it before the astonished school."

So long as Arnold was trying to make a place for himself among the British Poets—he was working in the first five or six years of his inspectorship at "Empedocles on Etna," "Tristam and Iseult," "Sohrab and Rustum," and "Balder Dead"—this uneasy and exhausting routine was a grievous interruption of his vocation. He managed to bring out the Empedocles volume in 1852; another volume containing "Sohrab and Rustum," later known as the *First Series,* in 1853; *Poems, Second Series,* 1855; and his classical tragedy, *Merope,* in 1858. After that there was no volume of poetry added till 1867, when *New Poems* was issued; this, however, is made up in considerable measure of reprinted pieces. When, in the seventh year of his occupation with the schools, *Merope* appeared, some of the critics suspected that his poetical vein was drying up; and Arnold himself admitted in an interesting letter to his sister that poetical composition was becoming almost painfully difficult: "People do not understand what a temptation there is, if you can not bear anything not *very good,* to transfer your operations to a region where form is everything. Perfection of a certain kind may there be attained, or at least approached, without knocking yourself to pieces, but to attain or approach perfection in the region of thought and feeling, and to unite with this perfection of form, demands not merely an effort and a labour, but an actual tearing of oneself to pieces, which one does not readily consent to (although one is sometimes forced to it) unless one can devote one's whole life to poetry. . . . Goethe is the only one, I think, of those who have had an *existence assujettie,* who has thrown himself with a great result into poetry. And even he felt what I say, for he could, no doubt, have done more, poetically, had he been freer; but it is not so light a matter, when you have other grave claims on your powers, to submit voluntarily to the exhaustion of the best poetical production in a time like this."

Even when Arnold had turned almost wholly to prose, which is perhaps a little less dependent than poetry upon continuity of mood, reading examination papers for two or three hours a day year after year must have been a dolorous task. Yet as he gradually relinquished the cherished enterprises for which his circumstances were unfavorable, and energetically applied himself to the undertakings which destiny seemed to have appointed for him, the amount of what he reckoned as actual drudgery diminished; what remained he learned to perform with despatch; and he bowed to the necessities of the hour with an ever more cordial smile. If the first choice was denied him, he had other resources. His philosophy taught him not to waste the energy of his spirit among his regrets, but cheerfully to embrace the "second best," and dance out the measure. There is not a particle of doubt that he was an effective inspector, nor that he became keenly interested in education and its practical problems as soon as he fully grasped their relation to the general changes which he wished to further in the social life of his times. Four months after his marriage he writes to his wife: "I think I shall get interested in the schools after a little time; their effects on the children are so immense, and their future effects in civilising the next generation of the lower classes, who, as things are going, will have most of the political power of the country in their hands, may be so important."

We are touching now upon the secret of the serene melancholy of Arnold's inner life and the blitheness of his outward demeanor. He did not without a pang suppress the lyric impulse of his youth—the purely individual passion for self-expression which is the birthright of every poet. But by the wise reading and earnest reflection of his early manhood he had made a clear, still, cool place at the center of his consciousness in which he saw the "realities of life" in their eternal aspects and with their permanent values. He had mastered the agitation and egotism of youth by meditating on the stream of human existence which keeps its general course and rapid fulness while its constituent elements sparkle, and spend themselves, and pass. From his perception that what is has been and will be again, he had acquired a wholesome tranquillity about the universe, a certain humility about his own function in it, and just that touch of superiority to transitory things—to the passing show—which enables a man of his rigorous social sense and fundamental seriousness to do his duty lightly and even gaily.

The union of a graceful and debonair manner with a grave and sustained purposefulness is not the commonest occurrence, and some of Arnold's contemporaries who were delighted with his fine ironical wit, his vivacious conversation, and his raillery quite misjudged the depth and steadiness of his keel.   Since his death, we have been permitted to look rather directly into—not his heart, perhaps—but into the subjects of the "meditations of his heart."   For thirty-seven years he kept little memorandum books in which he jotted down his engagements, lists of the works which he hoped to read in the ensuing year, and short extracts from English, French, German, Italian, Latin and Greek authors. If one dips anywhere into the published portion of the *Notebooks,* one finds one's self near the center of his intellectual and spiritual life.   The passages of his reading there recorded for daily pondering passed into his character and instructed his conduct. We shall form juster notions of the man's activity among the multitude if we look a little now into the occupations of his solitude.

It is a special mark of the family of minds to which he belongs that it tends to identify truth not with beauty, as it is identified in the famous line of Keats, but with God, as it is identified in the Gospels and in the works of poets of essentially religious rather than esthetic temper.   Arnold was a man who used his Bible, and made companions of the *Imitation,* the *Manual* of Bishop Wilson, the writings of Marcus Aurelius.   When his mother proposed sending him a ring for a birthday keepsake in 1871, he asked her, quite characteristically, to let him substitute for it a Bible, newly issued in Germany, containing the text in Hebrew, Greek, Latin and German; and he did not fail to let her know that the gift was in daily service. The religious undercurrent of his thoughts is attested in the *Notebooks*[4] by the abundance of such memoranda as these:

Les religions sortent à leur heure, sur un point donné du globe, du fonds inépuisable de l'esprit humain, que l'Etre infini sollicite sans cesse à s'élever graduellement vers lui. (Religions spring up at their hour, upon a given spot of the earth, from the inexhaustible deeps of the human spirit, which the infinite Being continuously invites to rise gradually toward him.)

L'âme d'homme est religieuse d'instinct, et dans tous les cultes on trouve un besoin commun de l'infini et de la félicité. (The soul of man is instinctively religious, and in all cults one finds a common need of the infinite and of felicity.)

People have no conception of the one only solid basis: inward truth, rectitude, and the fear of God.

Vera hominis felicitas et beatitudo in solâ sapientiâ et veri cognitione consistit. (The real happi-

---

[4] In frequent instances Arnold's quotations in foreign languages are grammatically defective.

ness and blessedness of man consists in wisdom alone and knowledge of the truth.)

All the paths of the Lord are mercy and truth unto such as keep his covenant.

I came, not to do mine own will, but the will of him that sent me.

From his favorite moralists and devotional writers Arnold acquired the arts and habits of deliberate self-discipline. He set apart an hour in the busiest day for reading and reflection. He examined himself and took himself to task for his "besetting sins." He put clearly before his mind some virtue which he felt in need of strengthening. He repeated his vows frequently to keep them fresh on his lips. With respect to his personal conduct and bearing, he seems particularly to have cultivated two not very closely related powers: the power of applying one's self intensely to sharply defined purposes, and the power of radiating geniality and charm. A reader of Dante, he knew what place in the Pit is reserved for those who are "sullen in the sweet air" *(tristi fummo nell'aer dolce che dal sol s'allegra);* and he strove not merely to check but quite to rout his temperamental tendency toward hypochondria. Positive indolence can never much have afflicted him, but his versatility exposed him to temptation to follow subordinate inclinations, and so to dissipate his talents. To correct his diffusiveness he took council of men of action:

Semper aliquid certi proponendum est. (Always place a definite purpose before thee.)

Omai convien che tu così ti spoltre. (Now it behooveth thee to free thyself from sloth.)

Es ist besser das geringste Ding von der Welt zu thun, als eine halbe Stunde für gering zu halten. (It is better to do the least thing in the world than to hold one half-hour of little account.)

Die Hauptsache ist, dass man lerne sich zu beherrschen. (The main thing is self-mastery.)

Was Friedrichen so gross und einzig gemacht hat, ist dass er jede bedeutende Sache, die er unternahm, so eifrig, so thätig betrieb als wenn sie die einzige wäre die ihn beschäftigte, und als hätte er noch nie was anderes zu Stande gebracht. (What made Frederick so great and unique is that every important thing which he undertook he carried on as eagerly, as energetically, as if it were his only concern, and as if he had never done anything else.)

Cum multa legeris et cognoveris, ad unum semper oportet redire principium. (When you have read and learned many things, always return to your leading idea.)

To correct his pensiveness he applied to his heart "tonic" maxims like these:

A merry heart doeth good like a medicine, but a broken spirit drieth the bones.

La gaieté clarifie l'esprit, surtout la gaieté littéraire. (Gaiety clears the mind, especially literary gaiety.)

Recherchons tout ce qui donne de la grâce, de la gaieté, du bonheur dans la vie. (Let us cultivate everything that can give grace, gaiety, joy in life.)

Une âme belle trouve un charme secret à satisfaire son génie bienfaisant et accessible. (A finely touched spirit secretly delights in showing himself gracious and approachable.)

Al lungo andare non piace e non è fortunata nel commercio degli uomini se non l'allegria. (In the long run one does not please nor prosper in human intercourse without gaiety.)

Ecce labora et noli contristari. (Work and lament not.)

Among these passages of somewhat intimately personal interest one finds scattered here and there quotations which mark the lines of Arnold's emergence from the solitude of individual life into the life of society. Here are the key-notes of his literary criticism, his poetry, his educational theory, his social gospel, his idea of the State:

It is too true that our own class, the guild of the

studious, does too little with the object of working upon the nation.

The aim is to understand myself and the age, to apprehend what is the need of each, and to administer according to our ability to that need.

La destination de l'homme est d'accroître le sentiment de la joie, de féconder l'énergie expansive, et de combattre, dans tout ce qui sent, le principe de l'avilissement et des douleurs. (Man's mission is to increase the feeling of joy, to fecundate the expansive energy, and to oppose, in every living thing, the principle of degradation and misery.)

Elever et cultiver les esprits, vulgariser les grand résultats des sciences naturelles et philologiques, tel est le seul moyen de faire comprendre et accepter les idées nouvelles de la critique. (To elevate and cultivate minds, to popularize the great results of the natural and philological sciences, such is the only means of gaining understanding and acceptance for the new critical ideas.)

Le but essentiel de l'art est d'élever l'homme audessus de la vie vulgaire, et de réveiller en lui le sentiment de son origine céleste. (The essential aim of art is to raise man above common life and to waken in him a sense of his celestial origin.)

La puissance de l'éducation consiste à augmenter le nombre des motifs dans l'esprit de l'individu, afin que leur conflit l'éclaire et le soustraie à la toute-puissance d'un motif unique. (The power of education consists in augmenting the number of motives in the mind of the individual, so that their conflict may enlighten him, and rescue him from the omnipotence of a single motive.)

Tout ce qui multiplie les noeuds qui attachent l'homme à l'homme le rend meilleur et plus heureux. (Whatever multiplies the bonds which unite man to man renders him better and happier.)

Un governement doit être un moteur de progrès, un organe de l'opinion publique, un protecteur de tous les droits légitimes, un initiateur de toutes les énergies qui constituent le génie national. (A government should be a progressive mover, an organ of public opinion, a protector of all legitimate rights, an initiator of all the energies which constitute the national spirit.)

The slightest reflection upon the foregoing groups of extracts will make clear that Arnold must soon have integrated his "bread-and-butter profession" of inspecting into his most serious life-work. Ultimately he not only approved of his own efforts in this direction, but also quite enjoyed many features of them. Despite some disavowals, he undeniably relished a controversy; and few subjects are more fruitful of controversy than education. He had compensation, too, for a good deal of tedious routine in his not infrequent official tours of investigation abroad. His official status as well as his personal reputation and connections obtained him unusual opportunities for becoming acquainted with dignitaries and celebrities in France, Germany, and Italy. His social gifts brightened with use, and he developed a keen zest for distinguished society. He even betrayed in time something of a partiality for the "good living" and the "grand style" which he found in great houses. Above all, he met in Paris the literary men of his time with whom he had most in common, his real *confrères* and coadjutors in the field of criticism. With all his hereditary and acquired earnestness he profoundly respected their literary conscientiousness; and he had sufficient flexibility of temper to savor their personal gaiety and gossip and worldliness. He liked and approved, moreover, the association in the French Academy of men of letters with savants in other realms and with men of rank in state and church.

Writing to his mother from Paris on August 16, 1859, he says: "This is my last appearance abroad as 'Monsieur le Professeur Docteur Arnold, Directeur-Général de toutes les Écoles de la Grand Bretagne,' as my French friends will have it that I am. I go to Berri on Sunday to see George Sand. I saw Prosper Mérimée this morning, a well-known author here, and a member of the French Academy. He is Private Secretary to the Empress, and a great favourite at Court. He asked me for a copy of my pamphlet to send to M. Fould, the Minister who is gone with the Emperor to Tarbes, that he might read it himself, and give it to the Emperor to read, if he thought fit."

Five days later he describes for his wife a memorable evening with Sainte-Beuve: "After writing to you on Friday, I strolled out a little, came back and dressed, and drove to Sainte-Beuve's. He had determined to take me to dine chez le Restaurant du Quartier, the only good one, he says, and we dined in the cabinet where G. Sand, when she is in Paris, comes and dines every day. Sainte-Beuve gave me an excellent dinner, and was in full vein of conversation, which, as his conversation is about the best to be heard in France, was charming. After dinner he took me back to his own house, where we had tea; and he showed me a number of letters he had had from G. Sand and Alf. de Musset at the time of their love affair, and then again at the time of their rupture. You may imagine how interesting this was after *Elle et Lui*. As for G. Sand and him, Sainte-Beuve says, '*Tout le mal* qu'ils ont dit l'un de l'autre est vrai.' But de Musset's letters were, I must say, those of a *gentleman* of the very first water. Sainte-Beuve rather advised me to go and see George Sand, but I am still disinclined 'to take so long a journey to see such a fat old Muse,' as M. de Circourt says in his funny English. . . . I stayed with Sainte-Beuve till midnight, and would not have missed my evening for all the world. I think he likes me, and likes my caring so much about his criticisms and appreciating his extraordinary delicacy of tact and judgment in literature."

In December of this same year, 1859, he writes to his sister: "I thought the other day that I would tell you of a Frenchman whom I saw in Paris, Ernest Renan, between whose line of endeavour and my own I imagine there is considerable resemblance, that you might have a look at some of his books if you liked. The difference is, perhaps, that he tends to inculcate *morality,* in a high sense of the word, upon the French nation as what they most want, while I tend to inculcate *intelligence,* also in a high sense of the word, upon the English nation as what they most want; but with respect both to morality and intelligence, I think we are singularly at one in our ideas, and also with respect both to the progress and the established religion of the present day. The best book of his for you to read, in all ways, is his *Essais de Morale et de Critique,* lately published. I have read few things for a long time with more pleasure than a long essay with which the book concludes—'Sur la poésie des race celtiques.' "

In order to bring Arnold's chief French friends together we may add here an extract from a letter of slightly later period (1865) : "On Friday I dined with the Scherers at Versailles. He is one of the most interesting men in France, and I think I have told you of him. He called his youngest boy *Arnold,*

after papa. . . . He interests me, from his connection with Vinet,[5] who has been occupying me a
good deal lately. . . . At his house I met several
of the writers in the *Journal des Débats.* Sainte-
Beuve, who is just made a senator, called for me at
half-past ten, and took me to the Princess Mathilde.
She received me very kindly, and said she knew that
in my knowledge of France and the French language and literature I was a 'Français'; to which
I replied that I had read the writings of M. Sainte-
Beuve, he being a great protégé of hers. The Prince
Napoleon was there, and a quantity of official and
diplomatic people, also several literary notabilities,
but none I cared very much for."

When Arnold announces in 1859 that his special
line of endeavor is to "inculcate intelligence" upon
the nation, one must recognize that the educator and
the critic are getting the upper hand of the poet. By
his election to the professorship of poetry at Oxford
in 1857 he had literary criticism thrust upon him at
precisely the right moment. His creative impulse
was ebbing, but his judgment was ripe, his principles established. He entered upon his lectureship
with adequate poetic feeling and imagination, with
taste cultivated by his own practise and by select but
wide reading, with habits of reflection and analysis,

---

[5] Vinet's idea of bringing forward "the rational side of
Christianity" appears in our chapter on Religion.

and with a high professional seriousness, strengthened by intercourse with men like Renan, Sainte-Beuve and Scherer. His letters in the decade from 1857 to 1867 are sprinkled with references to the composition and public reception of his lectures and essays. He published *On Translating Homer* in 1861, *Last Words On Translating Homer* in 1862, the first series of the *Essays in Criticism* in 1865, and *On the Study of Celtic Literature* in 1867. His talent for putting literary ideas in a clear light, his insistence upon their importance, and his pointed and positive manner of statement combined to evoke for nearly everything that he wrote the animated discussion which assures an author that he has not written in vain.

It is interesting to observe in his correspondence the sharpening of his appetite for fame and influence in this decade when his prose articles began to stir a public beyond the reach of his verse. He is delighted when Sainte-Beuve notices him in print: "I value his praise both in itself, and because it carries one's name through the literary circles of Europe in a way that no English praise can carry it." In a letter to his mother of July 30, 1861, he remarks: "I find people are beginning to know something about *me* myself, but I am still far oftener an object of interest as his [Thomas Arnold's] son than on my own account." Hints of this somewhat acutely personal ambition alternate with expressions of satis-

faction in having at last "got at" the British public
for its own good.   Speaking of an unfavorable notice in the *Guardian* in 1863, he says: "To an eminently *decorous* clerical journal my tendency to say
exactly what I think about things and people is thoroughly distasteful and disquieting.   However, one
cannot change English ideas so much as, if I live,
I hope to change them, without saying imperturbably
what one thinks and making a good many people uncomfortable."   As his reputation widened he became
a desired guest at notable dinner parties.   On June
16, 1863, he writes: "On Sunday night I dined
with Monckton Milnes, and met all the advanced
liberals in religion and politics, and a Cingalese in
full costume; so that having lunched with the Rothschilds, I seemed to be passing my day among Jews,
Turks, infidels, and heretics.   But the philosophers
were fearful!   G. Lewes, Herbert Spencer, a sort
of pseudo-Shelley called Swinburne, and so on.
Froude, however, was there, and Browning, and
Ruskin; the latter and I had some talk, but I should
never like him.   P— was there, too, tell Edward,
screaming away like a mill-wheel in full revolution."
Six months later he visits his great friend Lady de
Rothschild at Aston Clinton to meet Disraeli and
Bishop Wilberforce, with other notables.   After
dinner "Dizzy" approached him, remarking po-
litely that "he thought he had seen me somewhere."
"I said," continues Arnold, "Lord Houghton had

introduced me to him eight or nine years ago at a literary dinner among a crowd of other people. 'Ah, yes, I remember,' he said and then he went on: 'At that time I had a great respect for the name you bore, but you yourself were little known. Now you are well known. You have made a great reputation, but you will go further yet. You have a great future before you, and you deserve it.' "

Disrespectfully as Arnold sometimes spoke of this celebrated statesman, he was deeply gratified by his praise, and, as one surmises, he in a certain fashion rather envied him. Disraeli was a "charlatan," perhaps; but he was a charlatan with power, extensive worldly wisdom, ideas and brilliant wit. He had made a sensation both in literature and politics; and when he compared the rewards of the two professions he stimulated the undeniable love of influence and reputation in Arnold, which as yet was but very imperfectly satisfied. One side of Arnold's nature responded with the most delicate sympathy to the *schöne Seelen,* to the recluses and the sensitive, shrinking souls, to the Jouberts and the Amiels and the Wordsworths. But in the years of his maturity he had himself become a many-sided man; his admiration went out toward the Leopardis, the Goethes, even toward the Disraelis. Strongly developed impulses of his nature found imperfect expression in "mere literature."

With the exception of Clough, he seems to have

formed no close relationships with the more distinctly literary of his English contemporaries. Indeed his references to living writers of poetry and fiction, though less violent in expression than Carlyle's, are almost as steadily depreciatory. "I do not think Tennyson a great and powerful spirit in any line." "A sort of pseudo-Shelley called Swinburne." Ruskin is "dogmatic and wrong"—"the man and character too febrile, irritable, and weak to allow him to possess the *ordo concatenatioque veri.*" "Macaulay is to me uninteresting, mainly, I think, from a dash of intellectual vulgarity which I find in all his performance." Charlotte Bronte's mind contains nothing but "hunger, rebellion and rage." "I do not think Thackeray a great writer." His interest in Dickens may perhaps be sufficiently indicated, if one notes that he read *David Copperfield* for the first time in 1880, thirty years after it was published. The explanation of his rather disdainful attitude toward his fellow-craftsmen is partly that he had lived very little among the "writing class." His personal association was increasingly with members of the governing class. Quite legitimately he wrote at them, for it was primarily through them and the institutions controlled by them that he expected to influence the mind of the country. To present his ideas directly to the great middle class of Dickens' novel readers was beyond the scope of his ambition. The essential thing was to get a hearing among members of Parliament, the courts, the army, the church, the universities, and the thoughtful journals.

At the age of forty Arnold had pretty well ceased to hug to his heart the injunction of Epicurus, "Hide thy life." It is true that he planned in 1861 to "finish off" his critical writings by 1862, and to give the next ten years "earnestly to poetry." But however much he may have sighed for poetical seclusion between literary dinners, school inspections and reports, lectures, and articles for the magazines, he had, in the vulgar phrase, "too many irons in the fire, and more fish to fry." Having rounded off his poetry professorship by publishing his book *On the Study of Celtic Literature,* he began in *The Cornhill Magazine* the series of social and political essays which appeared in 1869 as *Culture and Anarchy.* This book went straight to the mark, achieving exactly the sort of success that its author desired. Shortly after its publication the Italian government proposed to Arnold that he "take charge of Prince Thomas of Savoy, the young Duke of Genoa," about whose acceptance of the throne of Spain there was soon an interesting discussion. The prince and the author of the new book were at once the recipients of much distinguished attention, faithfully chronicled in the letters of 1869. "When I was at the Athenæum yesterday, in the morning-room," he writes on the twenty-seventh of February,

"Alexander, the Bishop of Derry, came up and introduced himself to me, and while we were talking up came Magee, the Bishop of Peterborough, and joined us; and there I stood for a long time talking to my two bishops, to the amusement of some people in the room, which was very full." At a dinner of the Geological Society in February, at which the Duke of Argyll and Lord de Grey were present, "Huxley brought in my *Culture and Anarchy,* and my having made game of him in the Preface, very well in one of his speeches. . . . I have also had an interesting letter from Lord Lytton about the book." In May, Arnold and the prince are guests at Lord Lytton's place in Herfordshire. A few days later Arnold enjoys a couple of days of the Duke of Bedford's trout-fishing in Buckinghamshire. In June he writes from Harrow: "I heard the other day from Morier, the British Resident at Darmstadt, that the Princess Alice is quite fascinated with my *Culture and Anarchy,* uses all its phrases, and knows long bits by heart. The Crown Princess is reading the book." In July: "The Irish Lord Chancellor O'Hagan asked Sir John Simeon to introduce him to me the other day, and spoke to me in a way which astonished me of his interest in my works." In December he meets at dinner: "Disraeli and Lady Beaconsfield, Lord Stratford de Redcliffe, Count and Countess d'Apponyi, Lady Ashburton, Colonel Clifford, and Henry Cowper; Dizzy was in high force, and it was agreeable. He said to me across the table at dinner, *apropos* of something that was mentioned, 'Sweetness and light I call that, Mr. Arnold, eh?'" In the same letter he remarks that "nearly all the new periodicals have something or other about me, which shows how much more what I write is coming into vogue." On December thirteenth he adds an unconvinced princess to his list of royal readers: "Lady Augusta told me a pendant to the story I told you of Princess Alice. Princess Louise said to her the other day, 'Vicky (the Princess of Prussia) says she has no patience at all with Mr. Arnold.'" In June of 1870 he was presented for the degree of Doctor of Civil Law at Oxford by James Bryce (now Viscount Bryce). Lord Salisbury, Chancellor of the University, "told me afterwards it had been suggested to him, that he ought to have addressed me as *Vir dulcissime et lucidissime.*"

The pleasure of widening celebrity was tempered for Arnold in these years by a series of bitter personal losses. Between January 4, 1868, and February 16, 1872, he laid to rest in the Laleham churchyard three sons. His reaction to these successive blows may serve us as a measure of the depth of his feeling and of the perfection of his self-control. On the day of the first bereavement he wrote to his sister: "Poor little Basil died this

afternoon, a few minutes before one o'clock. I sat
up with him till four this morning, looking over my
papers, that Flu [Mrs. Arnold] and Mrs. Tiffin
might get some sleep, and at the end of every second paper I went to him, stroked his poor twitching
hand and kissed his soft warm cheek, and though
he never slept he seemed easy, and hardly moaned
at all. . . . And so this loss comes to me just
after my forty-fifth birthday, with so much other
'suffering in the flesh'—the departure of youth,
cares of many kinds, an almost painful anxiety
about public matters—to remind me that *the time
past of our life may suffice us!*—words which have
haunted me for the last year or two, and that we
'should no longer live the rest of our time in the
flesh to the lusts of men, but to the will of God.' "
When in November of this same year his eldest son,
Thomas, a boy of sixteen, followed his brother to
the grave, he made in his note-book this brief entry:
"*Tommy died.* Leva igitur faciem tuam in coelum!"
A week later he describes in a letter to Lady Rothschild his last moments with his boy: "The astonishing self-control which he had acquired in suffering was never shown more than in the last words
he said to me, when his breath grew shorter and
shorter, and from this, and the grieved face of the
doctor as he entered the room, he knew, I am sure,
that the end was come; and he turned to me, and—
his mamma, who was always with him, and whom he

adored, having gone into the next room for a moment—he whispered to me, in his poor labouring voice, 'Don't let mamma come in.' At his age that seems to me heroic self-control; and it was this patience and fortitude in him, joined to his great fragility and his exquisite turn for music, which interested so many people in him, and which bring us a sort of comfort now in all the tender things that are said to us of him." Of the third son, who died rather suddenly at Harrow at the age of eighteen, Arnold writes, "My main feeling about him is, I am glad to say, what I have put in one of my poems, the 'Fragment of a Dejaneira.'"

Mr. G. W. E. Russell, the editor of the *Letters,* who was with Arnold on the morning after the eldest son's death, says that he found the bereaved father consoling himself with Marcus Aurelius. A surer solace than stoic philosophy he had in the fulness of a mind too closely occupied from day to day with unavoidable labors and self-appointed tasks to give to the departed more than a soldier's farewell—a breathing space for grief and commemoration. Yet these poignant reminders of human fragility and mortality deepened, one suspects, the interest with which in the 'seventies Arnold turned toward the Eternal. After the publication of *Culture and Anarchy,* he had written to Lady Rothschild that he was "done with social and political essays for a long time to come." In 1870 he entered a new field of

his critical enterprises with *St. Paul and Protestantism.* Church, theology, and religion continued to
hold the foremost place in his attention for the next
six or seven years. The principal fruits of this excursion are preserved in *Literature and Dogma,*
1873; *God and the Bible,* 1875—an answer to the
critics of *Literature and Dogma;* and *Last Essays
on Church and Religion,* 1877. He set a good deal
of value also upon his *A Bible-Reading for Schools,*
1872, which reached a fourth edition in 1875, and
was reprinted in that year for general use with the
title, *The Great Prophecy of Israel's Restoration.*

His religious message delivered, he returned to
politics in a few essays on Ireland, the future of
the Liberals, and related topics; but the greater part
of his writing for the last ten years of his life belongs to more strictly literary criticism. Included
in his *Mixed Essays,* 1874, are "A French Critic On
Milton," "A French Critic On Goethe," and "George
Sand"—all three attesting his lifelong interest in
literary activity across the Channel. In 1878 he
brought out, with a suggestive preface, *The Six
Chief Lives From Johnson's 'Lives of the Poets.'*
For the *Golden Treasury Series* he made *con amore*
a selection of Wordsworth, with prefatory essay, in
1879; and a similar volume of Byron in 1881. For
Ward's *English Poets,* published in 1880, he wrote
the important introductory essay, "On The Study Of
Poetry," and the essays prefatory to the selections

from Gray and Keats. Among his latest productions are an article on Sainte-Beuve in *The Encyclopedia Britannica,* 1886; "Amiel" in *Macmillan's Magazine,* 1887; "Tolstoi" in *The Fortnightly Review,* 1887, and "Shelley" in *The Nineteenth Century,* 1888. The *Essays in Criticism, Second Series,* 1888, is a selection from articles and essays of this decade.

In addition to this work in the beaten path of criticism, we must record two books which proceeded out of Arnold's great adventure: *Discourses in America,* 1885, and *Civilization in the United States,* 1888. Having disdained the inhabitants of the United States for forty odd years, he resolved in his sixty-first year to have a look at them, to see what he could do for their salvation, and, incidentally, like Dickens and other English lecturers who have sniffed at the Yankee "greed for the dollar" at several hundred dollars a night, to reap the harvest of the American lecture circuit. His first expedition, on which he was accompanied by Mrs. Arnold and his daughter Lucy, extended from October, 1883, to March, 1884. There is something of comic flavor in the critic's reports of his travels.

One suspects that his impressions of our strange land before his advent in it were derived mainly from the reports of *ante-bellum* explorers like Harriet Martineau, Mrs. Trollope, and the dispassionate and "inimitable" Dickens. "I hate going to

America," he declared shortly before his departure; and it is evident that he expected to be dreadfully uncomfortable and dreadfully bored. He is pleased to learn from a newly published pamphlet that the "real America" is made up of owners and cultivators of the soil—"one hears so much of the cities, which do not seem tempting, and of the tendency of every American, farmer or not, to turn into a *trader,* and a trader of the 'cutest' and hardest kind. I do not think the bulk of the American nation at present gives one the impression of being made of fine enough clay to serve the highest purposes of civilization in the way you expect; they are what I call Philistines, I suspect, too many of them." He discovers at about the same time a man who prefers the American landscape to the English; and this is rather cheering—"I had fancied it quite monotonous." His English friends evidently made every effort to nerve him to face his ordeal smiling. A railway contractor, who had apparently not been across the water in vain, went so far as to assert that "all the railway porters and guides" had read Arnold's books. The only really disquieting information was this: "They say Lowell only knows at home Boston and Cambridge, and his advice as to social points cannot be followed for America generally."

In some respects he was pleasantly disappointed by America; in others, his experience only confirmed his preconceptions. The first view of New York from the harbor he found not half bad: "We were lying off Staten Island, a beautiful *orné* landscape with spires, villas, hills, and woods. 'Just like Richmond,' I said to some one by me, 'and not a single Mohican running about!' This precious speech has got into the newspapers here." He soon discovered, too, that the clubs were "capital," and that some of his entertainers, including Mr. Carnegie and members of the Vanderbilt, Astor, and Delano families, lived in a fair degree of comfort. Indeed he conceded that one or more of the houses in which he stayed were "as splendid as a house of the Rothschilds." He relished the shock of transition from such an establishment to the household of a Dartmouth professor "in a small way of life," or from a "great dinner with Phillips Brooks—venison and champagne"—to a simple tea with the President of Amherst—"rolls, broiled oysters, and preserved peaches—nothing else—and iced water or tea to wash it down. For once, this suits me perfectly well." But he is constrained to observe that "what we call a gentleman has a tremendous pull in the old world—or at any rate in England—over the gentleman here. . . . It is the best country for a Rothschild I ever knew, his superior pull is so manifest."

In New York City Mr. Carnegie gave him a "magnificent" reception, and he was gratified by atten-

tions from Henry Ward Beecher and General Grant.
In Hartford, Connecticut, "we had an immense reception"—every one from the governor down.   In
Boston he was introduced by O. W. Holmes, "a
dear little old man," and "dear old Whittier" came
to meet him at luncheon.   Writing from the Somer-
set Club on December sixth, he describes the
customary order of the day terminating with the
hand-shaking "function," and adds, "There was no
reception last night, however, thank God."   In Cambridge he was entertained by Charles Eliot Norton,
and remembered "a pleasant Professor Child."   Perhaps the only place in America which much ap-
pealed to his literary interest was Concord.   From
New England he went south as far as Richmond,
Virginia, where he was agreeably impressed by ves-
tiges of old English customs and "excellent Ma-
deira."   In Washington he had a pleasant interview
with the President, met the "really best men in Congress" at a dinner with "dear old Bancroft," noticed the "dirt, untidiness, and spitting" in the leg-
islative chambers, visited some of the colored
schools, and was astonished at the "line of demarca-
tion between the white and the negro."   Philadelphia
he pronounced the most attractive city he had seen
over here—"I prefer it to Boston."   As he moved
westward he thought the newspapers more and more
amusing: "A Detroit newspaper compared me, as
I stooped now and then to look at my manuscript

on a music stool, to 'an elderly bird pecking at grapes on a trellis'—that is the style of thing." Colonel John Hay and his wife brightened his stay in Cleveland. Chicago he describes as "a great uninteresting place of 600,000 inhabitants." A Chicago newspaper described him as follows: "He has harsh features, supercilious manners, parts his hair down the middle, wears a single eye-glass and ill-fitting clothes." St. Louis, he reported, had a small group of "wealthy and cultivated people, headed by General Sherman, who is quite delightful," and two large groups of Louisiana French and Germans, the latter more interested in their beer-gardens and sing-ing-halls than in culture. In St. Louis, speaking to audiences of only two hundred to three hundred fifty —the poorest since Baltimore!—he began to recognize "the truth of what an American told the Bishop of Rochester, that 'Denver was not ripe for Mr. Arnold.'"

It does not appear that as a result of this visit Arnold greatly modified his estimate of the typical American. He came to the country with a preconception that an aristocracy and a state church are indispensable training schools of national manners, and that Americans, never having undergone these disciplines, must necessarily be underbred. He detected some partial compensations ascribable to their lack of the molding force of an established upper class, but in general he found about what he had expected to find. Our poor fellow-countrymen's well-meant efforts to give him a "good time" gave him rather a somewhat erroneous impression of a terribly over-agitated social life. "I have seen no American yet," he wrote, a month after his arrival, "except Norton at Cambridge, who does not seem to desire constant publicity and to be on the go all the day long. It is very fatiguing." (If the good man had only known how "fatiguing" it is for the unseasoned American hunters to provide the British lion with the "publicity" which he spurns yet desires!) On the other hand he could not fail to be touched by the general stir he made—by the gracious hospitality and genuine admiration of a few individuals, the insatiable curiosity of the newspapers, the cordiality and bigness of the audiences. "They are very kind," he reports, "inconceivably kind, and one must have been accustomed to the total want of real popular interest among the English at home in anything but politics to feel the full difference of things here." It is creditable to his critical sense that he adds: "It is perfectly astounding, but there is not much real depth in it all." More questionable is his notion that the American people are characterized by a temperamental vivacity. "The whole family," he says, speaking of a Quaker household in Connecticut, "have, compared with our middle class at home, that buoyancy, enjoyment, and freedom from constraint which are everywhere in America, and which confirmed me in all I have said about the way in which the aristocratic class acts as an *incubus* upon our middle class at home." The absence of an established church presumably accounts for another American distinction: "The force of mere convention is much less strong here than in England. The dread of seeing and saying that what is old has served its time and must be displaced is much less." This was apropos of the reception of *Literature and Dogma,* which Arnold was a little surprised to discover did not greatly startle or shock educated Americans. Their relative freedom from the restraint of convention he notices in the political as well as in the religious field: "The political sense of the people here seems to be sounder than with us, and the soundest thing they have. To be sure, it is not confused by such a system of make-believes and conventions as ours." Yet despite all these qualifying circumstances, and despite certain sweet and lucid individuals whom he met in his travels, Arnold returned to England confirmed by experience in his conception of the average American as a hard uninteresting type of Philistine.

In the letters written in the few remaining years of his life, the sensitive reader will notice with interest Arnold's gradual perception that he was growing old. Allowing for the fact that many of these letters are to his wife and children, his tone is still significantly less intense, gentler, and more

effusive than in the earlier part of the correspondence. He is as full of business and social engagements as ever, perhaps, but he is no longer making
plans for work very far ahead. He chats about his
fruit trees, the family pets, botanical discoveries,
and other trivialities, "forgetting the bright speed
he had," and lingering with a certain affectionate-
ness over little things. In May of 1885 he writes
that he has been having a "horrid pain" across his
chest; has been dieted for indigestion, though he
had feared the trouble was with his heart; and that
he felt "very unlike lawn-tennis, as going fast or
going up hill gives me the sense of having a mountain on my chest; luckily in fishing, one goes slow
and stands still a great deal." A few days later he
writes to his daughter Lucy (who had married Mr.
F. W. Whitridge of New York and made her home
in America) that he can not get rid of the ache
across his chest, and has to stop "half a dozen times
in going up to Pains Hill! What a mortifying
change. But so one draws to one's end."

This feeling that he was entering his "last period"
was doubtless accentuated by the fact that in July,
1885, he was especially busy in finishing up his work
in the Education Department in preparation for his
retirement. In October, however, his superannua-
tion was pleasantly postponed by a request from
the Education Office that he go to Berlin and Paris
to get information for them with regard to free

schools. He liked these official tours—"one has the opportunity of learning so much"; and he had not been in Germany for twenty years. This mission gave him five or six weeks on the Continent in November and December, and a couple of months early in 1886. Besides attending to official business, he improved the opportunity to hear Wagnerian opera; went to the theater every night when not otherwise engaged; had a pleasant talk with the old historian Mommsen, who impressed him as a blend of Voltaire with Newman; heard Bismarck speak for an hour in the Reichsrath; and was presented to the King of Prussia, with whom he conversed in French. "His Majesty and I," he reports to his daughter, "talked it in much the same manner, neither of us like Frenchmen, but with perfect fluency and solidity of grammar." He also had several conversations with the crown prince and princess. The conferences with the princess seem to have been especially delightful; for, as he tells his younger daughter, "I kissed her hand this time both on coming and going, and really she is so nice that to kiss her hand is a pleasure." Unquestionably Arnold had a way with princesses.

In April, 1886, soon after his return from the Continent, he became the grandfather of an American girl. It is a pleasure to record that he accepted the little Philistine radiantly. On hearing the news he addressed Mrs. Arnold, who had gone to her daughter in New York, as "My Sweet Granny." With all despatch he finished up his report on foreign schools, and on May 22 sailed for the second time to America. His behavior as a grandfather was exemplary. When he was staying with his daughter at Stockbridge, he made a visit to the "dear baby" the first thing in the morning: "At that time she is lying awake in her little crib, enchanted to see visitors, and always receives me with a smile or two. The other day she snatched a five dollar note out of my hand, and waved it in triumph like a true little Yankee." Arnold's idea that the American has a turn for accumulating money was perhaps reënforced in the course of this summer by a three days' stay at the cottage of Mr. Carnegie and an inspection of his works at Pittsburg. He says nothing about the steel works, but reports that he made the "magnate" stop the team, when they were driving through the Alleghanies, while he got out and gathered rhododendrons. To Sir Mountstuart Grant Duff he writes: "You should read Carnegie's book *Triumphant Democracy*. He and most Americans are simply unaware that nothing in the book touches the capital defect of life over here: namely, that compared with life in England it is so uninteresting, so without savour and without depth." Arnold spent July and August in the Berkshires, and found some pleasant things to say of the hills and the wild flowers, but by the end of August he was sighing for his home in Surrey and civilization: "The great relief will be to cease seeing the American newspapers. . . . Their badness and ignobleness are beyond belief."

To an American friend he wrote on January 29, 1887, some months after his return to England: "One should try to bring oneself to regard death as a quite natural event, and surely in the case of the old it is not difficult to do this. For my part, since I was sixty I have regarded each year, as it ended, as something to the good beyond what I could naturally have expected. This summer in America I began to think that my time was really coming to an end, I had so much pain in my chest, the sign of a malady which had suddenly struck down in middle life, long before they came to my present age, both my father and grandfather." The next year in April he was looking eagerly forward to a visit from his American granddaughter and her mother, and on the fourteenth of the month went to Liverpool to meet them. The family malady struck him down suddenly before the meeting took place. He died on the fifteenth of April, 1888, in his sixty-sixth year. In his note-book under that date he had written: "Weep bitterly over the dead, as he is worthy, and then comfort thyself; drive heaviness away: thou shalt not do him good, but hurt

thyself."   He had also written in a sentence for
the following Sunday: "When the dead is at rest,
let his remembrance rest; and be comforted for him
when his spirit is departed from him."

CHAPTER II

"The fact is, however, that the state of mind expressed in many of the poems is one that is becoming more common." —*Letters,* I, 59.

ARNOLD himself, in a much quoted letter to his mother of June 5, 1869, made an extraordinarily high claim in behalf of his own poems. "They represent," he said, "on the whole, the main movement of mind in the last quarter of a century, and thus they will probably have their day as people become conscious to themselves of what that movement of mind is, and interested in the literary productions which reflect it. It might be fairly urged that I have less poetical sentiment than Tennyson, and less intellectual vigour and abundance than Browning; yet, because I have perhaps more of a fusion of the two than either of them, and have more regularly applied that fusion to the main line of modern development, I am likely enough to have my turn, as they have had theirs." If Arnold had written an essay on his own poetry, it would probably have been an expansion of this passage.

As we look back now over the quarter of a century, or a little more, previous to 1869, "the main movement of mind" through the period is not difficult to trace. In all phases of human activity we discern the forward pressure of reason, flushed still with the excitement of the French Revolution, temporarily checked and thwarted in some quarters, but steadily besieging and undermining the position held by tradition, prescription, and the deep inarticulate powers of feeling. In the political field the Reform Bills, the Chartist Movement, the European revolutions of 1848 were signs of its advance. In science Darwin's *Origin of Species,* published in 1859, was its most conspicuous monument. In religion and philosophy the Utilitarians, the Positivists, the "higher criticism" of the Bible, Strauss's *Leben Jesu,* 1835, and Renan's *Vie de Jésus,* 1863, were various manifestations of the same spirit. In literature the displacement of the romanticism of Godwin and Sir Walter Scott by the Victorian realism of Dickens, Thackeray, George Eliot, and Anthony Trollope attested the popularity of the desire to see the "facts of life." The main movement of mind, then, was democratic, scientific, critical, realistic—directed, in short, toward the extension of the sway of reason over all things.

Arnold's poems reflect that movement in a peculiarly fascinating because in an intimately personal way. The conflict of aristocratic with democratic impulses, of traditional belief and dogma with scientific knowledge, of romantic inclination with classical discipline and conviction, of emotion with intelligence, he not only perceived in the world around him but also felt very sharply within himself. He felt these conflicts and he expressed them poetically. He betrays thus a somewhat unhappily divided personality, yet a personality very resolutely divided. His reason commands him to march in the "main movement of mind"; and he obeys with undeviating loyalty what he is constrained to accept as the supreme authority. But as he advances toward the Truth, keeping step with his convictions, his innermost self turns again and again, like the homesick heart of a soldier, to bid a reluctant farewell to his sympathies. With most of the finest spirits of his time he felt the pathos and the melancholy of disillusion.

In his youth, as we have noted, he was somewhat prone to indulge his low spirits, to be interested in them, and even to seek food for them in the outpourings of other disillusioned souls—Rousseau, Chateaubriand, Senancour, Byron, Leopardi; and a sense of kinship drew him late in life to the world-weary Amiel. From this state of depression he emerged, however, by deliberate self-discipline, by a happy marriage, and by the manifold activities of his maturity; and took refuge from his feelings in his "morality and character." Without any special reference to chronology, we can find the record in his poems of a gradual spiritual pilgrimage through disillusions to ennui and despair, thence to resignation and stoical endurance, and ultimately to a new kind of courage and hope, denoting a pretty complete moral recovery.

His disillusionment had, as is commonly enough the case with young men crossing the threshold of manhood, three distinct phases: a disillusionment about love and human relationships; a disillusionment about his powers and his career; and a disillusionment about God and the universe. Of the three failures of reality to correspond with desire, the first was for him apparently the least important, and the poems commemorating it are not the best of his work. They throw a certain light, nevertheless, upon an otherwise unilluminated aspect of his inner life, and two or three of them lift the theme to the level of universal feelings.

We need not pry into the biographical background of the series of seven poems entitled "Switzerland" or the shorter series called "Faded Leaves." What appears on the surface is that Arnold met on the Continent, assuredly at some period anterior to his marriage, a French girl who exercised over him for a while a very considerable fascination; that in the first spell of this attraction he dreamed of that perfect union of harmonious spirits which poets celebrate and realistic novelists tell us does not exist;

and that experience proved him mistaken in the object of his romantic devotion. It is hinted that "Marguerite's" affection flagged, and that the lovers parted by mutual agreement. The appealing passages of the series are those which express the poet's sense of the hopeless fragility of human passion, his vague shame at his emotional abandonment, his final consciousness of spiritual isolation:

IV. ISOLATION. TO MARGUERITE

We were apart: yet, day by day,
I bade my heart more constant be.
I bade it keep the world away,
And grow a home for only thee;
Nor feared but thy love likewise grew,
Like mine, each day, more tried, more true.

The fault was grave! I might have known,
What far too soon, alas! I learned,—
The heart can bind itself alone,
And faith may oft be unreturned.
Self-swayed our feelings ebb and swell.
Thou lov'st no more. Farewell! Farewell!

Farewell!—And thou, thou lonely heart,
Which never yet without remorse
Even for a moment didst depart
From thy remote and spherèd course
To haunt the place where passions reign,—
Back to thy solitude again!

Back! with the conscious thrill of shame
Which Luna felt, that summer-night,
Flash through her pure immortal frame,
When she forsook the starry height
To hang over Endymion's sleep
Upon the pine-grown Latmian steep.

Yet she, chaste queen, had never proved
How vain a thing is mortal love,
Wandering in heaven, far removed;
But thou hast long had place to prove
This truth,—to prove, and make thine own:
"Thou hast been, shalt be, art, alone."

Or, if not quite alone, yet they
Which touch thee are unmating things,—
Ocean and clouds and night and day;
Lorn autumns and triumphant springs;
And life, and others' joy and pain,
And love, if love, of happier men.

Of happier men; for they, at least,
Have *dreamed* two human hearts might blend
In one, and were through faith released
From isolation without end
Prolonged; nor knew, although not less
Alone than thou, their loneliness.

V. TO MARGUERITE.   CONTINUED

Yes! in the sea of life enisled,
With echoing straits between us thrown,
Dotting the shoreless watery wild,
We mortal millions live *alone*.
The islands feel the enclasping flow,
And then their endless bounds they know.

But when the moon their hollows lights,
And they are swept by balms of spring,
And in their glens, on starry nights,
The nightingales divinely sing;
And lovely notes, from shore to shore,
Across the sounds and channels pour,—

Oh! then a longing like despair
Is to their farthest caverns sent;
For surely once, they feel, we were
Parts of a single continent!
Now round us spreads the watery plain:
Oh, might our marges meet again!

Who ordered that their longing's fire
Should be, as soon as kindled, cooled?
Who renders vain their deep desire?—
A God, a God their severance ruled!
And bade betwixt their shores to be
The unplumbed, salt, estranging sea.

To bring out still more clearly the conflicting
forces in Arnold's nature let us take first a passage
from "Faded Leaves" in which one feels the pang
and hears the cry of the heart uttered in pure lyrical
abandon:

LONGING

Come to me in my dreams, and then
By day I shall be well again!
For then the night will more than pay
The hopeless longing of the day.

Come, as thou cam'st a thousand times,
A messenger from radiant climes,
And smile on thy new world, and be
As kind to others as to me!

Or, as thou never cam'st in sooth,
Come now, and let me dream it truth;
And part my hair, and kiss my brow,
And say, *My love! why sufferest thou?*

Come to me in my dreams, and then
By day I shall be well again!
For then the night will more than pay
The hopeless longing of the day.

Now let us have a single stanza from "Absence," the Switzerland series which seems to sum up the comment of Arnold's reason upon the sweet tumult of the emotional life:

I struggle towards the light; and ye,
Once-long'd-for storms of love!
If with the light ye cannot be,
I bear that ye remove.

These same lines might be employed, with slight modification, to illustrate Arnold's final attitude in the religious field; for there is a curious parallelism between his experiences and his disillusionments with respect to human and with respect to divine intimacy.

The primary fact in his religious experience was

his consciousness of his own *soul*. One speaks in these days with a good deal of hesitation about the nature of the soul; and Arnold himself is not too explicit. What he does make clear is his conviction that the true center of one's being is not in the life of the senses, nor in the shifting waves of emotion, nor in the activities of the discursive intellect. Deeper than all these, judging all these, unsatisfied with all these, the spiritual self sits apart, hungering and thirsting for its own felicity in the perfect, the absolute, the divine. The sensual, emotional, reasoning man becomes aware of this innermost organ when the pain of its inappeasable desire throbs into the consciousness, as it intermittently does, through the anodynes of mortal love and toil. Thence the melancholy which has its sovereign shrine in the "very temple of delight." Arnold describes its visitations in "The Buried Life:"

> Light flows our war of mocking words; and yet
> Behold, with tears mine eyes are wet!
> I feel a nameless sadness o'er me roll.
> Yes, yes, we know that we can jest,
> We know, we know that we can smile!
> But there's a something in this breast,
> To which thy light words bring no rest,
> And thy gay smiles no anodyne;
> Give me thy hand, and hush awhile,
> And turn those limpid eyes on mine,
> And let me read there, love! thy inmost soul.

Alas! is even love too weak
To unlock the heart, and let it speak?
Are even lovers powerless to reveal
To one another what indeed they feel?

I knew the mass of men concealed
Their thoughts, for fear that if revealed
They would by other men be met
With blank indifference, or with blame reproved;
I knew they lived and moved
Tricked in disguises, alien to the rest
Of men, and alien to themselves—and yet
The same heart beats in every human breast!

But we, my love! doth a like spell benumb
Our hearts, our voices? must we too be dumb?

Ah! well for us, if even we,
Even for a moment, can get free
Our heart, and have our lips unchained;
For that which seals them hath been deep-ordained!

Fate, which foresaw
How frivolous a baby man would be,—
By what distractions he would be possessed,
How he would pour himself in every strife,
And well-nigh change his own identity,—
That it might keep from his capricious play
His genuine self, and force him to obey
Even in his own despite his being's law,
Bade through the deep recesses of our breast
The unregarded river of our life
Pursue with indiscernible flow its way;

And that we should not see
The buried stream, and seem to be
Eddying at large in blind uncertainty,
Though driving on with it eternally.

But often, in the world's most crowded streets,
But often, in the din of strife,
There rises an unspeakable desire
After the knowledge of our buried life;
A thirst to spend our fire and restless force
In tracking out our true, original course;
A longing to inquire
Into the mystery of this heart which beats
So wild, so deep in us,—to know
Whence our lives come, and where they go.
And many a man in his own breast then delves,
But deep enough, alas! none ever mines.
And we have been on many thousand lines,
And we have shown, on each, spirit and power;
But hardly have we, for one little hour,
Been on our own line, have we been ourselves,—
Hardly had skill to utter one of all
The nameless feelings that course through our breast,
But they course on forever unexpressed.
And long we try in vain to speak and act
Our hidden self, and what we say and do
Is eloquent, is well—but 'tis not true!
And then we will no more be racked
With inward striving, and demand
Of all the thousand nothings of the hour
Their stupefying power;
Ah, yes, and they benumb us at our call!

Yet still, from time to time, vague and forlorn,
From the soul's subterranean depth upborne
As from an infinitely distant land,
Come airs, and floating echoes, and convey
A melancholy into all our day.

Only—but this is rare—
When a belovèd hand is laid in ours,
When, jaded with the rush and glare
Of the interminable hours,
Our eyes can in another's eyes read clear,
When our world-deafened ear
Is by the tones of a loved voice caressed,—
A bolt is shot back somewhere in our breast,
And a lost pulse of feeling stirs again.
The eye sinks inward, and the heart lies plain,
And what we mean, we say, and what we would, we
     know.
A man becomes aware of his life's flow,
And hears its winding murmur, and he sees
The meadow where it glides, the sun, the breeze.

And there arrives a lull in the hot race
Wherein he doth forever chase
The flying and elusive shadow, rest.
An air of coolness plays upon his face,
And an unwonted calm pervades his breast;
And then he thinks he knows
The hills where his life rose,
And the sea where it goes.

This poem gives us the point of departure, so to
speak, for Arnold's religious disillusion. It shows

him to begin with innately and profoundly religious. That is to say, he felt in the depths of his being the need of a being outside himself—supreme, beneficent, eternal—to whose continuous effort through the ages he might unite his own will and workings, and so redeem them from insignificance and quick perdition. He lived, however, in an age when the power and the consolation which come from certitude in this great matter were not easily to be had. The medieval architecture of religious faith appeared to his candid eye to have crumbled into a Gothic ruin. His poetic feelings hovered fondly and regretfully about it; but he could not, like Newman and the Oxford "medievalizers," worship in it. In his poem "The Grand Chartreuse," written in consequence of his visit to a Carthusian monastery, he reveals clearly enough why the Oxford Movement, however much he admired its leader, left him cold:

> For rigorous teachers seized my youth,
> And purged its faith, and trimmed its fire,
> Showed me the high, white star of Truth,
> There bade me gaze, and there aspire.
> Even now their whispers pierce the gloom:
> *What dost thou in this living tomb?*
>
> Forgive me, masters of the mind!
> At whose behest I long ago
> So much unlearned, so much resigned:
> I come not here to be your foe!

I seek these anchorites, not in ruth,
To curse and to deny your truth;

Not as their friend, or child, I speak!
But as, on some far northern strand,
Thinking of his own gods, a Greek
In pity and mournful awe might stand
Before some fallen Runic stone;
For both were faiths, and both are gone.

Wandering between two worlds, one dead,
The other powerless to be born,
With nowhere yet to rest my head,
Like these, on earth I wait forlorn.
Their faith, my tears, the world deride:
I come to shed them at their side.

Oh, hide me in your gloom profound,
Ye solemn seats of holy pain!
Take me, cowled forms, and fence me round,
Till I possess my soul again;
Till free my thoughts before me roll,
Not chafed by hourly false control!

The main movement of mind, Arnold well knew, was not, in his time, cloisterward. It was clearing the ground for another edifice, still to be designed. Remorseless reason enjoined it upon him not to archaize but to spend his labor on the foundation of the new temple of the religious spirit. With arms outstretched in farewell to the faith of his fathers, he seems to say:

If with the light ye cannot be,
I bear that ye remove.

His renunciation of what he held to be intellectually illegitimate consolations left him for a time in a cheerless spiritual isolation in a harsh and spiritually meaningless world. This is the major mood of "Dover Beach," in which, however, there blends the pathos of the merely human affections of lovers clinging to each other like children lost in the night:

> The sea is calm to-night.
> The tide is full, the moon lies fair
> Upon the straits; on the French coast, the light
> Gleams and is gone; the cliffs of England stand,
> Glimmering and vast, out in the tranquil bay.
> Come to the window, sweet is the night-air!
> Only, from the long line of spray
> Where the sea meets the moon-blanched sand,
> Listen! you hear the grating roar
> Of pebbles which the waves draw back, and fling,
> At their return, up the high strand,
> Begin and cease, and then again begin,
> With tremulous cadence slow, and bring
> The eternal note of sadness in.
>
> Sophocles long ago
> Heard it on the Ægean, and it brought
> Into his mind the turbid ebb and flow
> Of human misery: we
> Find also in the sound a thought,
> Hearing it by this distant northern sea.
>
> The sea of faith
> Was once, too, at the full, and round earth's shore
> Lay like the folds of a bright girdle furled.

But now I only hear
Its melancholy, long, withdrawing roar,
Retreating, to the breath
Of the night-wind, down the vast edges drear
And naked shingles of the world.

Ah, love, let us be true
To one another! for the world, which seems
To lie before us like a land of dreams,
So various, so beautiful, so new,
Hath really neither joy, nor love, nor light,
Nor certitude, nor peace, nor help for pain;
And we are here as on a darkling plain
Swept with confused alarms of struggle and flight,
Where ignorant armies clash by night.

Arnold went a long step further with the expression of the bleakness of religious disillusion. In *Empedocles on Etna* he wrote a philosophical drama of despair. Though the Greek philosopher who is the nominal subject of the piece flourished about 500 B. C., and though Arnold protested against the identification of his personal ideas with those of his dramatic protagonist, the poem is manifestly saturated with his own thoughts and feelings about life. His own tendency, if unchecked, would have carried him near to the leaping-off place of his hero.

On a fair summer morning, which has lost its fairness for him, the old philosopher, weary of the world and of his wisdom, climbs to the crest of the volcano, and seats himself on the verge of the glowing crater. There he pours out his last reflection

upon himself and upon the destiny of mortals. He
has outlived his capacity for joy, his hopes, his
faith in a divine order. He feels himself but a link
in a mechanical universe. The stars that come out
above him as evening draws on seem no longer as
they were of yore "rejoicing, intelligent sons of
heaven," but

> . . . lonely, cold-shining lights,
> Unwilling lingerers
> In the heavenly wilderness
> For a younger ignoble world.

He deems his "ineffable longing for the life of
life," knowledge of the absolute, "baffled forever;"
nor does he desire in some new incarnation to return

> Back to this meadow of calamity,
> This uncongenial place, this human life.

Allegiance to reason, which he had taken for the
noblest human faculty, has poorly rewarded him.
In his arid philosophical mind the image of the
world and of himself is repellent. Having stripped
himself of the consolatory emotions, he is now con-
sumed by an impotent passion for his lost power of
magnanimous feeling:

> Oh that I could glow like this mountain!
> Oh that my heart bounded with the swell of the sea!
> Oh that my soul were full of light as the stars!
> Oh that it brooded over the world like the air!

But no, this heart will glow no more; thou art
A living man no more, Empedocles!
Nothing but a devouring flame of thought,—
But a naked, eternally restless mind!

One thought at the end feebly comforts him: he has not been the "slave of sense." He has served the mind—perhaps has been the slave of the mind. Faithful to what we think of as the new spirit of modern scientific investigation, he has followed truth wherever it led him, and whatever its consequences. The following lines Darwin might have spoken, or Huxley. In them one recognizes the austerity, the bitterness, and the pride of the uncompromising intellect:

Yea, I take myself to witness
That I have loved no darkness,
Sophisticated no truth,
Nursed no delusion,
Allowed no fear.

Clutching this iron consolation to his breast, Empedocles leaps headlong into the fiery crater of the volcano, and soon, like Ethan Brand in Hawthorne's melancholy tale, is a heap of white lime—tragic symbol of intellectual frustration and despair.

A man who, at the age of thirty, feels and thinks as Empedocles does may be saved from his utter despondency by the discovery of fresh interests; but it is not likely that he will long continue to produce poetry. The spirit of modern scientific inquiry and criticism has brought forth abundant fruits in its own field; but it has been no poet's Muse. On this point Arnold himself was perhaps at first a little deceived. He condemned the poetry of most of his contemporaries because it lacked intellectual content; because it did not make him think. In his sonnet on the "Austerity of Poetry" he represents the Muse as wearing "a robe of sackcloth next the smooth, white skin:"

> Such, poets, is your bride, the Muse! young, gay,
> Radiant, adorned outside; a hidden ground
> Of thought and of austerity within.

He conceived of his critical labors for some time as a preparation for a period of richer and more important poetical activity. His disillusionment was to find that as his intellectual vision widened his emotional powers contracted; that as the discipline of his feelings approached completion there was relatively little feeling left to discipline. Not in "Empedocles" only but in a dozen other places he laments the cessation in himself of the powerful throb of emotional impulse which he felt in his youth—a cessation which is the innermost explanation of his abandonment of his poetical career. The loss of lyrical power is a dreary subject for song, yet this theme can not be passed over in any adequate representation of Arnold's personal poetry. The three passages that follow will sufficiently illustrate it. The first is from "Growing Old," and is in answer to the question, "What is it to grow old?"

'Tis not to see the world
As from a height, with rapt prophetic eyes,
And heart profoundly stirred;
And weep, and feel the fulness of the past,
The years that are no more.

It is to spend long days,
And not once feel that we were ever young;
It is to add, immured
In the hot prison of the present, month
To month with weary pain.

It is to suffer this,
And feel but half, and feebly, what we feel.
Deep in our hidden heart
Festers the dull remembrance of a change,
But no emotion,—none.

DESPONDENCY

The thoughts that rain their steady glow
Like stars on life's cold sea,
Which others know, or say they know,—
They never shone for me.

Thoughts light, like gleams, my spirit's sky,
But they will not remain.
They light me once, they hurry by,
And never come again.

THE PROGRESS OF POESY

A VARIATION

Youth rambles on life's arid mount,
And strikes the rock, and finds the vein,
And brings the water from the fount,—
The fount which shall not flow again.

The man mature with labor chops
For the bright stream a channel grand,
And sees not that the sacred drops
Ran off and vanished out of hand.

And then the old man totters nigh,
And feebly rakes among the stones.
The mount is mute, the channel dry;
And down he lays his weary bones.

We have considered now Arnold's three major
disillusionments. While it is the quality of poetry
to eternalize these depressing experiences, it is the
quality of the human heart to live through them, and
even to forget them. Actually Arnold was not long
a broken-hearted lover. He was never a desiccated
old man. He did not make the leap of Empedocles.
He only in his early speculative melancholy contem-
plated and imagined it. He seems to have passed
out of his darker moods, as his contemporaries John
Stuart Mill and Thomas Carlyle did, through a
"center of indifference" and by a gradual displace-

ment in his consciousness of the "me" by the "not-me"—the classical method of salvation.

Among his more personal utterances is a group of poems expressing the idea that one ought to *endure* life even if one can not enjoy it; that one ought to endure life—if for no higher motive, then because the individual self is too insignificant a matter to dignify by an interruption of the ordinary course of nature.   Readers of *Sartor Resartus* will recall the kind of solace that Teufelsdröckh found in self-humiliation as with "calcined" heart he looked up out of the shadows of the valley of despair at the eternal starry splendor of the heavens: "Thousands of human generations, all as noisy as our own, have been swallowed-up of Time, and there remains no wreck of them any more; and Arcturus and Orion and Sirius and the Pleiades are still shining in their courses, clear and young, as when the Shepherd first noted them in the plain of Shinar.   Pshaw! what is all this paltry little Dog-cage of an earth; what art thou that sittest whining there?"   Similar reflections, similarly induced, fixed in Arnold the wholesome bitterness of an inward and spiritual humility, which may be illustrated by an extract from "Resignation":

> The world in which we live and move
> Outlasts aversion, outlasts love,
> Outlasts each effort, interest, hope,
> Remorse, grief, joy; and, were the scope

Of these affections wider made,
Man still would see, and see dismayed,
Beyond his passion's widest range,
Far regions of eternal change.
Nay, and since death, which wipes out man,
Finds him with many an unsolved plan,
With much unknown, and much untried,
Wonder not dead, and thirst not dried,
Still gazing on the ever full
Eternal mundane spectacle,—
The world in which we draw our breath,
In some sense, Fausta, outlasts death.

Enough, we live! and if a life
With large results so little rife,
Though bearable, seem hardly worth
This pomp of worlds, this pain of birth;
Yet, Fausta, the mute turf we tread,
The solemn hills around us spread,
This stream which falls incessantly,
The strange-scrawled rocks, the lonely sky,
If I might lend their life a voice,
Seem to bear rather than rejoice.
And even could the intemperate prayer
Man iterates, while these forbear,
For movement, for an ampler sphere,
Pierce Fate's impenetrable ear;
Not milder is the general lot
Because our spirits have forgot,
In action's dizzying eddy whirled,
The something that infects the world.

Wordsworthian though Arnold professed himself, the voice that he lends to the "solemn hills" has a far grimmer message than that delivered by the sage of Cockermouth. There is no gusto or exultation in it. The enthusiastic and entranced author of "Tintern Abbey" perceived, or thought he perceived, in nature a divine and consoling spirit, a moral guide and teacher. By the middle of the nineteenth century serious poets could hardly entertain such conceptions. They spoke rather of nature "red in tooth and claw," devouring her own sweet brood; for the younger generation had its sentimental illusions of harmony and order in the natural world shattered by overwhelming evidences of an ugly and more or less meaningless "struggle for existence." When Arnold attributes personality to the non-human forces of the universe, he seldom speaks of the "mighty Mother" flatteringly. To him she is enigmatic, a dark-browed sphinx, a cruel or rather indifferent spectator, mocking the vain fever of man's small activities. Thus in his sonnet inscribed "to a preacher":

"In harmony with Nature?" Restless fool,
Who with such heat dost preach what were to thee,
When true, the last impossibility,—
To be like Nature strong, like Nature cool!

Know, man hath all which Nature hath, but more,
And in that *more* lie all his hopes of good.
Nature is cruel, man is sick of blood;
Nature is stubborn, man would fain adore;

Nature is fickle, man hath need of rest;
Nature forgives no debt, and fears no grave;
Man would be mild, and with safe conscience blest.

Man must begin, know this, where Nature ends;
Nature and man can never be fast friends.
Fool, if thou canst not pass her, rest her slave!

As these lines indicate, he was emphatically not a nature-worshiper in the Wordsworthian sense. His "Scholar-Gipsy" and his "Thyrsis" show him keenly sensitive to pastoral beauty; but his feeling for nature's more winsome aspects is nearer to that of Keats in the odes and to that of the Greek idyllists than to that of Wordsworth. He is deeply penetrated with the sentiment of the Cumner Hills near Oxford; and he renders with charming delicacy and suggestiveness the impressions which he has received from woods and rivers and flowering fields. The emotion which pervades these pieces is, however, a relatively simple and sensuous delight in the consoling loveliness of the external features of rural life—a loveliness sufficient for an hour to make the scholar forget his books, and to free the thinker from the pain of thought. The emotion is modified in each case not by the heightening of mystical communion but by a return to Arnold's habitual world of thought and morality. Now, to speak it frankly, the thought in these much-praised elegies is a bit too thin to bear triumphantly the weight of all the flowers which Arnold has strung upon it. He presents in them both an appearance, an unwonted appearance, of dallying by the wayside, of digressing, of indulging in a moral holiday. So that, though they are perfectly sincere and delightful, they represent their author inadequately—as "L'Allegro" inadequately represents Milton; they are a little aside from his central tendency.

Let us have first a few stanzas from "Thyrsis," the monody written to commemorate his friend, Arthur Hugh Clough, and the haunts of their Oxford days:

> Too rare, too rare, grow now my visits here,
>   But once I knew each field, each flower, each stick;
>   And with the country-folk acquaintance made
>   By barn in threshing-time, by new-built rick.
>   Here, too, our shepherd-pipes we first assayed.
>   Ah me! this many a year
>   My pipe is lost, my shepherd's holiday
>   Needs must I lose them, needs with heavy heart
>   Into the world and wave of men depart,
>   But Thyrsis of his own will went away.
>
> It irked him to be here, he could not rest.
>   He loved each simple joy the country yields,
>   He loved his mates; but yet he could not keep,
>   For that a shadow lowered on the fields,
>   Here with the shepherds and the silly sheep.
>   Some life of men unblest

He knew, which made him droop, and filled his head.
  He went; his piping took a troubled sound
  Of storms that rage outside our happy ground;
He could not wait their passing; he is dead.

So, some tempestuous morn in early June,
  When the year's primal burst of bloom is o'er,
    Before the roses and the longest day,—
  When garden-walks, and all the grassy floor,
    With blossoms red and white of fallen May,
      And chestnut-flowers, are strewn,—
  So have I heard the cuckoo's parting cry,
    From the wet field, through the vexed garden-trees,
    Come with the volleying rain and tossing breeze:
  The bloom is gone, and with the bloom go I!

Too quick despairer, wherefore wilt thou go?
  Soon will the high midsummer pomps come on,
    Soon will the musk carnations break and swell,
  Soon shall we have gold-dusted snapdragon,
    Sweet-william with his homely cottage-smell,
      And stocks in fragrant blow;
  Roses that down the alleys shine afar,
    And open, jasmine-muffled lattices,
    And groups under the dreaming garden-trees,
  And the full moon, and the white evening star.

He hearkens not! light comer, he is flown!
  What matters it? next year he will return,
    And we shall have him in the sweet spring-days,
  With whitening hedges, and uncrumpling fern,
    And bluebells trembling by the forest-ways,
      And scent of hay new-mown.

> But Thyrsis never more we swains shall see,—
>> See him come back, and cut a smoother reed,
>> And blow a strain the world at last shall heed;
> For Time, not Corydon, hath conquered thee!

In the "Scholar-Gipsy" Arnold plays much of the same pastoral music which he evokes in "Thyrsis"; but the poem has this additional interest, that it betrays his poetical sympathy with an impulse which in his own conduct he severely checked—the impulse to drift and wander irresponsibly. According to an old story of Glanvil's, a lad in the University of Oxford left his studies and joined a band of vagabond gipsies. While the poet is under the spell of the Cumner Hills and the vagrant memories of his own youth, he is content to idealize the life of the scholarly truant:

> Oh, born in days when wits were fresh and clear,
>> And life ran gayly as the sparkling Thames;
>>> Before this strange disease of modern life,
>> With its sick hurry, its divided aims,
>>> Its heads o'ertaxed, its palsied hearts, was rife,—
>>>> Fly hence, our contact fear!
> Still fly, plunge deeper in the bowering wood!
>> Averse, as Dido did with gesture stern
>> From her false friend's approach in Hades turn,
> Wave us away, and keep thy solitude!

> Still nursing the unconquerable hope,
>> Still clutching the inviolable shade,
>>> With a free, onward impulse brushing through,
>> By night, the silvered branches of the glade,—

> Far on the forest-skirts, where none pursue,
>   On some mild pastoral slope
> Emerge, and resting on the moonlit pales
>   Freshen thy flowers as in former years
>   With dew, or listen with enchanted ears,
> From the dark dingles, to the nightingales!
>
> But fly our paths, our feverish contact fly!
>   For strong the infection of our mental strife,
>   Which, though it gives no bliss, yet spoils for rest;
>   And we should win thee from thy own fair life,
>   Like us distracted, and like us unblest.
>   Soon, soon thy cheer would die,
>   Thy hopes grow timorous, and unfixed thy powers,
>   And thy clear aims be cross and shifting made:
>   And then thy glad perennial youth would fade,
>   Fade, and grow old at last, and die like ours.

Both the famous elegies are in Arnold's "Doric mood;" and that, we say, is not his most characteristic mood. It is the mood of a transient though poignant nostalgia.

Some aspects of the natural world he thought exemplary and edifying, particularly the march of the stars in their courses, and the silent swinging of the earth through its lonely course around the sun. To speak of the exemplary and edifying aspects of nature is on the whole more characteristic of him than to speak of her consoling loveliness.

There is little or nothing mystical for him in the sweet influence of the Pleiades. It is simply that the planetary and stellar motions appear to him matchless patterns of quiet eternal activity. Illustrations may be found in "A Summer Night," "Self-Dependence," and in "Quiet Work"—two of which are quoted below:

A SUMMER NIGHT

In the deserted, moon-blanch'd sheet,
How lonely rings the echo of my feet!
Those windows, which I gaze at, frown,
Silent and white, unopening down,
Repellent as the world;—but see,
A break between the housetops shows
The moon! and, lost behind her, fading dim
Into the dewy dark obscurity
Down at the far horizon's rim,
Doth a whole tract of heaven disclose!

And to my mind the thought
Is on a sudden brought
Of a past night, and a far different scene.
Headlands stood out into the moonlit deep
As clearly as at noon;
The spring-tide's brimming flow
Heaved dazzlingly between;
Houses, with long white sweep,
Girdled the glistening bay;
Behind, through the soft air,
The blue haze-cradled mountains spread away.
That night was far more fair—
But the same restless pacings to and fro,
And the same vainly throbbing heart was there,
And the same bright, calm moon.

And the calm moonlight seems to say,—
Hast thou, then, still the old unquiet breast,
Which neither deadens into rest,
Nor ever feels the fiery glow
That whirls the spirit from itself away,
But fluctuates to and fro,
Never by passion quite possessed,
And never quite benumbed by the world's sway?
And I, I know not if to pray
Still to be what I am, or yield, and be
Like all the other men I see.

For most men in a brazen prison live,
Where, in the sun's hot eye,
With heads bent o'er their toil, they languidly
Their lives to some unmeaning task-work give,
Dreaming of naught beyond their prison-wall.
And as, year after year,
Fresh products of their barren labor fall
From their tired hands, and rest
Never yet comes more near,
Gloom settles slowly down over their breast.
And while they try to stem
The waves of mournful thought by which
        they are prest,
Death in their prison reaches them,
Unfreed, having seen nothing, still unblest.

And the rest, a few,
Escape their prison, and depart
On the wide ocean of life anew.
There the freed prisoner, where'er his heart
Listeth, will sail;
Nor doth he know how there prevail,

Despotic on that sea,
Trade-winds which cross it from eternity.
Awhile he holds some false way, undebarred
By thwarting signs, and braves
The freshening wind and blackening waves.
And then the tempest strikes him; and between
The lightning-bursts is seen
Only a driving wreck,
And the pale master on his spar-strewn deck
With anguished face and flying hair,
Grasping the rudder hard,
Still bent to make some port, he knows not where,
Still standing for some false, impossible shore.
And sterner comes the roar
Of sea and wind; and through the deepen-
      ing gloom
Fainter and fainter wreck and helmsman loom,
And he too disappears, and comes no more.

Is there no life, but these alone?
Madman or slave, must man be one?

Plainness and clearness without shadow of stain!
Clearness divine!
Ye heavens, whose pure dark regions have no sign
Of languor, though so calm, and, though so great,
Are yet untroubled and unpassionate;
Who, though so noble, share in the world's toil,
And, though so task'd, keep free from dust and soil!
I will not say that your mild deeps retain
A tinge, it may be, of their silent pain
Who have long'd deeply once, and long'd in vain—
But I will rather say that you remain

A world above man's head, to let him see
How boundless might his soul's horizon be
How vast, yet of what clear transparency!
How it were good to abide there, and breathe free;
How fair a lot to fill
Is left to each man still.

QUIET WORK

One lesson, Nature, let me learn of thee,
One lesson which in every wind is blown,
One lesson of two duties kept at one
Though the loud world proclaim their enmity,—

Of toil unsevered from tranquillity;
Of labor, that in lasting fruit outgrows
Far noisier schemes, accomplished in repose,
Too great for haste, too high for rivalry.

Yes, while on earth a thousand discords ring,
Man's senseless uproar mingling with his toil,
Still do thy quiet ministers move on,

Their glorious tasks in silence perfecting;
Still working, blaming still our vain turmoil,
Laborers that shall not fail, when man is gone.

If the stars have any voice, it says: "Endure, and
go about your business quietly and diligently." In
general, however, Arnold feels that man needs not,
and had better not, look to nature for moral guidance. There is one law for things and another law
for man. "Man must begin, know this, where na-

ture ends." The stars perform their appointed tasks tranquilly and effortlessly indeed; but, after all, the effort and the earnestness of man are his special human distinctions, the signs of his morality, the marks which show his alliance with God:

MORALITY

We cannot kindle when we will
The fire which in the heart resides;
The spirit bloweth and is still,
In mystery our soul abides.
　But tasks in hours of insight willed
　Can be through hours of gloom fulfilled.

With aching hands and bleeding feet
We dig and heap, lay stone on stone;
We bear the burden and the heat
Of the long day, and wish 'twere done.
　Not till the hours of light return,
　All we have built do we discern.

Then, when the clouds are off the soul,
When thou dost bask in Nature's eye,
Ask how *she* viewed thy self-control,
Thy struggling, tasked morality,—
　Nature, whose free, light, cheerful air,
　Oft made thee, in thy gloom, despair.

And she, whose censure thou dost dread,
Whose eye thou wast afraid to seek,
See, on her face a glow is spread,
A strong emotion on her cheek!
　"Ah, child!" she cries, "that strife divine,
　Whence was it, for it is not mine?

"There is no effort on *my* brow;
I do not strive, I do not weep:
I rush with the swift spheres, and glow
In joy, and when I will, I sleep.
  Yet that severe, that earnest air,
  I saw, I felt it once—but where?

"I knew not yet the gauge of time,
Nor wore the manacles of space;
I felt it in some other clime,
I saw it in some other place.
  'Twas when the heavenly house I trod,
  And lay upon the breast of God."

It is clearly Arnold's conviction that the appointed places for man to hear his oracle are in human history, in the inspired books, in the lives of his fellow men, and in his own heart. There he will find the ideals of truth, justice, courage, gentleness and love of which the non-human world, which we call nature, gives no token.

Some superficial observers have remarked that Arnold the critic and Arnold the poet are two different persons. No one will come to such a conclusion who has the tact to distinguish the poems in which a vagrant fancy is indulged from those through which his central thought and feeling flow. For example, the author of the *Notebooks,* the poem called the "Buried Life," and the volumes of biblical criticism is clearly one and the same person. What element have these three works in common? They

have in common a strong sense that the center of
man's being is an inward monitor, the heart of his
moral and spiritual nature, and that his true prosperity in life depends upon his listening to that, depends upon his being ruled by that. The two sonnets
quoted below are not finer poetry than many of the
stanzas describing the roving of the Scholar-Gipsy
through dew-drenched English lanes; but they are
much closer to the center of Arnold's thought and
feeling at maturity:

EAST LONDON

'Twas August, and the fierce sun overhead
Smote on the squalid streets of Bethnal Green,
And the pale weaver, through his windows seen
In Spitalfields, looked thrice dispirited.

I met a preacher there I knew, and said,—
"Ill and o'erworked, how fare you in this scene?"
"Bravely!" said he; "for I of late have been
Much cheered with thoughts of Christ, *the living bread.*"

O human soul! as long as thou canst so
Set up a mark of everlasting light,
Above the howling senses' ebb and flow,

To cheer thee, and to right thee if thou roam,—
Not with lost toil thou laborest through the night!
Thou mak'st the heaven thou hop'st indeed thy home.

THE BETTER PART

Long fed on boundless hopes, O race of man,
How angrily thou spurn'st all simpler fare!
"Christ," some one says, "was human as we are;
No judge eyes us from heaven, our sin to scan;

"We live no more, when we have done our span."
"Well, then, for Christ," thou answerest, "who can care?
From sin which Heaven records not, why forbear?
Live we like brutes our life without a plan!"

So answerest thou; but why not rather say,—
"Hath man no second life? *Pitch this one high!*
Sits there no judge in heaven, our sin to see?

"More strictly, then, the inward judge obey!
Was Christ a man like us? Ah! let us try
If we then, too, can be such men as he!"

It is a curious and significant fact that Arnold is
most bracing when he stands by a grave; his most
inspiriting lines are his commemorative poems: the
prayer at the end of "Heine's Grave;" the "Memo-
rial Verses" for Wordsworth; "Westminster Abbey," written in commemoration of Dean Stanley;
"A Southern Night," occasioned by the death of a
brother; and, above all, "Rugby Chapel," in which
he pays to his father's memory an almost religious
veneration.

In the latter part of "Rugby Chapel" one feels the presence of that powerful stream of moral energy which flowed from father to son, preserving him through the sandy and desert places of his thought, and making him at length a positive and shining force in the world. Let us conclude our consideration of his personal poems with the exultant notes of this tribute:

> And through thee I believe
> In the noble and great who are gone;
> Pure souls honored and blest
> By former ages, who else—
> Such, so soulless, so poor,
> Is the race of men whom I see—
> Seemed but a dream of the heart,
> Seemed but a cry of desire.
> Yes! I believe that there lived
> Others like thee in the past,
> Not like the men of the crowd
> Who all round me to-day
> Bluster or cringe, and make life
> Hideous and arid and vile;
> But souls tempered with fire,
> Fervent, heroic, and good,
> Helpers and friends of mankind.
>
> Servants of God!—or sons
> Shall I not call you? because
> Not as servants ye knew
> Your Father's innermost mind,
> His who unwillingly sees

One of his little ones lost,—
Yours is the praise, if mankind
Hath not as yet in its march
Fainted and fallen and died.

See! In the rocks of the world
Marches the host of mankind,
A feeble, wavering line.
Where are they tending? A God
Marshalled them, gave them their goal.
Ah, but the way is so long!
Years they have been in the wild:
Sore thirst plagues them; the rocks,
Rising all round, overawe;
Factions divide them; their host
Threatens to break, to dissolve.
Ah! keep, keep them combined!
Else, of the myriads who fill
That army, not one shall arrive;
Sole they shall stray; on the rocks
Batter forever in vain,
Die one by one in the waste.

Then, in such hour of need
Of your fainting, dispirited race,
Ye like angels appear,
Radiant with ardor divine.
Beacons of hope, ye appear!
Languor is not in your heart,
Weakness is not in your word,
Weariness not on your brow.
Ye alight in our van! at your voice,
Panic, despair, flee away.
Ye move through the ranks, recall

The stragglers, refresh the outworn,
Praise, re-inspire the brave.
Order, courage, return.
Eyes rekindling, and prayers,
Follow your steps as ye go.
Ye fill up the gaps in our files,
Strengthen the wavering line,
Stablish, continue our march,
On, to the bound of the waste,
On, to the City of God.

CHAPTER III

"To be less and less *personal* in one's desires and workings is the great matter, and this too I feel, I am glad to say, more deeply than I did, but for progress in the direction of the 'seeketh not her own' there is always room."—*Letters,* I, 400.

THE impulse to express spiritual desolation, to which Arnold yielded in "Empedocles" and numerous shorter pieces, was almost from the outset in conflict with his own theory of the function of poetry. The true end of all art, he held, and of poetry especially is, like that of religion, to strengthen and uphold the heart with high inspirations and consolations. The great poet—this one learns of Homer, Sophocles, Virgil, Dante, Shakespeare—does not pour into the world the unchecked flood of his personal emotions. He rises above his individual passions and affairs to survey the wide course of human life; to feel and comment upon its permanent and significant aspects; to illustrate the fortitude and the moral splendor with which man may confront the indignity of his lot. In "Resignation," published in 1849 in the first volume of his verse, Arnold, describing the character of the poet,

writes an indirect condemnation of many of his
more intimate effusions:

> The poet, to whose mighty heart
> Heaven doth a quicker pulse impart,
> Subdues that energy to scan
> Not his own course, but that of man.

> .   .   .   .   .   .

> Lean'd on his gate, he gazes—tears
> Are in his eyes, and in his ears
> The murmur of a thousand years.
> Before him he sees life unroll,
> A placid and continuous whole—
> That general life, which does not cease,
> Whose secret is not joy, but peace.

It is noteworthy that Arnold recognized the incon-
sistency of "Empedocles" with his critical principles,
and withdrew it from circulation. In the important
preface to his poetical volume of 1853 he explains
both why he had been attracted to the subject and
why on reflection he suppressed the work. The discussion provides us an interesting approach to his
other long poems. He had been drawn to Empedocles by that sense of kinship in philosophic melancholy which drew him to Senancour and Amiel. "I
intended to delineate," he says, "the feelings of one
of the last of the Greek religious philosophers, one
of the family of Orpheus and Musæus, having sur-
vived his fellows, living on into a time when the

habits of Greek thought and feeling had begun fast
to change, character to dwindle, the influence of the
Sophists to prevail. Into the feelings of a man so
situated there entered much that we are accustomed
to consider as exclusively modern; how much the
fragments of Empedocles himself which remain to
us are sufficient at least to indicate. What those who
are familiar only with the great movements of early
Greek genius suppose to be its exclusive characteristics, have disappeared; the calm, the cheerfulness,
the disinterested objectivity have disappeared; the
dialogue of the mind with itself has commenced;
modern problems have presented themselves; we
hear already the doubts, we witness the discourage-
ment, of Hamlet and of Faust."

The faithful delineation of such feelings may be
interesting, as it adds to our knowledge; but it is
depressing, and therefore falls short of the highest
poetical quality. That a work commands interest is
something; "but, if the representation be a poetical
one, more than this is demanded. It is demanded
not only that it shall interest, but also that it shall
inspirit and rejoice the reader; that it shall convey a
charm, and infuse delight. For the Muses, as
Hesiod says, were born that they might be 'a forget-
fulness of evils, and a truce from cares': and it is not
enough that the poet should add to the knowledge of
men, it is required of him also that he should add to
their happiness. 'All art,' says Schiller, 'is dedicated

to joy, and there is no higher and no more serious problem than how to make men happy. The right art is that alone which creates the highest enjoyment.' "

This important principle, Arnold hastens to add, by no means excludes the poet from the treatment of tragic themes. The world could afford no better subjects, he says, than *Macbeth,* or *Romeo and Juliet,* or *Othello.*

"In presence of the most tragic circumstances, represented in a work of art, the feeling of enjoyment, as is well known, may still subsist; the representation of the most utter calamity, of the liveliest anguish, is not sufficient to destroy it; the more tragic the situation, the deeper becomes the enjoyment; and the situation is more tragic in proportion as it becomes more terrible.

"What then are the situations, from the representation of which, though accurate, no poetical enjoyment can be derived? They are those in which the suffering finds no vent in action; in which a continuous state of mental distress is prolonged, unrelieved by incident, hope, or resistance; in which there is everything to be endured, nothing to be done. In such situations there is inevitably something morbid, in the description of them something monotonous. When they occur in actual life they are painful, not tragic; the representation of them in poetry is painful also.

"To this class of situations, poetically faulty as it appears to me, that of Empedocles, as I have endeavoured to represent him, belongs; and I have therefore excluded the poem from the present collection."

The rest of this admirable preface is occupied with the development of another central critical doctrine: that the choice of a poetical subject is all-important. Here again Arnold speaks as a sound classicist, protesting against the modern demand for modern themes, and decrying the romantic emphasis upon the "treatment" as distinguished from the "subject" and upon detail as distinguished from design:

"The poet, then, has in the first place to select an excellent action; and what actions are the most excellent? Those, certainly, which most powerfully appeal to the great primary human affections: to those elementary feelings which subsist permanently in the race, and which are independent of time. These feelings are permanent and the same; that which interests them is permanent and the same also. The modernness or antiquity of an action, therefore, has nothing to do with its fitness for poetical representation; this depends upon its inherent qualities. To the elementary part of our nature, to our passions, that which is great and passionate is eternally interesting; and interesting solely in proportion to its greatness and to its passion. A great human action of a thousand years ago is more interesting to it than a smaller human action of to-day, even though upon the representation of this last the most consummate skill may have been expended, and though it has the advantage of appealing by its modern language, familiar manners, and contemporary allusions, to all our transient feelings and interests. These, however, have no right to demand of a poetical work that it shall satisfy them; their claims are to be directed elsewhere.   Poetical works belong to the domain of our permanent passions; let them interest these, and the voice of all subordinate claims upon them is at once silenced.   .   .   .

"The date of an action, then, signifies nothing; the action itself, its selection and construction, this is what is all-important.   This the Greeks understood far more clearly than we do.   The radical difference between their poetical theory and ours consists, as it appears to me, in this: that, with them, the poetical character of the action in itself, and the conduct of it, was the first consideration; with us, attention is fixed mainly on the value of the separate thoughts and images which occur in the treatment of an action.   They regarded the whole; we regard the parts.   With them the action predominated over the expression of it; with us the expression predominates over the action.   Not that they failed in expression, or were inattentive to it; on the contrary, they are the highest models of expression, the unapproached masters of the *grand style*."

Now, when Arnold, obeying the injunction of the Elizabethan sonneteer, looked in his heart and wrote, he was constrained to record the poetical experience which he found there, such as it was.   When, on the other hand, he deliberately chose a subject in the external world, he was actuated more and more, as his critical ideas grew clearer, by a desire to represent in English the spirit of the ancient classics—to show what a poem should be. If one considers his longer pieces in the order of their publication, one becomes conscious of a progressive diminution in them of the purely biographical and contemporaneous interest, a development in the direction of objectivity. "Empedocles on Etna" and "Tristram and Iseult" appeared together in 1852; "Sohrab and Rustum" in 1853; "Balder Dead" in 1855; and "Merope" in 1858. "Empedocles" so obviously springs from the author's personal relations with mid-nineteenth century thought that we have treated it in the preceding chapter as a "biographical document."

In "Tristram and Iseult" he attains a certain dramatic detachment from the emotions which he depicts, yet he is still fascinated, as in the "Switzerland" lyrics by a subject very close to his bosom—the counter-claims of passion and reason. Critics have remarked upon the curious prominence that he gives to Tristram's wife, Iseult of Brittany, in consequence of which the unity of the poem suffers, the interest quite passing, at the end of the second section, from the lovers to her. One suspects that the poet, not yet altogether disenthralled from the magic of medieval romance though more than half in love with classic beauty, was not absolutely certain where the center of his subject lay, was not entirely sure what effect he wished to produce. His personal poems repeatedly prove that there was a period in his life in which he was drawn to and fro by his hunger for passion and his hunger for peace. Youth, as he declares in "Youth and Calm," hears an inner voice crying "Calm's not life's crown, though calm is well." At any rate he exhibits here, apparently with intense sympathy, passion, in Tristram and Iseult of Ireland, wearing life to a shadow; and then with equal sympathy he exhibits in Iseult of Brittany the image of a life self-contained, resigned, calm as a waxen effigy. Both pictures are beautiful and both are profoundly sad; the poet stands between them with divided affections. To the dead lovers he bids farewell with the compassion few can withhold from frustrated and perished loveliness :

> Cheer, cheer thy dogs into the brake,
> O hunter! and without a fear
> Thy golden-tasselled bugle blow,
> And through the glades thy pastime take—
> For thou wilt rouse no sleepers here!
> For these thou seest are unmoved;
> Cold, cold as those who lived and loved
> A thousand years ago.

There can be no doubt, however, that in the long run Arnold, like the gods, approved "the depth and not the tumult of the soul;" nor that the last canto, presenting the life of Iseult and her children in Brittany, is incomparably the finest third of the poem.

In the fresh idyllic charm of its landscape, its touching humanity, its tone of tranquil melancholy, and its metrical regularity, the graver, collected, habitual feelings of the poet find expression seldom surpassed by him or by any of his contemporaries:

ISEULT OF BRITTANY

A year had flown, and o'er the sea away,
In Cornwall, Tristram and Queen Iseult lay;
In King Marc's chapel, in Tyntagel old:
There in a ship they bore those lovers cold.

The young surviving Iseult, one bright day,
Had wandered forth. Her children were at play
In a green circular hollow in the heath
Which borders the seashore; a country path
Creeps over it from the tilled fields behind.
The hollow's grassy banks are soft-inclined;
And to one standing on them, far and near
The lone unbroken view spreads bright and clear
Over the waste. This cirque of open ground
Is light and green; the heather, which all round
Creeps thickly, grows not here; but the pale grass
Is strewn with rocks and many a shivered mass
Of veined white-gleaming quartz, and here and there
Dotted with holly-trees and juniper.
In the smooth centre of the opening stood
Three hollies side by side, and made a screen,
Warm with the winter-sun, of burnished green
With scarlet berries gemmed, the fell-fare's food.
Under the glittering hollies Iseult stands,
Watching her children play: their little hands

Are busy gathering spars of quartz, and streams
Of stagshorn for their hats; anon, with screams
Of mad delight they drop their spoils, and bound
Among the holly-clumps and broken ground,
Racing full speed, and startling in their rush
The fell-fares and the speckled missel-thrush
Out of their glossy coverts; but when now
Their cheeks were flushed, and over each hot brow,
Under the feathered hats of the sweet pair,
In blinding masses showered the golden hair,
Then Iseult called them to her, and the three
Clustered under the holly-screen, and she
Told them an old-world Breton history.

Warm in their mantles wrapped, the three stood there,
Under the hollies, in the clear still air,—
Mantles with those rich furs deep glistering
Which Venice ships do from swart Egypt bring.
Long they stayed still, then, pacing at their ease,
Moved up and down under the glossy trees;
But still, as they pursued their warm dry road,
From Iseult's lips the unbroken story flowed,
And still the children listened, their blue eyes
Fixed on their mother's face in wide surprise.
Nor did their looks stray once to the sea-side,
Nor to the brown heaths round them, bright and wide,
Nor to the snow, which, though 'twas all away
From the open heath, still by the hedgerows lay,
Nor to the shining sea-fowl, that with screams
Bore up from where the bright Atlantic gleams,
Swooping to landward; nor to where, quite clear,
The fell-fares settled on the thickets near.
And they would still have listen'd, till dark night
Came keen and chill down on the heather bright;

But, when the red glow on the sea grew cold,
And the grey turrets of the castle old
Look'd sternly through the frosty evening-air,
Then Iseult took by the hand those children fair,
And brought her tale to an end, and found the path
And led them home over the darkening heath.

And is she happy? Does she see unmoved
The days in which she might have lived and loved
Slip without bringing bliss slowly away,
One after one, to-morrow like to-day?
Joy has not found her yet, nor ever will—
Is it this thought which makes her mien so still,
Her features so fatigued, her eyes, though sweet,
So sunk, so rarely lifted save to meet
Her children's? She moves slow; her voice alone
Hath yet an infantine and silver tone,
But even that comes languidly; in truth,
She seems one dying in a mask of youth.
And now she will go home, and softly lay
Her laughing children in their beds, and play
Awhile with them before they sleep; and then
She'll light her silver lamp, which fishermen
Dragging their nets through the rough waves, afar,
Along this iron coast, know like a star,
And take her broidery-frame, and there she'll sit
Hour after hour, her gold curls sweeping it;
Lifting her soft-bent head only to mind
Her children, or to listen to the wind.
And when the clock peals midnight, she will move
Her work away, and let her fingers rove
Across the shaggy brows of Tristram's hound,
Who lies, guarding her feet, along the ground;

Or else she will fall musing, her blue eyes
Fixed, her slight hands clasped on her lap; then rise,
And at her prie-dieu kneel, until she have told
Her rosary-beads of ebony tipped with gold;
Then to her soft sleep—and to-morrow'll be
To-day's exact repeated effigy.

Yes, it is lonely for her in her hall.
The children, and the grey-haired seneschal,
Her women, and Sir Tristram's aged hound,
Are there the sole companions to be found.
But these she loves; and noisier life than this
She would find ill to bear, weak as she is.
She has her children, too, and night and day
Is with them; and the wide heaths where they play,
The hollies, and the cliff, and the sea-shore,
The sand, the sea-birds, and the distant sails,
These are to her dear as to them; the tales
With which this day the children she beguiled
She gleaned from Breton grandames, when a child,
In every hut along this sea-coast wild;
She herself loves them still, and, when they are told,
Can forget all to hear them, as of old.

Dear saints, it is not sorrow, as I hear,
Not suffering, which shuts up eye and ear
To all that has delighted them before,
And lets us be what we were once no more.
No, we may suffer deeply, yet retain
Power to be moved and soothed, for all our pain,
By what of old pleased us, and will again.
No, 'tis the gradual furnace of the world,
In whose hot air our spirits are upcurl'd
Until they crumble, or else grow like steel—

Which kills in us the bloom, the youth, the spring—
Which leaves the fierce necessity to feel,
But takes away the power—this can avail,
By drying up our joy in everything,
To make our former pleasures all seem stale.
This, or some tyrannous single thought, some fit
Of passion, which subdues our souls to it,
Till for its sake alone we live and move—
Call it ambition, or remorse, or love—
This too can change us wholly, and make seem
All which we did before, shadow and dream.

And yet, I swear, it angers me to see
How this fool passion gulls men potently;
Being, in truth, but a diseased unrest,
And an unnatural overheat at best.
How they are full of languor and distress
Not having it; which when they do possess,
They straightway are burnt up with fume and care,
And spend their lives in posting here and there
Where this plague drives them; and have little ease,
Are furious with themselves, and hard to please.
Like that bold Cæsar, the famed Roman wight,
Who wept at reading of a Grecian knight
Who made a name at younger years than he;
Or that renown'd mirror of chivalry,
Prince Alexander, Philip's peerless son,
Who carried the great war from Macedon
Into the Soudan's realm, and thundered on
To die at thirty-five in Babylon.

What tale did Iseult to the children say,
Under the hollies, that bright winter's day?

She told them of the fairy-haunted land
Away the other side of Brittany,
Beyond the heaths, edged by the lonely sea;
Of the deep forest-glades of Broce-liande,
Through whose green boughs the golden sunshine
      creeps,
Where Merlin by the enchanted thorn-tree sleeps.
For here he came with the fay Vivian,
One April, when the warm days first began.
He was on foot, and that false fay, his friend,
On her white palfrey; here he met his end,
In these lone sylvan glades, that April-day.
This tale of Merlin and the lovely fay
Was the one Iseult chose, and she brought clear
Before the children's fancy him and her.

Blowing between the stems, the forest-air
Had loosened the brown locks of Vivian's hair,
Which played on her flushed cheek, and her blue eyes
Sparkled with mocking glee and exercise.
Her palfrey's flanks were mired and bathed in sweat,
For they had travelled far and not stopped yet.
A brier in that tangled wilderness
Had scored her white right hand, which she allows
To rest ungloved on her green riding-dress;
The other warded off the drooping boughs.
But still she chatted on, with her blue eyes
Fixed full on Merlin's face, her stately prize.
Her 'haviour had the morning's fresh clear grace,
The spirit of the woods was in her face;
She look'd so witching fair, that learned wight
Forgot his craft, and his best wits took flight,
And he grew fond, and eager to obey
His mistress, use her empire as she may.

They came to where the brushwood ceased, and day
Peer'd 'twixt the stems; and the ground broke away,
In a sloped sward down to a brawling brook.
And up as high as where they stood to look
On the brook's farther side was clear; but then
The underwood and trees began again.
This open glen was studded thick with thorns
Then white with blossom; and you saw the horns,
Through last year's fern, of the shy fallow-deer
Who come at noon down to the water here.
You saw the bright-eyed squirrels dart along
Under the thorns on the green sward; and strong
The blackbird whistled from the dingles near,
And the weird chipping of the woodpecker
Rang lonelily and sharp; the sky was fair,
And a fresh breath of spring stirr'd everywhere.
Merlin and Vivian stopp'd on the slope's brow,
To gaze on the light sea of leaf and bough
Which glistering plays all round them, lone and mild,
As if to itself the quiet forest smiled.
Upon the brow-top grew a thorn, and here
The grass was dry and moss'd, and you saw clear
Across the hollow; white anemonies
Starr'd the cool turf, and clumps of primroses
Ran out from the dark underwood behind.
No fairer resting-place a man could find.
"Here let us halt," said Merlin then; and she
Nodded, and tied her palfrey to a tree.

They sate them down together, and a sleep
Fell upon Merlin, more like death, so deep.
Her finger on her lips, then Vivian rose,
And from her brown-locked head the wimple throws,

And takes it in her hand, and waves it over
The blossomed thorn-tree and her sleeping lover.
Nine times she waved the fluttering wimple round,
And made a little plot of magic ground.
And in that daisied circle, as men say,
Is Merlin prisoner till the judgment-day;
But she herself whither she will can rove—
For she was passing weary of his love.

Fine as "Tristram and Iseult" is in parts, it is less vigorously integrated than "Sohrab and Rustum," and it falls short of the high seriousness of the later poem. "Sohrab," combining freshness and charm of treatment with austerity of design and mood, probably approaches as closely as anything in Arnold's works to his own poetic ideal. On completing it he wrote to his mother in May, 1853: "All my spare time has been spent on a poem which I have just finished, and which I think by far the best thing I have yet done, and that it will be generally liked, though one never can be sure of this. I have had the greatest pleasure in composing it—a rare thing with me, and, as I think, a good test of the pleasure what you write is likely to afford to others; but then the story is a very noble and excellent one." The nucleus of the story, told in Sir John Malcolm's *History of Persia,* is as follows: The great warrior Rustum, fighting as the champion of the Persians, unwittingly kills in single combat his long-lost son

Sohrab, the champion of the Tartars, who has been seeking his father through the world.

The incident impressed Arnold as being of Homeric or Miltonic quality, and he treated it in the "grand style" as an epic episode. It was admirably adapted to enforce his doctrine on the choice of a subject; for though the persons and places and the period of history involved are far remote from the common interests and knowledge of Occidental readers, the nature of the action is such as to appeal powerfully to some of the most elementary human feelings—the feelings of fatherhood and sonship, and, let us add, the feeling which almost every mother's son knows soon or late, the feeling of irretrievable disaster. Without indulging in oversubtlety, we may surmise that the narrative peculiarly engaged the sympathies of the poet as a striking fragment of the evidence about human affairs which led him in "Dover Beach" to declare that

> We are here as on a darkling plain
> Swept with confused alarms of struggle and flight,
> Where ignorant armies clash by night.

In its pervading temper, however, "Sohrab and Rustum" differs significantly from the temper of "Dover Beach" and still more, from the temper of the condemned "Empedocles." It is poignantly sad, but it is not depressing; for it is in the heroic mood. The distressfulness of the action is relieved by the splendid courage and magnanimity of the participants, and their bitter conflict ends not in despondency but in a solemn peace, which affects the reader with a curious sense of liberation, enlargement, and exaltation. It yields, in short, the special joy of the truly tragic: a sense of something transcending the individual life, of something in the world nobler than nature, of something in the heart which destiny can not break—a sense, in the presence of death, of deathless things.

This final effect, the highest which poetry can produce, is procured by various more or less definable means. For example, the temporary importance and at the same time the ultimate insignificance of the champions is magnificently emphasized by the Homeric marshaling of the contending Persian and Tartar hosts, so that all barbaric Asia seems to seethe behind the individual combatants:

> The sun by this had risen, and cleared the fog
> From the broad Oxus and the glittering sands.
> And from their tents the Tartar horsemen filed
> Into the open plain: so Haman bade,—
> Haman, who next to Peran-Wisa ruled
> The host, and still was in his lusty prime.
> From their black tents, long files of horse, they
>   streamed;
> As when some gray November morn the files,
> In marching order spread, of long-necked cranes
> Stream over Casbin and the southern slopes
> Of Elburz, from the Aralian estuaries,

Or some frore Caspian reed-bed, southward bound
For the warm Persian seaboard,—so they streamed.
The Tartars of the Oxus, the king's guard,
First, with black sheep-skin caps and with long spears;
Large men, large steeds, who from Bokhara come
And Khiva, and ferment the milk of mares.
Next, the more temperate Toorkmuns of the south,
The Tukas, and the lances of Salore,
And those from Attruck and the Caspian sands;
Light men and on light steeds, who only drink
The acrid milk of camels, and their wells.
And then a swarm of wandering horse, who came
From far, and a more doubtful service owned,—
The Tartars of Ferghana, from the banks
Of the Jaxartes, men with scanty beards
And close-set skull-caps; and those wilder hordes
Who roam o'er Kipchak and the northern waste,
Kalmucks and unkempt Kuzzaks, tribes who stray
Nearest the Pole, and wandering Kirghizzes,
Who come on shaggy ponies from Pamere,—
These all filed out from camp into the plain.
And on the other side the Persians formed,—
First a light cloud of horse, Tartars they seemed,
The Ilyats of Khorassan; and behind,
The royal troops of Persia, horse and foot,
Marshall'd battalions bright in burnish'd steel.

The terrific grandeur of the combat is magnified
by the representation of nature as an angry spectator
or a participant in it; yet the heroes are superbly at
the center of the poem, and in the hottest fury of
their encounter their personal relationship is the

center of the interest, and its disclosure the turning
point of the action:

> And you would say that sun and stars took part
> In that unnatural conflict: for a cloud
> Grew suddenly in heaven, and darked the sun
> Over the fighters' heads; and a wind rose
> Under their feet, and moaning swept the plain,
> And in a sandy whirlwind wrapped the pair.
> In gloom they twain were wrapped, and they alone;
> For both the on-looking hosts on either hand
> Stood in broad daylight, and the sky was pure,
> And the sun sparkled on the Oxus stream.
> But in the gloom they fought, with bloodshot eyes
> And laboring breath. First Rustum struck the shield
> Which Sohrab held stiff out; the steel-spiked spear
> Rent the tough plates, but failed to reach the skin,
> And Rustum plucked it back with angry groan.
> Then Sohrab with his sword smote Rustum's helm,
> Nor clove its steel quite through; but all the crest
> He shore away, and that proud horse-hair plume,
> Never till now defiled, sank to the dust;
> And Rustum bowed his head. But then the gloom
> Grew blacker, thunder rumbled in the air,
> And lightnings rent the cloud; and Ruksh the horse,
> Who stood at hand, uttered a dreadful cry:
> No horse's cry was that, most like the roar
> Of some pained desert-lion, who all day
> Has trailed the hunter's javelin in his side,
> And comes at night to die upon the sand;
> The two hosts heard that cry, and quaked for fear,
> And Oxus curdled as it crossed his stream.
> But Sohrab heard, and quailed not, but rushed on,
> And struck again; and again Rustum bowed

His head; but this time all the blade, like glass,
Sprang in a thousand shivers on the helm,
And in the hand the hilt remained alone.
Then Rustum raised his head; his dreadful eyes
Glared, and he shook on high his menacing spear,
And shouted: *Rustum!*—Sohrab heard that shout,
And shrank amazed: back he recoil'd one step,
And scann'd with blinking eyes the advancing form;
And then he stood bewilder'd, and he dropp'd
His covering shield, and the spear pierced his side.
He reel'd, and staggering back, sank to the ground,
And then the gloom dispersed, and the wind fell,
And the bright sun broke forth, and melted all
The cloud; and the two armies saw the pair;—
Saw Rustum standing, safe upon his feet,
And Sohrab, wounded, on the bloody sand.

While the stricken Sohrab declares himself, the
father, still unconvinced, yet touched by the abstract
pity of the young man's fate, lets his mind travel
back to the days of his youth:

. . . . yet he listen'd plunged in thought;
And his soul set to grief, as the vast tide
Of the bright rocking ocean sets to shore
At the full moon; tears gathered in his eyes;
For he remembered his own early youth,
And all its bounding rapture; as, at dawn,
The shepherd from his mountain-lodge descries
A far, bright city, smitten by the sun,
Through many rolling clouds,—so Rustum saw
His youth; saw Sohrab's mother in her bloom;
And that old king, her father, who loved well

His wandering guest, and gave him his fair child
With joy; and all the pleasant life they led,
They three, in that long-distant summer-time,—
The castle, and the dewy woods, and hunt
And hound, and morn on those delightful hills
In Ader-baijan.   And he saw that youth,
Of age and looks to be his own dear son,
Piteous and lovely, lying on the sand;
Like some rich hyacinth which by the scythe
Of an unskilful gardener has been cut,
Mowing the garden grass-plots near its bed,
And lies, a fragrant tower of purple bloom,
On the mown, dying grass,—so Sohrab lay,
Lovely in death, upon the common sand.
And Rustum gazed on him with grief, and said,—

   "O Sohrab, thou indeed art such a son
Whom Rustum, wert thou his, might well have loved!
Yet here thou errest, Sohrab, or else men
Have told thee false: thou art not Rustum's son."

When Sohrab produces unmistakable proof of his identity, Rustum in utter remorse and desperation clutches his sword "to draw it, and forever let life out."   But Sohrab, uncomplaining, resigned, and blissful, speaks out of the strength and magnanimity of a great love:

   "Father, forbear! for I but meet to-day
The doom which at my birth was written down
In Heaven, and thou art Heaven's unconscious hand.
Surely my heart cried out that it was thou,
When first I saw thee; and thy heart spoke too,
I know it!   But fate trod those promptings down

Under its iron heel; fate, fate engaged
The strife, and hurled me on my father's spear.
But let us speak no more of this. I find
My father, let me feel that I have found!
Come, sit beside me on this sand, and take
My head betwixt thy hands, and kiss my cheeks,
And wash them with thy tears, and say, *My son!*
Quick, quick! for numbered are my sands of life,
And swift; for like the lightning to this field
I came, and like the wind I go away,—
Sudden, and swift, and like a passing wind;
But it was writ in Heaven that this should be."

So said he; and his voice released the heart
Of Rustum, and his tears broke forth; he cast
His arms round his son's neck, and wept aloud,
And kissed him. And awe fell on both the hosts,
When they saw Rustum's grief; and Ruksh, the horse,
With his head bowing to the ground, and mane
Sweeping the dust, came near, and in mute woe
First to the one, then to the other, moved
His head, as if inquiring what their grief
Might mean; and from his dark, compassionate eyes,
The big warm tears rolled down, and caked the sand.

．　　．　　．　　．　　．　　．　　．

But, with a grave mild voice, Sohrab replied:
"Desire not that, my father! thou must live.
For some are born to do great deeds, and live
As some are born to be obscured, and die.
Do thou the deeds I die too young to do,
And reap a second glory in thine age;
Thou art my father, and thy gain is mine."

It is suggestive to place beside Empedocles' "criticism of life"—uttered in the hot fit of a fevered intellect—as an "uncongenial place," a "meadow of calamity," the lines describing the passage of Sohrab's unconquerable soul, the busy resumption of routine by the Persian and Tartar hosts, and the starry tranquillity of nature which succeeds, faintly hinting at a far-off peace in the union of the Many with the One.

> Unwillingly the spirit fled away,
> Regretting the warm mansion which it left,
> And youth, and bloom, and this delightful world.
>   So, on the bloody sand, Sohrab lay dead;
> And the great Rustum drew his horseman's cloak
> Down o'er his face, and sate by his dead son.
> As those black granite pillars, once high-reared
> By Jemshid in Persepolis, to bear
> His house, now 'mid their broken flights of steps
> Lie prone, enormous, down the mountain side,—
> So in the sand lay Rustum by his son.
>   And night came down over the solemn waste,
> And the two gazing hosts, and that sole pair,
> And darkened all; and a cold fog, with night,
> Crept from the Oxus. Soon a hum arose,
> As of a great assembly loosed, and fires
> Began to twinkle through the fog; for now
> Both armies moved to camp, and took their meal;
> The Persians took it on the open sands
> Southward, the Tartars by the river-marge;
> And Rustum and his son were left alone.

But the majestic river floated on,
Out of the mist and hum of that low land,
Into the frosty starlight, and there moved,
Rejoicing, through the hushed Chorasmian waste,
Under the solitary moon; he flowed
Right for the polar star, past Orgunjè,
Brimming, and bright, and large; then sands begin
To hem his watery march, and dam his streams,
And split his currents; that for many a league
The shorn and parcelled Oxus strains along
Through beds of sand and matted rushy isles,—
Oxus, forgetting the bright speed he had
In his high mountain cradle in Pamere,
A foiled circuitous wanderer,—till at last
The longed-for dash of waves is heard, and wide
His luminous home of waters opens, bright
And tranquil, from whose floor the new-bathed stars
Emerge, and shine upon the Aral Sea.

Two years after the appearance of "Sohrab and
Rustum" Arnold brought out his "Balder Dead."
He hoped that it would "consolidate the peculiar sort
of reputation" which he had made by his treatment
of the Persian episode. Why it missed the popular
success attained by its predecessor is partly revealed
in Arnold's own apology for it. Writing to Pal-
grave in 1869 regarding the first collected edition
of his poems, then in the press, he says: " 'Balder'
perhaps no one cares much for except myself; but
I have always thought, though very likely I am
wrong, that it has not had justice done to it; I consider that it has a natural *propriety* of diction and

rhythm which is what we all prize so much in Virgil, and which is not common in English poetry. For instance, Tennyson has in the *Idylls* something dainty and *tourmenté* which excludes this natural propriety; and I have myself in 'Sohrab' something, not dainty, but *tourmenté* and Miltonically *ampoullé*, which excludes it. . . . We have enough Scandinavianism in our nature and history to make a short *conspectus* of the Scandinavian mythology admissible."[1]

The apologist has temporarily forgotten his preface of 1853. The relative failure of "Balder" is not due to its "Scandinavianism" any more than the success of "Sohrab" is due to its Orientalism. The trouble with "Balder" is in the subject itself—in the action, which is excessively fantastic, and in the characters, who are gods and notoriously difficult to handle. The subject does not "powerfully appeal to the great primary human affections"; it is deficient in "greatness" and "passion." If it possessed these qualities, it would hold us, though the manners were Patagonian. For the absence of these qualities we find in a poem of nearly twelve hundred lines no adequate compensation in "a natural propriety of diction" and "a short conspectus of the Scandinavian mythology."

This is not to deny the work interest and charm. It has the interest of its fantastic story—its mytho-

---

[1] Quoted in G. W. E. Russell's *Matthew Arnold*, p. 42.

logical interest. It has the charm of its rather dulcet
style and its Virgilian echoes, singularly out of
place, the captious will say, in a poem drawn from
the Norse *Edda*. One can not believe that it originated in the heat and light of an intense imaginative
experience, for its effect is not cumulative and uni-
fied; it has fine passages which one can excerpt
without feeling conscience-stricken, as specimens of
its quality. Let us have the beautiful speech of Regner over the dead body of Balder, and the description of the funeral pyre and the burial ship. When
Arnold wrote the tribute to Balder's singing it is a
fair guess that he was thinking of Wordsworth:

> "Balder, there yet are many scalds in heaven
> Still left, and that chief scald, thy brother Brage,
> Whom we may bid to sing, though thou art gone.
> And all these gladly, while we drink, we hear,
> After the feast is done, in Odin's hall;
> But they harp ever on one string, and wake
> Remembrance in our soul of wars alone,
> Such as on earth we valiantly have waged,
> And blood, and ringing blows, and violent death.
> But when thou sangest, Balder, thou didst strike
> Another note, and, like a bird in spring,
> Thy voice of joyance minded us, and youth,
> And wife, and children, and our ancient home.
> Yes, and I too remembered then no more
> My dungeon, where the serpents stung me dead,
> Nor Ella's victory on the English coast;
> But I heard Thora laugh in Gothland Isle,
> And saw my shepherdess, Aslauga, tend

Her flock along the white Norwegian beach.
Tears started to mine eyes with yearning joy.
Therefore with grateful heart I mourn thee dead."
  So Regner spake, and all the heroes groaned.
But now the sun had passed the height of heaven,
And soon had all that day been spent in wail;
But then the Father of the ages said,—
  "Ye gods, there well may be too much of wail!
Bring now the gathered wood to Balder's ship;
Heap on the deck the logs, and build the pyre."
  But when the gods and heroes heard, they brought
The wood to Balder's ship, and built a pile,
Full the deck's breadth, and lofty; then the corpse
Of Balder on the highest top they laid,
With Nanna on his right, and on his left
Hoder, his brother, whom his own hand slew.
And they set jars of wine and oil to lean
Against the bodies, and stuck torches near,
Splinters of pine-wood, soaked with turpentine;
And brought his arms and gold, and all his stuff,
And slew the dogs who at his table fed,
And his horse, Balder's horse, whom most he loved,
And threw them on the pyre; and Odin threw
A last choice gift thereon, his golden ring.
The mast they fixed, and hoisted up the sails;
Then they put fire to the wood; and Thor
Set his stout shoulder hard against the stern
To push the ship through the thick sand; sparks flew
From the deep trench she ploughed, so strong a god
Furrowed it; and the water gurgled in.
And the ship floated on the waves, and rocked.
But in the hills a strong east-wind arose,
And came down moaning to the sea; first squalls
Ran black o'er the sea's face, then steady rushed

The breeze, and filled the sails, and blew the fire.
And wreathed in smoke the ship stood out to sea.
Soon with a roaring rose the mighty fire,
And the pile crackled; and between the logs
Sharp quivering tongues of flame shot out, and leapt,
Curling and darting, higher, until they licked
The summit of the pile, the dead, the mast,
And ate the shrivelling sails; but still the ship
Drove on, ablaze above her hull with fire.
And the gods stood upon the beach, and gazed.
And while they gazed, the sun went lurid down
Into the smoke-wrapped sea, and night came on.
Then the wind fell, with night, and there was calm;
But through the dark they watch'd the burning ship
Still carried o'er the distant waters on,
Farther and farther, like an eye of fire.

Readers who wish to become fond of Arnold's
poetry should postpone "Merope," his last elaborate
work, till they have acquired a decided taste for him
—which is no more than one might say of Milton
and his "Samson Agonistes." Critics generally regard this tragedy in the Greek manner as a quite un-
inspired performance—perfunctory, cold, destitute
of poetical beauty. If its production was a mistake,
it was, however, a mistake that Arnold was doomed
to make. The heavenly Muse was perhaps absent
during its composition, but the critical spirit drove
him to the task. He had come out as the exponent
of classical principles in poetry. He looked upon
Homer and Sophocles as the supreme exemplars in
their respective fields of epic poetry and tragedy.

He had in his "Sohrab" represented the Homeric manner in English.   He felt under obligation to do the same service for Sophocles, and would not have felt less so if Swinburne had already captivated the public with such glamourous corruptions of Greek form and Greek feeling as "Atalanta in Calydon." The really enthusiastic admiration that he entertained for his model and his desire to communicate that admiration through his imitation imparted to the experiment a special interest which is piquantly revealed in his letters.

On July 25, 1857, he writes: "I am well in the middle of my *Merope,* and please myself pretty well, though between indolence and nervousness I am a bad worker.   What I learn in studying Sophocles for my present purpose is, or seems to me, wonderful, so far exceeding all that one would learn in years' reading of him without such a purpose.   And what a man!   What works!   I must read *Merope* to you.   I think and hope it will have what Buddha called the 'character of *Fixity,* that true sign of the Law.'"   When the reviews appeared early in the following year, he was a good deal disappointed: "Instead of reading it for what it is worth, everybody begins to consider whether it does not betray a design to substitute tragedies *à la Grecque* for every other kind of poetical composition in England, and falls into an attitude of violent resistance to such an imaginary design.   What I meant them was to see in it a specimen of the world created by the Greek imagination. This imagination was different from our own, and it is hard for us to appreciate, even to understand it; but it had a peculiar power, grandeur, and dignity, and these are worth trying to get an apprehension of. But the British public, prefer, like all obstinate multitudes, to 'die in their sins,' and I have no intention to keep preaching in the wilderness." On February 9, 1858, he writes to his sister: "I am anxious to explain to you that you are not the least bound to like her ["Merope"], as she is calculated rather to inaugurate my Professorship with dignity than to move deeply the present race of *humans*. No one is more sensible of this than I am, only I have such a real love for this form and this old Greek world that perhaps I infuse a little soul into my dealings with them which saves me from being entirely *ennuyeux,* professorial, and pedantic; still you will not find in *Merope* what you wish to find, and I excuse you beforehand for wishing to find something different, and being a little dissatisfied with me."

Later in the year came a letter from Froude begging Arnold to "discontinue the *Merope* line"; apropos of which Arnold avowed to his sister the terrible difficulty and strain which he experienced, under the pressure of his other occupations, in poetical productions of his best sort. The Greek tragedy is firmly designed and executed; but the gusto and freshness of the poet's voice have almost vanished. In the main it is the contrivance of an austere and intelligent artisanship without the warmth and vital rhythm of the authentic creative impulse. The English reader who desires a hint of the charm of Sophocles will find more of it in a good prose translation of the "Oedipus" than in many "Meropes." Yet for us who are studying the English poet's development it is worth while to pause for a moment over a specimen of his severest manner. Let us take the comment of the Chorus on—what shall we say?—Carlyle's theory of hero-worship, perhaps, or Bismarck's belief in the superiority of a benevolent autocracy, or, if we will, some more recent and more tragic political egotism, not yet fully chastened by the indignant gods:

THE CHORUS

Much is there which the sea
Conceals from man, who cannot plumb its depths.
Air to his unwing'd form denies a way,
And keeps its liquid solitudes unscaled.
Even earth, whereon he treads,
So feeble is his march, so slow,
Holds countless tracts untrod.

But more than all unplumb'd,
Unscaled, untrodden, is the heart of man.
More than all secrets hid, the way it keeps.
Nor any of our organs so obtuse,
Inaccurate, and frail,

As those wherewith we try to test
Feelings and motives there.

Yea, and not only have we not explored
That wide and various world, the heart of others,
But even our own heart, that narrow world
Bounded in our own breast, we hardly know,
Of our own actions dimly trace the causes.
Whether a natural obscureness, hiding
That region in perpetual cloud,
Or our own want of effort, be the bar.

Therefore—while acts are from their motives judged,
And to one act many most unlike motives,
This pure, that guilty, may have each impell'd—
Power fails us to try clearly if that cause
Assign'd us by the actor be the true one;
Power fails the man himself to fix distinctly
The cause which drew him to his deed,
And stamp himself, thereafter, bad or good.

The most are bad, wise men have said.
Let the best rule, they say again.
The best, then, to dominion hath the right.
Rights unconceded and denied,
Surely, if rights, may be by force asserted—
May be, nay should, if for the general weal.
The best, then, to the throne may carve his way,
And strike opposers down,
Free from all guilt of lawlessness,
Or selfish lust of personal power;
Bent only to serve virtue,
Bent to diminish wrong.
And truly, in this ill-ruled world,

Well sometimes may the good desire
To give to virtue her dominion due!
Well may he long to interrupt
The reign of folly, usurpation ever,
Though fenced by sanction of a thousand years!
Well thirst to drag the wrongful ruler down;
Well purpose to pen back
Into the narrow path of right
The ignorant, headlong multitude,
Who blindly follow, ever,
Blind leaders, to their bane!

But who can say, without a fear:
That best, who ought to rule, am I;
The mob, who ought to obey, are these,
I the one righteous, they the many bad?
Who, without check of conscience, can aver
That he to power makes way by arms,
Sheds blood, imprisons, banishes, attaints,
Commits all deeds the guilty oftenest do,
Without a single guilty thought,
Arm'd for right only, and the general good?

Therefore, with censure unallay'd
Therefore, with unexcepting ban,
Zeus and pure-thoughted Justice brand
Imperious self-asserting violence;
Sternly condemn the too bold man, who dares
Elect himself Heaven's destined arm;
And, knowing well man's inmost heart infirm,
However noble the committer be,
His grounds however specious shown,
Turn with averted eyes from deeds of blood.

This chorus admirably complements Arnold's two sonnets "To a Republican Friend," illuminates the basis of his qualified Liberalism, and the statement in one of his letters—"I should never myself vote for a Tory." To the writer of this present chapter the chorus seems far from *ennuyeux*. Though it is quite without the fluent melancholy and passion of "Tristram," the somber and splendid imagery of "Sohrab," or the studied grace and decoration of "Balder," its wisdom and gravity and starkness of expression give it a kind of sincere and naked beauty of another order—the beauty of important thought compactly and lucidly uttered. The "present race of humans" differs from Arnold and the Greeks most signally in this: that it ranks above beauty of thought every other poetical beauty, and is quite willing to dispense with thinking altogether, provided its emotions are sufficiently engaged. When it is asked to read poetry, it prefers to any amount of sheer intellectual edification the music and glamour of a piece like "The Forsaken Merman," which, with all its metrical seductions, throbs with a perpetually enchanting "human interest."

"The Forsaken Merman" appeared in Arnold's first volume, published in 1849. To read it immediately after the chorus from "Merope," published in 1858, should give one a sharp impression of the range of the poet's activities in his nine or ten fruitful years. Those who find no virtue in "Merope," and no validity in the ideas which the tragedy was designed to illustrate will of course seize the occasion to say that here is a melancholy illustration of the disaster in store for a poet who sets out on his progress attended by an inspector of schools, a professor and a critic.

THE FORSAKEN MERMAN

Come, dear children, let us away;
Down and away below!
Now my brothers call from the bay,
Now the great winds shoreward blow,
Now the salt tides seaward flow;
Now the wild white horses play,
Champ and chafe and toss in the spray.
Children dear, let us away!
This way, this way!

Call her once before you go,—
Call her once yet!
In a voice that she will know,—
"Margaret! Margaret!"
Children's voices should be dear
(Call once more) to a mother's ear;
Children's voices, wild with pain,—
Surely she will come again!
Call her once, and come away;
This way, this way!
"Mother dear, we cannot stay!

The wild white horses foam and fret."
Margaret! Margaret!

Come, dear children, come away down:
Call no more!
One last look at the white-walled town,
And the little grey church on the windy shore;
Then come down!
She will not come, though you call all day;
Come away, come away!

Children dear, was it yesterday
We heard the sweet bells over the bay,—
In the caverns where we lay,
Through the surf and through the swell,
The far-off sound of a silver bell?
Sand-strewn caverns, cool and deep,
Where the winds are all asleep;
Where the spent lights quiver and gleam,
Where the salt weed sways in the stream,
Where the sea-beasts, ranged all round,
Feed in the ooze of their pasture-ground;
Where the sea-snakes coil and twine,
Dry their mail and bask in the brine;
Where great whales come sailing by,
Sail and sail, with unshut eye,
Round the world for ever and aye?
When did music come this way?
Children dear, was it yesterday?

Children dear, was it yesterday
(Call yet once) that she went away?
Once she sate with you and me,
On a red gold throne in the heart of the sea,
And the youngest sate on her knee.

She comb'd its bright hair, and she tended it well,
When down swung the sound of a far-off bell.
She sigh'd, she look'd up through the clear green sea;
She said: "I must go, for my kinsfolk pray
In the little grey church on the shore to-day.
'Twill be Easter-time in the world—ah me!
And I lose my poor soul, Merman! here with thee."
I said: "Go up, dear heart, through the waves;
Say thy prayer, and come back to the kind sea-caves!"
She smiled, she went up through the surf in the bay.
Children dear, was it yesterday?

Children dear, were we long alone?
"The sea grows stormy, the little ones moan;
Long prayers," I said, "in the world they say;
Come!" I said; and we rose through the surf in the bay.
We went up the beach, by the sandy down
Where the sea-stocks bloom, to the white-wall'd town;
Through the narrow paved streets, where all was still,
To the little grey church on the windy hill.
From the church came a murmur of folk at their prayers,
But we stood without in the cold blowing airs.
We climb'd on the graves, on stones worn with rains,
And we gazed up the aisle through the small leaded
        panes.

She sate by the pillar; we saw her clear:
"Margaret, hist! come quick we are here!
Dear heart," I said, "we are all alone;
The sea grows stormy, the little ones moan."
But, ah, she gave me never a look,
For her eyes were seal'd to the holy book!
Loud prays the priest; shut stands the door.
Come away, children, call no more!
Come away, come down, call no more!

Down, down, down!
Down to the depths of the sea!
She sits at her wheel in the humming town,
Singing most joyfully.
Hark what she sings: "O joy, O joy,
For the humming street, and the child with its toy
For the priest, and the bell, and the holy well;
For the wheel where I spun,
And the blessed light of the sun!"
And so she sings her fill,
Singing most joyfully,
Till the spindle drops from her hand,
And the whizzing wheel stands still.
She steals to the window, and looks at the sand,
And over the sand at the sea;
And her eyes are set in a stare;
And anon there breaks a sigh,
And anon there drops a tear,
From a sorrow-clouded eye,
And a heart sorrow-laden,
A long, long sigh,
For the cold strange eyes of a little mermaiden,
And the gleam of her golden hair.

Come away, away, children;
Come, children, come down!
The hoarse wind blows colder;
Lights shine in the town.
She will start from her slumber
When gusts shake the door:
She will hear the winds howling,
Will hear the waves roar.
We shall see, while above us
The waves roar and whirl,

A ceiling of amber,
A pavement of pearl.
Singing: "Here came a mortal,
But faithless was she!
And alone dwell for ever
The kings of the sea."

But, children, at midnight,
When soft the winds blow,
When clear falls the moonlight,
When spring-tides are low;
When sweet airs come seaward
From heaths starr'd with broom,
And high rocks throw mildly
On the blanch'd sands a gloom;
Up the still, glistening beaches,
Up the creeks we will hie,
Over banks of bright seaweed
The ebb-tide leaves dry.
We will gaze, from the sand-hills,
At the white, sleeping town;
At the church on the hill-side—
And then come back down.
Singing: "There dwells a loved one,
But cruel is she!
She left lonely for ever
The kings of the sea."

CHAPTER IV

"I think the moment is, on the whole, favourable for the Essays; and in going through them I am struck by the admirable riches of human nature that are brought to light in the group of persons whom they treat, and the sort of unity that as a book to stimulate the better humanity in us the volume has."—*Letters*, I, 286-7.—January, 1865.

MUCH of what passes for literary criticism is a very perishable branch of literature. Most of Arnold's essays in this kind remain as sound, vital and interesting to-day as when they were written. By their virtue he probably exercises thirty years after his death a more constant and important influence upon current literary opinion and taste than any English critic living. The persistence of his critical force in literature is ascribable in the main to three causes. The first of these is clearly brought out in the passage of the letter quoted above: he did not attempt a chronicle of all the popular and transitory work issuing from the press; he carefully selected for comment men and books which he thought had some mark of immortality about them; he assembled, as he says, a group of

132

persons illustrating the "admirable riches of human nature." In the second place, he conveyed along with the firm and delicate delineations of his subjects an irresistibly stimulating sense of his own fine delight in them—that indispensable personal gusto of the interpreter which excites the envy of the reader, stimulates his curiosity, and makes him feel that, until he shares it, he is excluded from one of the exquisite pleasures of the world. The third and perhaps most distinctive cause of Arnold's durability is in the number and the soundness of the literary principles and the general ideas which he states and illustrates. Let us review in order: his more important general ideas; his critical method; and the principal subjects of his criticism.

The first question which we ask, in these days of world-wide war, regarding any one who ventures an opinion of European politics is whether he is "pro-Ally" or "pro-German." The waves of prejudice and passion set in motion by the great conflict wash every coast; and we find it difficult to conceive of any disinterested commentator. At the present moment it seems to some sensitive souls as if the statesmen of every nation, the poets, the historians, even the men of science, were all patriotically engaged in lying, at home and abroad, for their countries. The cynically philosophical tell us that the now inflamed and apparent mendacity of mankind is only a magnification of our normal and habitual disinclination and incapacity for telling the truth. What is truth but some definite person's impression formed at some definite point of view? "Name the person and the point of view," says the cynic, "and I shall know how to value his 'truth.'" Arnold, a seeker for truth, bows to the impressionists and acknowledges the tantalizing "relativity" of our knowledge in the preface to his first series of *Essays in Criticism*: "To try and approach truth on one side after another, not to strive or cry, nor to persist in pressing forward, on any one side, with violence and self-will,—it is only thus, it seems to me that mortals may hope to gain any vision of the mysterious Goddess, *whom we shall never see except in outline, but only thus even in outline.*" He, too, would agree that the value of "truth" depends upon the perceiver and the point of view.

To indicate Arnold's point of view is therefore fundamental to our consideration of his criticism. His culture had given him a strong sense of the *community* of the civilized world; in literary matters he was an avowed cosmopolitan. "Let us conceive," he says in his essay on Wordsworth, "of the whole group of civilized nations as being, for intellectual and spiritual purposes, one great confederation, bound to a joint action and working towards a common result; a confederation whose members have a due knowledge both of the past, out of which they all proceed, and of one another. This was the ideal of Goethe, and it is an ideal which will impose itself upon the thoughts of our modern societies more and more."[1] Taken together, these two passages sufficiently indicate Arnold's position: We can not attain absolute truth; but by taking civilized humanity as our center we can at least avoid the errors due to political, religious, national, or racial partisanship.

To *seek* the absolute truth, not in this world to behold it face to face, but to press steadily nearer to it, this, as he understands it, is the sovereign business of criticism. In his important essay, "The Function of Criticism at the Present Time," he enforces the idea in a series of memorable definitions. The first of these seems cold, dispassionate, disinterested, like the purest aspirations of the "scientific spirit": "It is the business of the critical power . . . to see the object as in itself it really is." Lest this offend the "relativists," he follows it up with the qualification that the critical power never quite completes its business: "It tends to establish an order of ideas, if not absolutely true, yet true by comparison with that which it displaces; to make the best ideas prevail. Presently these ideas reach society, the touch of truth is the touch of life, and there is a stir and growth everywhere; out of this stir and growth come the creative epochs of literature."

_____

[1] An earlier formulation of this idea occurs in "The Function of Criticism," *Essays in Criticism,* First Series, N. Y., 1903, p. 39.

Criticism's positive and fructifying element he emphasizes in a second definition of its function: "Its business is . . . simply to know the best that is known and thought in the world, and by in its turn making this known, to create a current of true and fresh ideas." To this, probably the most frequently quoted, formulation of its mission he adds a third: its "best spiritual work" is "to keep man from a self-satisfaction which is retarding and vulgarizing, to lead him towards perfection, by making his mind dwell upon what is excellent in itself, and the absolute beauty and fitness of things." By this time, one will observe, Arnold has passed far beyond the cold dispassionate curiosity "to see the object as in itself it really is." Criticism's supreme object is still truth; but criticism now glows with esthetic and moral passion, is responsible, interested, purposeful, devoted to the advancement of human welfare. Yet as Arnold understands the matter the third definition is, so to speak, an implication of the first— seek first the kingdom of truth, and all these other things shall be added unto you.

Abstractly considering, no sensible being can object to the operations of a force so benignant. It is only when the current of "true and fresh ideas" scatters the musty straw in which we have made our beds and disturbs the slumber of our old habits and our settled prejudices that we grow uneasy. Arnold, knowing that his readers will assent without reflec-

tion unless he a little offends their sensibilities,
names, with deliberately irritating iteration of the
charge, some of the most ancient and honored organs of British opinion as offenders against the new
critical spirit of which he is the spokesman: "What
is the bane of criticism in this country? It is that
practical considerations cling to it and stifle it. It
subserves interests not its own. Our organs of
criticism are organs of men and parties having practical ends to serve, and with them those practical
ends are the first thing and the play of mind the second; so much play of mind as is compatible with
the prosecution of those ends is all that is wanted.
. . . We have the *Edinburgh Review*, existing as
an organ of the old Whigs, and for as much play
of the mind as may suit its being that; we have the
Quarterly Review, existing as an organ of the
Tories, and for as much play of the mind as may
suit its being that; we have the *British Quarterly
Review*, existing as an organ of the political Dissenters, and for as much play of the mind as may
suit its being that; we have the *Times*, existing as
an organ of the common, satisfied, well-to-do Englishman, and for as much play of mind as may suit
its being that." These organs of partisan opinion
we shall no doubt always have with us; "but it would
be well, too, that there should be a criticism, not the
minister of these interests, not their enemy, but
absolutely and entirely independent of them."

Arnold develops this idea in his essay on "The Literary Influence of Academies." Precisely because his criticism is not cold and detached and absolutely disinterested but human and social and passionate, he is not contented with a mere *knowledge* of the best; he is bent upon making the best *prevail* in society, and he turns, inquiringly, to the Academy as an instrument for accomplishing this purpose— for making the best authoritative. The occasion for his illuminating discussion was offered by a new edition of Pellison and D'Olivet's history of the French Academy. Reading this work causes Arnold to reflect upon the absence of any such institution in England. "A thousand voices," he says, "will be ready to tell us that this absence is a signal mark of our national superiority; that it is in great part owing to this absence that the exhilarating words of Lord Macaulay, lately given to the world by his very clever nephew, Mr. Trevelyan, are so profoundly true: 'It may safely be said that the literature now extant in the English language is of far greater value than all the literature which three hundred years ago was extant in all the languages of the world together.'" "I daresay this is so;" continues Arnold with his characteristic insinuating irony, "only, remembering Spinoza's maxim that the two great banes of humanity are self-conceit and the laziness coming from self-conceit, I think it may do us good, instead of resting in our pre-eminence with perfect security, to look a little more closely why this is so, and whether it is so without any limitations."

The French Academy had its origin, Arnold reminds his readers, at about 1629 in a group of seven or eight persons in Paris who met at one another's houses to "discuss literary matters." Cardinal Richelieu, then the all-powerful minister, saw the possibility of developing this little society into a powerful institution for the elevation and standardization of literary taste in France; and in 1637 the Parliament gave it a corporate and official public character. Its statutes of foundation expressed its purpose as follows: "The Academy's principal function shall be to work with all the care and all the diligence possible at giving sure rules to our language, and rendering it pure, eloquent and capable of treating the arts and sciences." This, however, was not the full scope of Richelieu's intention, nor of the actual activities of the Academicians: "The new Academy, now enlarged to a body of forty members, and meant to contain all the chief literary men of France, was to be a *literary tribunal.* The works of its members were to be brought before it previous to publication, were to be criticised by it, and finally, if it saw fit, to be published with its declared approbation. The works of other writers, not members of the Academy, might also, at the request of these writers themselves, be passed under the Academy's review. Besides this, in essays and discussions the Academy examined and judged works already published, whether by living or dead authors, and literary matters in general."

Now, an effort to oppose the slovenliness and mediocrity in which the majority of men are sufficiently comfortable can never be a thoroughly popular movement. "An effort to set up a recognized authority, imposing on us a high standard in matters of intellect and taste, has," as Arnold truly says, "many enemies in human nature. We all of us like to go our own way, and not to be forced out of the atmosphere of commonplace habitual to most of us; —*'was uns alle bändigt'*, says Goethe, *'das Gemeine'*. . . . But if the effort to limit this freedom of our lower nature finds, as it does and must find, enemies in human nature, it finds also auxiliaries in it. Out of the four great parts, says Cicero, of the *honestum*, or good, which forms the matter on which *officium*, or human duty, finds employment, one is the fixing of a *modus* and an *ordo*, a measure and order, to fashion and wholesomely constrain our action, in order to lift it above the level it keeps if left to itself, and to bring it nearer to perfection. . . . Other creatures submissively follow the law of their nature; man alone has an impulse leading him to set up some other law to control the bent of his nature." The influence of an Academy is to fortify this special human impulse toward measure and order; it is to lift us out of the indolence of our natures by holding up ideas of excellence and of glory and golden opinions to be won by excellence alone.

The English people, undisciplined by Academic influences, are constantly in danger, Arnold intimates, of being pleased without just cause! " 'In France,' says M. Sainte-Beuve, 'the first consideration for us is not whether we are amused and pleased by a work of art or mind, nor is it whether we are touched by it. What we seek above all to learn is, whether *we were right* in being amused with it, and in applauding it, and in being moved by it.' Those are very remarkable words, and they are, I believe, in the main quite true. A Frenchman has to a considerable degree, what one may call a conscience in intellectual matters; he has an active belief that there is a right and a wrong in them, that he is bound to honour and obey the right, that he is disgraced by cleaving to the wrong. All the world has, or professes to have, this conscience in moral matters. The word *conscience* has become almost confined, in popular use, to the moral sphere, because this lively susceptibility of feeling is, in the moral sphere, so far more common than in the intellectual sphere. . . . Well, now we are on the road to see why the French have their Academy and we have nothing of the kind."

Continuing his sinuous attack upon English self-satisfaction, Arnold ascribes the "note of provinciality" in English literature to the same cause that was responsible for the English lack of a "conscience in intellectual matters." "In the bulk of the intellectual work of a nation which has no centre, no intellectual metropolis like an Academy, like M. Sainte-Beuve's 'sovereign organ of opinion,' like M. Renan's 'recognized authority in matters of tone and taste'—there is observable a *note of provinciality*. Now to get rid of provinciality is a certain stage of culture; a stage the positive result of which we must not make of too much importance, but which is, nevertheless, indispensable, for it brings us on to the platform where alone the best and highest intellectual work can be said fairly to begin. Work done after men have reached this platform is *classical;* and that is the only work which, in the long run, can stand. All the *scoriæ* in the work of men of great genius who have not lived on this platform are due to their not having lived on it. Genius raises them to it by moments, and the portions of their work which are immortal are done at these moments; but more of it would have been immortal if they had not reached this platform at moments only, if they had had the culture which makes men live there."

At the conclusion of a long discourse on the advantages of an Academy and the disadvantages of being without one, the reader may perhaps be a little surprised to find that Arnold does not advocate the establishment of an institution in England parallel to the French Academy; that, in fact, he dismisses the idea as foreign to the liberty-loving genius of the English. A people like the English, he feels, or, may we add, like the Americans, can not be bullied into the kingdom of Heaven—to say nothing of being regimented and legislated into a love of high excellence in matters of intellect and taste. The adroit and effective appeal to a people long accustomed to wilfulness and freedom must be made through the subtle passions of jealousy and envy. In dealing with a democratic society the reformer who discreetly touches these powerful springs of human action can work miracles with the Pied Piper of Hamlin. Arnold has this magical touch! What he has done in the essay on Academies is perhaps sufficient: by a skilful use of the comparative method he has made the possessions of the French people— their standard of high excellence, their conscience in intellectual matters, their freedom from provinciality—seem *enviable*. National jealousy, without an official organization of forty Immortals, can possibly be trusted, once thoroughly aroused, to give force to these ideas, even in a democracy.

That Arnold was in the broad sense of the word a classicist is manifest in his discourses on the critical and the academic ideals. In his inaugural address as Professor of Poetry at Oxford, "On the Modern Element in Literature,"[2] he declares himself

---

[2] *Essays in Criticism,* Third Series, Boston, 1910.

a classicist in a more restricted sense of the term. That is to say, when he compares the great literatures, ancient and modern, he reaches the conclusion that the literature of Greece is on the whole the soundest, the most admirable, the most worthy of emulation that has as yet been produced in the world. He desired no slavish imitation of Greek models. His attitude toward foreign influences is well indicated in a letter of January 21, 1865: "I hate all over-preponderance of single elements, and all my efforts are directed to enlarge and complete us by bringing in as much as possible of Greek, Latin, Celtic authors. More and more I see hopes of fruit by steadily working in this direction. To be too much with the Americans is like living with somebody who has all one's own bad habits and tendencies." In English literature he recognized peculiar virtues of energy and sincerity and imaginative splendor, but also peculiar vices and deficiencies of provincialism, whim, caprice, eccentricity, and verbal and emotional incontinence, notably exemplified by writers like Ruskin, Carlyle, Sterne, Swinburne, Shelley, and even, to some extent, by writers so near supremacy as Milton and Shakespeare. The special corrective for the inherent faults of the English temper, Arnold believed, was to be found in ever-renewed contacts with literatures showing a natural instinct, like that of the

Greeks, or an acquired taste, like that of the French, for form, order and measure.

It is a misfortune of English criticism that whenever one breathes a word of a "classical restoration," some one exclaims "Pope!"—and the public yawns. Pope is an admirable and delightful writer, who has been quoted and calumniated for more than a hundred years by romantic critics and schoolboys. Some day it will be thought an ill omen to speak disrespectfully of Pope. But Arnold did not come to restore Pope. For the pseudo-classicism of the Queen Anne period he had as little real liking as had the belligerent romanticists of the early nineteenth century. In Pope's poverty of feeling he saw the excesses of restraint just as in Keats's superabundance of it he saw the excesses of freedom. As a true classicist he wishes to mediate between them. The clearness, good sense, and continence which are the special excellences of the pseudo-classicist he wishes to preserve and unite with the passion and exaltation which are the peculiar glories of the romanticist. No poetry which falls short of such a union can be entirely "adequate"—can wholly satisfy our desire for an art which represents human life in its integrity. Has such a union been accomplished?

Yes, Arnold tells us, it was accomplished in Greece; and thither we must still turn for light and leading.   "Now, the peculiar characteristic of the highest literature—the poetry—of the fifth century in Greece before the Christian era, is its *adequacy;* the peculiar characteristic of the poetry of Sophocles is its consummate, its unrivalled *adequacy;* that it represents the highly developed human nature of that age—human nature developed in a number of directions, politically, socially, religiously, morally developed—in its completest and most harmonious development in all these directions; while there is shed over this poetry the charm of that noble serenity which always accompanies true insight.   If in the body of Athenians of that time there was, as we have said, the utmost energy of mature manhood, public and private; the most entire freedom, the most unprejudiced and intelligent observation of human affairs—in Sophocles there is the same energy, the same maturity, the same freedom, the same intelligent observation; but all these idealized and glorified by the grace and light shed over them from the noblest poetical feeling.   And therefore I have ventured to say of Sophocles, that he 'saw life steadily, and saw it whole.' "

If Sophocles "saw life steadily and saw it whole," why then he saw "the object as in itself it really is."   But this—seeing the object as in itself it really is—as Arnold tells us in another place is the function of *criticism.*   Are then the functions of poetry and criticism the same?   To the distress of some of his readers, Arnold would reply that, in great part, they are. One of his most discussed definitions or descriptions of poetry occurs in his essay on Wordsworth: "It is important, therefore, to hold fast to this: that poetry is at bottom a criticism of life; that the greatness of a poet lies in his powerful and beautiful application of ideas to life— to the question: How to live. Morals are often treated in a narrow and false fashion. . . . We find attraction, at times, even in a poetry of revolt against them. . . . Or we find attraction in a poetry indifferent to them. . . . We delude ourselves in either case; and the best cure for our delusion is to let our minds rest upon that great and inexhaustible word *life,* until we learn to enter into its meaning. A poetry of revolt against moral ideas is a poetry of revolt against *life;* a poetry of indifference to moral ideas is a poetry of indifference towards *life.*" We need inquire no further into Arnold's position with respect to the tiresome but still-mooted question of the relation of art to morals. Poetry, he holds, which represents human life adequately is by necessity, by the nature of human life, moral.

If we infer from this position that he thought the best poetry the best morality, we shall not be far from the track of his own reasoning. Indeed, we may go further and say that he thought the best poetry the best religion, also. In his essay on "The

Study of Poetry" he justifies this identification as follows: "The future of poetry is immense, because in poetry, where it is worthy of its high destinies, our race, as time goes on, will find an ever surer and surer stay. There is not a creed which is not shaken, not an accredited dogma which is not shown to be questionable, not a received tradition which does not threaten to dissolve. Our religion has materialized itself in the fact, in the supposed fact; it has attached its emotion to the fact, and now the fact is failing it. But for poetry the idea is everything; the rest is a world of illusion, of divine illusion. Poetry attaches its emotion to the idea; the idea *is* the fact. The strongest part of our religion to-day is its unconscious poetry. . . . More and more mankind will discover that we have to turn to poetry to interpret life for us, to console us, to sustain us. Without poetry, our science will appear incomplete; and most of what now passes with us for religion and philosophy will be replaced by poetry."

Arnold here makes great claims for poetry; but it is to be remembered that the only poetry which much interests him is great poetry. What constitutes poetical greatness, however, is a topic which he seldom discussed abstractly, and probably never discussed to the satisfaction of modern estheticians. We have seen clearly enough what he sought in the *substance* of poetry: "the application of ideas to

life," truth and high seriousness, the finer spirit of
science, morality, and religion. He sought also
in the *manner* of poetry—in its diction and movement—"the grand style." When critics asked him
what he meant by "the grand style," he gave, in his
lectures on translating Homer, what they must have
considered an evasive answer. To those who questioned him mockingly, he retorted mockingly, "Ye
shall die in your sins." To those who questioned him
earnestly he did not however declare directly what
"the grand style" is. He only pointed to a specimen
of it, and formulated the conditions under which
it appears: "I think it will be found that the grand
style arises in poetry, *when a noble nature, poetically
gifted, treats with simplicity or with severity a serious subject.* I think this definition will be found
to cover all instances of the grand style in poetry
which present themselves. I think it will be found
to exclude all poetry which is not in the grand style.
And I think it contains no terms which are obscure,
which themselves need defining. Even those who
do not understand what is meant by calling poetry
noble, will understand, I imagine, what is meant by
speaking of a noble nature in a man. But the noble
or powerful nature—the *bedeutendes individuum* of
Goethe—is not enough. For instance, Mr. Newman has zeal for learning, zeal for thinking, zeal
for liberty, and all these things are noble, they en-
noble a man; but he has not the poetical gift; there

must be the poetical gift, the 'divine faculty,' also. And, besides all this, the subject must be a serious one (for it is only by a kind of license that we can speak of the grand style in comedy); and it must be treated *with simplicity or severity*." Many years later he returned to the subject, in "The Study of Poetry," and emphasized the inseparability of style and substance: "So far as high poetic truth and seriousness are wanting to a poet's matter and substance, so far also, we may be sure, will a high poetic stamp of diction and movement be wanting to his style and manner." But after he had labored through a couple of pages in an effort to be abstract and theoretical he declared, with a touch of characteristic impatience over abstractions: "So stated, these are but dry generalities: their whole force lies in their application."

This brings us inevitably to a consideration of Arnold's special method in criticism. His type is not very easy to define, for it is a composite of three methods which we may designate in order of their appearance as: the judicial or classical method; the impressionistic or romantic method; and the historical or naturalistic method. Arnold's composition of all these methods into a method of his own may be explained more clearly if we first indicate a little more distinctly the character of each of them separately.

The judicial method was established by Aristotle,

who in his *Poetics* attempted to set forth the principles of sound poetical composition which he had derived from the practise of the great Greek poets. The enduring influence of the principles enunciated by Aristotle was at bottom due to their conformity in general with the principles of "right reason" and human psychology. His followers for many ages accepted the *Poetics* quite literally as the supreme authority. The primary object of their criticism was to bring a work of art into the Aristotelian court, and to judge it, and to rank it by literary law. The first question with all such critics is not, "Does the work please us?", but "Has it a right to please us?" Such, in the main, is the criticism of Horace, Scaliger, Vida, Ben Jonson, Rymer, Boileau, Pope, Addison, and, with some important qualifications, of Doctor Johnson, for whom, by the way, Arnold felt a very great respect.

The impressionistic method has no such illustrious origin nor descent nor continuity of development. Historians of literature may, if they please, trace it to Longinus; but for England, at any rate, it originated in the eighteenth century. It originated in a growing interest and satisfaction in the Middle Ages, the romantic tradition, the works of Spenser and Shakespeare, which, in many important respects, were quite indefensible before a literal interpretation of the Aristotelian law. It originated in a protest against "criticism by rules." It rose in response to a demand for some one who would dare to be pleased without giving a reason why. The excellence of an impressionistic critic is not in his judgment but in his sensibility. His business with a work of art is to feel keenly its charm, to describe accurately the impression that it has made upon him, and so to transmit his pleasure to the reader. He speaks little or nothing of rules but much of *taste*. "Mrs. M.'s conversation," says Hazlitt—one of the keenest of the impressionists, "is as fine cut as her features, and I like to sit in the room with that sort of coronet face. What she said leaves a flavor, like fine green tea. H—t's is like champagne, and N—'s like anchovy sandwiches." Of Lamb, a rival in the use of the impressionistic method, Hazlitt exclaims: "But with what a gusto would he describe his favorite authors, Donne, or Sir Philip Sidney, and call their most crabbed passages *delicious!* He tried them on his palate as epicures taste olives, and his observations had a *smack* in them, like a roughness on the tongue." There is impressionism piquantly described and exemplified by a master. Lamb, Hazlitt and Hunt constitute the most winsome group of English impressionists; Swinburne and Pater are others. They appeal to no authority outside themselves; they are ambassadors plenipotentiary from the poet to the reader; such power and persuasion as they exercise are dependent upon their individual personality, style, and gusto.

The historical method, not fully developed till the nineteenth century, got fairly under way in eighteenth-century England, and in a rather curious relation with impressionism. To put the matter simply, early practitioners, like Joseph and Thomas Warton, beginning with a lively relish for work in the romantic tradition, dignified their inclinations and satisfied their curiosity by exploring and bringing to light the English and Continental origins of romance. In other words, they gave to their scholarship the task of explaining and, to that extent, of justifying their taste. This ulterior purpose becomes, however, in typical modern historical criticism, negligible. Its supreme object is not to judge a work of art and fix its absolute value, like the criticism by rule and reason; nor to relish it and communicate its pleasure, like the impressionistic criticism; but to understand and explain it. In this sense, to understand and explain it is to note at what time and under what circumstances it originated, what personal and "environmental" forces "produced" it, its relation to the author and his other works, the author's relation to his contemporaries and predecessors, the influence of nation, race, etc.—in short, to set forth its "evolution." To a man like Taine, who was perhaps the most brilliant exponent of the historical method in its rigor and vigor, this seems the *only* serious form of criticism. Other methods were the methods of pedants or dilettantes; this alone was "scientific." The Frenchmen whom Arnold most admired—Sainte-Beuve, Renan, and Scherer—all utilized it impressively, though not exclusively, and always with a more sensitive tact than Taine exhibited.

Now if the question is asked whether Arnold's criticism is judicial, the answer must indubitably be in the affirmative. The discrimination of values is the final object of all his work; and no critic judges more steadily and vigorously and severely than he. This indeed, is one of his shining distinctions: that his discussion of a principle or a poem or a man always comes to a point, always terminates in a decision, usually pronounced with a tone of finality and authority which insures its making a lasting impression even upon those who do not accept it. What makes his decisions generally so weighty is one's consciousness that he seldom speaks, as the impressionist often does, out of a whim or a crochet or a mere personal inclination. His sovereign assurance is not due to arrogant self-confidence. It is due rather to confidence in an authority higher than himself, of which he has made himself the representative and interpreter. He speaks with emphasis and certitude because he speaks for the classical spirit and the classical tradition. He is not a pedantic follower of the letter of the law; yet, whenever he can, he will cite Aristotle and the Greeks, even, as in the case of "Empedocles," against himself—the finest proof of judicial integrity. He checks his instinctive estimate, furthermore, by constantly comparing the work in hand with the undisputed master works of similar kind in various tongues. Finally, he looks for authority outside himself in concurrent opinions of other qualified judges. The way to test the goodness of a translation of Homer, he says, is to ask how it affects scholars "who possess, at the same time with knowledge of Greek, adequate poetical taste and feeling." He will hesitate to hold an opinion alone in the great "intellectual federation" of modern nations, for it may be only an English opinion; it may even be only an Arnoldian opinion. But if he finds that Goethe and Sainte-Beuve are on his side, he is strongly disposed to believe that right is there, too.

Deference to the reasons underlying classical rules; constant reference to the body of classical literature, ancient and modern; habitual recourse to the opinions of the most eminent modern critics:—these are the features of Arnold's criticism which give it centrality, weight, and authority. They add immensely to his personal force. But what of the personal force itself? Tradition and society are admirable disciplinarians, are powerful allies, of individual talent; but they are not a substitute for it.

In the work of criticism, as Arnold would be the first to declare, the value of sound principles and great examples "lies in their application." To what extent does his own treatment of books and authors depend upon the element of "divine grace"—palate, taste, an immediate personal relish for the excellencies that are set before him? Richard Garnett asserts, in the *Dictionary of National Biography,* that the literary organ, so notably present in Lamb and Hazlitt, is in Arnold inadequately developed: "His great defect as a critic is the absence of a lively æsthetic sense; the more exquisite beauties of literature do not greatly impress him unless as vehicles for the communication of ideas." We may freely admit that he cared little for form without substance; but, on the other hand, he cared little for substance without form! The charge that he lacked a "lively æsthetic sense" will not stand examination.

One of the constant marks of the critic of taste is the citation of passages. Lamb and Hazlitt, for example, are great quoters; they are always placing before you specimens of the "beauties" which they have come upon in their explorations, to which they affix their personal certificates of high excellence. This is the warrant of their good faith—the token that the report of their esthetic ecstasies was not mere windy vaporing. Adducing an exquisite fragment, "Here," they say in effect, "is precisely what moved us; try it for yourself!" Does Arnold commit himself in this fashion—does he offer to his readers the concrete material by which they may verify for themselves the quality of his taste? Unquestionably he does. Take, for example, in the essay on "The Influence of Academies," his discussion of the "classical" and the "provincial" in the form and in the substance of prose. There is a bit out of Jeremy Taylor to show exactly what he means by the provincial in form; a bit out of Bossuet to show exactly what he means by the classical in form; a bit out of Addison to show exactly what he means by provincial commonplace in ideas; and a bit of Joubert to show exactly what he means by classical elevation and distinction in ideas.

Nothing, indeed, more clearly vouches for the liveliness of Arnold's taste and his reliance upon it than his often avowed preference of concrete illustration to definition. In "The Function of Criticism" he tells us that it is not as an abstract lawgiver that the critic "will generally do most good to his readers;" even on the occasions when an enunciation and detailed application of principles are necessary, "the safeguard is never to let oneself become abstract, always to retain an intimate and lively consciousness of the truth of what one is saying, and, the moment this fails us, to be sure that something is wrong." Take, for example, in his essay on "The Study of Poetry," his discussion of "the characters of a high quality of poetry." "There can be no more useful help," he says, "for discovering what poetry belongs to the class of the truly excellent, and can therefore do us most good, than to have always in one's mind lines and expressions of the great masters, and to apply them as a touchstone to other poetry. Of course we are not to require this other poetry to resemble them; it may be very dissimilar. But if we have any tact we shall find them, when we have lodged them well in our minds, an infallible touchstone for detecting the presence or absence of high poetic quality, and also the degree of this quality, in all other poetry which we may place beside them." To show precisely what kind of poetry he himself employs as a touchstone, he presents three lines of Homer, half a dozen from Dante, as many from Shakespeare, and three various bits from Milton. "These few lines, if we have tact and can use them, are enough even of themselves to keep clear and sound our judgments about poetry, to save us from fallacious estimates of it, to conduct us to a real estimate." Here are classical authority and personal taste met together. The "touchstones" will "save" us—yes, "if we have tact and can use them!" But taste must function in choosing them, and taste must keep on functioning in using them; there is no automatic mode of registering the reaction to them of inferior work.

It is primarily as a critic of taste, throughout this

very fascinating essay on "The Study of Poetry,"
that Arnold takes up the *Chanson de Roland,* Chré-
tien de Troyes, Chaucer, Villon, Dryden, Pope,
Burns; and, with a sample of poetic ore from each
lying on the table before us, applies his touchstones
for high beauty, worth and power.   It is as a critic
of taste that he appears in his lectures "On Translating Homer"; for the value of the discussion depends from point to point upon the drawing and
concrete illustration of fine distinctions of personal
feeling in the mysterious matter of style.   It is as
a critic of taste that he ventures among pundits in
his essay "On Celtic Literature," in which his problem is not so much to assay for the "grand style"
as to recognize, isolate and describe that perilously
elusive and intangible element, the Celtic spirit.
That surely was not a task to be performed by rule,
for there were no rules; it was a task to be performed by "divine grace."   And so we might multiply illustrations; for, much as he emphasizes the
importance of fresh information, there is hardly
one of the *Essays in Criticism* in which the conclusion is reached by an effort of intellect and knowledge, unassisted by esthetic sensibility.   In most of
them, the really decisive part is played by personal
taste, functioning, to be sure, under classical discipline.

His treatment of Wordsworth is typical of his
procedure.   He has the whole body of the poet's

work before him. He picks up one piece of it after another, inquiring whether it exhibits the special power and virtue of its author. He rejects three-fourths of it as below the level of high excellence which Wordsworth attained at his best. He rejects the portions of it in which Wordsworth introduces his metaphysical system; in which he flatly moralizes; in which he "proses" about the future of science. He preserves the portion of it that has been rendered crystalline and radiant by the poet's special faculty, which, according to his custom, he compactly defines: "Wordsworth's poetry is great because of the extraordinary power with which Wordsworth feels the joy offered to us in nature, the joy offered to us in the simple primary affections and duties; and because of the extraordinary power with which, in case after case, he shows us this joy, and renders it so as to make us share it." The definition of Wordsworth's power is a task of thought and reflection; but the selection of the passages in which the power is exhibited is the task of taste.

We come now to the question of Arnold's relation to the type of criticism which concerns itself primarily with understanding and explaining the genesis and evolution of a great work of art. To what extent does he resort to the historical method? We may say in general that such historical elucidation as appears in his literary essays is quite subordinate to other ends. The suggestively sympa-

thetic essay on Thomas Gray is exceptional; it is
perhaps primarily an attempt to "explain" Gray's
sterility with reference to his age.   In the "Hein-
rich Heine," also, there is an extended effort to
show the poet's connection with the main current
of European ideas and his reaction against German
Philistinism; but the essay terminates with the
characteristic verdict: "A half-result, for want of
moral balance, and of nobleness of soul and character"—a judgment in which historical explication
is not concerned.   In the essay on Byron we find
two or three pages occupied with an account of the
British Philistinism of the early nineteenth century,
against which Byron reacted; the final object of the
discussion, however, is not to "explain" his work
and career, but to define his special qualities and to
assign him his rank among modern poets.   In the
"Milton" the reference of the "dead wood" in *Para-
dise Lost* to contemporary theology and the *Zeit-
geist* is quite incidental to the chief purpose of the
discourse, which is to declare that, for English readers, Milton's poetry has an absolute value as its
supreme illustration of the grand style, as the best
modern equivalent to the manner of the ancient
classics.   For the relatively slight use which Arnold
made of the historical method, the really distinctive
critical method of his time, we may offer two very
different explanations.

It may be said first that, though he was a man of

deep and varied culture, he had not the minute and exhaustive erudition which is—theoretically, at least —required for the successful use of the historical method. He was not even one of the old-fashioned "giant readers"—like Coleridge or James Russell Lowell. For omnivorous "browsing," he had neither leisure nor inclination. In his early manhood he began quite deliberately to restrict his excursions, to live with the world's classics, to confine himself more and more strictly to the reading of works which are permanently important and of intrinsic interest and merit. A critic whose culture has taken this course must tread warily among our modern historical investigators or run the risk of being tripped up by annotators without a hundredth part of his learning or judgment. Any student of the Elizabethan drama, for example, will undertake to revise and *improve* the "roll of our chief poetical names, besides Shakespeare and Milton, from the age of Elizabeth downwards," which Arnold gives in his essay on Wordsworth: "Spenser, Dryden, Pope, Gray, Goldsmith, Cowper, Burns, Coleridge, Scott, Campbell, Moore, Byron, Shelley, Keats [and Wordsworth]." What, one exclaims, Tom Moore a greater poetical glory than Jonson, Campbell a greater poetical glory than Marlowe, Goldsmith a greater poetical glory than Webster, Cowper or Scott a greater poetical glory than Beaumont and Fletcher! Arnold speaks elsewhere to be sure, of the Elizabethan as a great poetical age, but this roll of honor, with its amazing predominance of men whose works fall after 1750, is pretty conclusive evidence that he was not intimately acquainted with it. One is almost tempted to suggest that, in "getting up" the period, he selected Spenser and Shakespeare as its best representatives, and let the rest go. So, too, when generalizing about eighteenth-century poetry, he declares that the heroic couplet was the inevitable vehicle for a large work, one feels that he has his eye on Pope; but one has grave doubts whether he has really envisaged at all the simply innumerable long pieces in blank verse and Spenserian stanza which that age produced. Lapses like these a critic can never be sure of avoiding, who has not explored an immense wilderness of forgotten, obscure, and, from a strictly esthetic point of view, almost worthless and entirely negligible literature. The work of taste and judgment will never rest in complete security unless it rests upon the work of a thorough historical investigation. Of Arnold's lapses we may say, as he said of Johnson's *Lives,* "Such is the common course and law of progress; one thing is done at a time, and other things are sacrificed to it. We must be thankful for the thing done, if it is valuable, and we must put up with the temporary sacrifice of other things to this one. The other things will have their turn sooner or later."

The second and chief reason why Arnold does not

much employ the historical method is that he is not
primarily interested in its results.   It is when he
touches upon medieval literature that he most distinctly sets his own work off from the work of the
historical scholar.   "Yet it is now all gone," he says
in "The Study of Poetry," "this French romance
poetry, of which the weight of substance and the
power of style are not inadequately represented by
this extract from Christian of Troyes.   Only by
means of the historical estimate can we persuade
ourselves now to think that any of it is of historical
importance."   This sweeping condemnation would
impress one as more authoritative, more likely to
be final, if one felt sure that Arnold possessed,
along with his poetical taste and judgment, the
medieval eruditeness of Gaston Paris or Professor
Bédier.   If he had been on intimate terms with
French romantic poetry, no doubt he would have
found something in it which deserved to be saved
for the "high seriousness" of its matter and its manner.   His statement is over-emphatic; yet it is sufficiently illustrative.   If a modern defender of the
Middle Ages, however learned, asserted the "poetical
importance of Christian of Troyes," Arnold would
feel qualified and called upon to dispute the point.
If, on the other hand, the medieval champion took
his stand, not upon the intrinsic worth of things like
the *Chanson de Roland,* the *Ivain, Gawain and the
Green Knight,* or the *Romance of the Rose,* but

upon the importance of these works in the evolution
of poetry and the history of culture, Arnold would
not offer combat. He would say: "We have no
quarrel. To you, who are studious of the origins
and evolutions and relations of literary species,
third and fourth rate poetry, may be just as significant as the best. To me, who am studious only
of literary works which subsist absolutely—without
reference to the time or place of their production,
third and fourth rate poetry of a bygone age hardly
exists. Let us go our separate ways: you, the way
of the historian, the naturalist, the man of science,
if you please; I, the way of the literary critic."

In more than one place, however, Arnold inserts
a caution against imagining that historical explication can do the work of esthetic and moral criticism.
The caution was timely, because leading exponents
of the newly perfected "historical method" were en-
deavoring to destroy the credit of both the "classical
method" and the "impressionistic method." From
this attack the worst sufferers were probably these
who judged by taste or "divine grace." To men of
letters who were fascinated by the methods and aims
of modern science the discussion of one's likings and
dislikings in the field of literature seemed a trifling
and somewhat contemptible effusion of personal
feeling. Even Arnold's friend Scherer took his
stand against it. In "A French Critic on Milton,"
Arnold explains Scherer's belief in the "historical

method," and then pretty definitely expresses his own belief that without taste the historical method is as sounding brass and tinkling cymbal:

"He [Scherer] sees very clearly how vain is Lord Macaulay's sheer laudation of Milton, or Voltaire's sheer disparagement of him. Such judgments, M. Scherer truly says, are not judgments at all. They merely express a personal sensation of like or dislike. And M. Scherer goes on to recommend, in the place of such 'personal sensations,' the method of historical criticism—that great and famous power in the present day. He sings the praises of 'this method at once more conclusive and equitable, which sets itself to understand things rather than to class them, to explain rather than to judge them; which seeks to account for a work from the genius of its author, and for the turn which this genius has taken from the circumstances amidst which it was developed;'—the old story of 'the man and the *milieu*,' in short. 'For thus,' M. Scherer continues, 'out of these two things the analysis of the writer's character and the study of his age, there spontaneously issues the right understanding of his work. In place of an appreciation thrown off by some chance comer, we have the work passing judgment, so to speak, upon itself, and assuming the rank which belongs to it among the productions of the human mind.'

"The advice to study the character of an author and the circumstances in which he has lived, in order to account to oneself for his work is excellent. But it is a perilous doctrine, that from such a study the right understanding of his work will 'spontaneously issue.' In a mind qualified in a certain manner it will—not in all minds. It cannot be said that Macaulay had not studied the character of Milton, and the history of the times in which he lived. But a right understanding of Milton did not 'spontaneously issue' therefrom in the mind of Macaulay, because Macaulay's mind was that of a rhetorician, not of a disinterested critic. Let us not confound the method with the result intended by the method. The critic who rightly appreciates a great man or a great work, and who can tell us faithfully—life being short, and art long, and false information very plentiful—what we may expect from their study and what they can do for us: he is the critic we want, by whatever methods, intuitive or historical, he may have managed to get his knowledge."

We have now considered the measure of Arnold's participation in the judicial, the impressionistic, and the historical methods of criticism. We have seen that his own method is marked by the constant functioning of his personal taste, constantly disciplined by standards and authorities outside himself, and assisted, in a subordinate degree, by the processes of historical elucidation. We do not, however, touch upon the really distinguishing characteristic of his criticism while we are speaking of his method. We touch upon his distinguishing characteristic when we speak of his object. We have noticed earlier in the chapter several of his own statements of the "function of criticism." Bringing them and their implications all together, we may say that Arnold's object in criticism is: to make us know the best, to make us love it, and to make us practise it. As he advanced in years his distaste increased to impatience with knowledge which is not amiable, with amiability which is unintelligent, and with both knowledge and amiability which lead to nothing. He desired ever more earnestly to get people to honor his truths by using them; he drove ever more steadily at the incorporation of ideas in character and at their expression in the conduct of life. He wanted to see something more of the grand style in the manner and something more of truth and seriousness in the substance of the men of his time. This is what he might have called the "keynote" of his criticism.

If we keep this keynote in mind, we shall understand the choice of most of his subjects. In the opening paragraph of his essay "On the Modern Element in Literature" he quotes a saying of Buddha to one of his disciples: "Go then, O Pourna, having been delivered, deliver; having been consoled, console; being arrived at the farther bank, enable others to arrive there also." Arnold applies the utterance to the "intellectual deliverance" which a man achieves who attains a central position in the mundane spectacle, and "sees life steadily, and sees it whole." In this particular essay he is commending the literature of the Greeks as a means to such intellectual deliverance; but, as we have seen, he does not declare that the *only* "means of grace." A man is on the road to salvation when he loves the best, devotes himself wholly to the pursuit of it, and for its sake is indifferent to the second-rate, the mediocre, the unsound. To be freed from all the thousand seductions and distractions of inferior interests—*was uns alle bändigt, das Gemeine,* to quote Arnold's favorite phrase from Goethe—that is indeed, an intellectual deliverance. All facts are interesting—this he concedes to the omnivorous scientific curiosity of the age; but some are so much more interesting, more valuable, more "edifying" than others! If we had the leisure of a Methuselah we should perhaps have appetite for them all. But we have not; and if we are unwilling to pass through the brief span of life in a state of bewilderment and dizziness at the whirl and variety and glitter of the show, we must reject its indiscriminated multiplicity, we must make our own choices. There is enough of high and permanent excellence to engage us. Why accept anything else? Pronouncing his last word on Goethe, whom he considered the wisest of modern men, Arnold says: "There rises to mind this sentence: '*Die Gestalt dieser Welt vergeht; und ich möchte mich nur mit dem beschäftigen, was bleibende Verhältnisse sind.*' 'The fashion of this world passeth away; and I would fain occupy myself only with the abiding.'   There is the true Goethe, and with that Goethe we would end."

Now it is Arnold's devotion to "the abiding" that makes his volumes of literary criticism a kind of center and refuge and stronghold for—let us not say, the professed student; let us say, for the general reader, for the man of affairs, for any man who, conscious of the breadth and brevity of life, wishes a guide to the highlands and mountain tops of literature—wishes death, when it overtakes him, to find him in good company, and noble occupation. And what an admirable center for such excursions these volumes constitute!   There are not many of them.   The two volumes of the *Essays in Criticism* which Arnold himself collected should be on every "five-foot shelf."   If to these we add the volume containing "On the Study of Celtic Literature" and "On Translating Homer;" the "Emerson" in *Discourses in America;* half a dozen of the *Mixed Essays;* and the "third series" of *Essays in Criticism* collected in 1910 by Mr. Edward J. O'Brien, we shall have the substance of his work in this kind.[3] Let us consider rather more closely some of the ways in which it offers us help.

Remembering his strong sense of the community

[3] It must be admitted that his Biblical criticism might fairly be included in this kind; and the inclusion of it here would perhaps profitably emphasize his essentially "literary" approach to the Bible.   To give importance to the religious department of his thought rather than to mark a division of literary kinds, I have treated it in a later chapter.

of mankind, his literary cosmopolitanism, his
avowed hatred of "over-preponderance of single
elements," one notices first perhaps how many paths,
radiating how widely into the literature of the
world, converge in these books. Toward the Greeks
one is directed by "On the Modern Element in Literature," "On Translating Homer," the preface to
the poems of 1853, "Pagan and Mediæval Religious
Sentiment," "A Speech at Eton," and by innumerable incidental references. Toward the Romans one
is directed by "Marcus Aurelius" and by reiterated
incidental references to Virgil. Toward the Persians, by "A Persian Passion Play"—probably more
persuasively, by "Sohrab and Rustum." Toward
the Celts, by "On the Study of Celtic Literature."
Toward the Italians, by "Dante and Beatrice" and
—certainly far more persuasively in this case—by
incidental praise and illustration of Dante's "grand
style" in its "simplicity" and in its "severity." Toward, let us say, the wandering Jew, by "Spinoza
and the Bible." Toward the Germans, by "Hein-
rich Heine," "A French Critic on Goethe," and by
continual reference to Goethe. Toward the French
by "Maurice de Guérin," "Eugénie de Guérin,"
"Joubert," "Amiel," "Obermann," "George Sand,"
Scherer on Milton and on Goethe, "Renan," "Sainte-
Beuve," and by almost ubiquitous reference. Toward the Russians, by "Tolstoi." Toward the
Americans, by "Emerson." Toward the English, by

"The Study of Poetry," "Milton," "Johnson's Lives," "Thomas Gray," "John Keats," "Wordsworth," "Byron," "Shelley." We should have prized a formal deliverance on Shakespeare:—yet here is a goodly company—all distinguished, though not all equally important—of poets, philosophers, novelists and critics, assembled from the four quarters of the earth with the deliberate purpose of suggesting to the reader that, if he wishes to know the best that has been said and thought in the world, he should not settle indolently down with the writers of his own day and nation.

Disparagers of Arnold's criticism not infrequently complain that, though he goes far and wide for subjects, he is monotonous in his discoveries, because he is interested only in "moral ideas" of fatiguing "high seriousness." The field of "moral ideas," if one really understands the words, is not such a narrow field, nor such a dull field, as some of the younger critics would have us believe. But that Arnold was exclusively interested in it is an error so serious as to warrant some pains in its removal. Four volumes or forty of "literary criticism" are of little more help to the student of literature than so many volumes of sermons, if they stimulate only his moral centers, if they do not quicken his *literary* sensibility.

Any one who reads Arnold thoughtfully and thoroughly without feeling an immense quickening of his literary sensibility has, in all probability, no literary sensibility to quicken. The quickening force of the esthetic interest is present to a greater or less degree in everything that Arnold wrote. But it is present with conspicuous and irresistible power in one of the works, which by its title is perhaps a little forbidding to the unprofessional reader—the lectures "On Translating Homer." Readers whom the title deters with the apprehension of something very professional, technical, and pedantic should be assured that, though they may be so unfortunate as to feel no special interest in Homer and absolutely none in translating him, they are likely to find these lectures one of the most instructively delightful of Arnold's works. Occasioned by two recent English translations of the Greek poet, they afford to the relics of savagery in most of us a continuous illicit pleasure in the skilful pitiless flaying of Mr. Francis Newman, the worst of the translators. This performance, it will be acknowledged, exhilarates by no *moral* appeal—except, perhaps to a sense that Mr. Newman deserved what was administered to him.

The destruction of Mr. Wright and Mr. Newman, however, is quite incidental to the main purposes, which are to establish the stylistic qualities of Homer, and, further than that, to establish the idea of the "grand style." Now in establishing his idea of the grand style by his "touchstone" method Arnold sharply challenges us, in the course of a hundred and fifty vivacious pages, to feel, mark, and compare with him the stylistic qualities in specific lines from: Homer, Newman, Cowper, Pope, Chapman, the romance of Richard Coeur de Leon, Milton, the Popular Ballads, Shakespeare, the Bible, Doctor Maginn, Scott, Virgil, Dante, Spenser, Tennyson, Horace, Hawtrey, Spedding, Wordsworth and Macaulay. If you compare all these passages as you are directed to compare them, if you make an earnest effort to perceive the stylistic distinctions which Arnold tells you are there, you will find the process highly exciting to your esthetic sensibility; you will undergo an esthetic discipline which you will never forget, and which will leave you with a sense of augmented power in these matters. That you can not always agree with your guide nor feel what he feels is of comparatively little moment. That he has induced in you a sustained effort of feeling and discrimination—there is the precious virtue of his discipline. In this connection one can not resist borrowing from Arnold, Joubert's exquisite appreciation of a Greek disciplinarian of the mind who achieved by similar methods similar results: "Plato shows us nothing, but he brings brightness with him; he puts light into our eyes, and fills us with a clearness by which all objects afterwards become illuminated. He teaches us nothing; but he prepares us, fashions us, and makes us ready to know all. Somehow or other, the habit of reading him augments in us the capacity for discerning and entertaining whatever fine truths may afterwards present themselves. Like mountain-air, it sharpens our organs, and gives us an appetite for wholesome food."

It is pretty generally agreed that Arnold's discourses on Celtic literature are not so sound as his lectures on Homer. He had little or no acquaintance with Celtic works in the original languages; and his determination of national and racial characteristics is rather a matter of divination than of science. His method of detecting the presence of "Celtic Magic" in English poetry is itself a magical method, reminding one of the method of New England wellfinders with their hazel dipping-sticks. Professor Saintsbury, the erudite and animated historian of criticism, remarks severely: "With bricks of ignorance and mortar of assumption you can build no critical house." This is taking Arnold's effort just a bit too seriously. He himself openly avows his superficial acquaintance with the monuments of Celtic culture, and frequently reminds his readers that his opinions are conjectural and speculative. He writes as an "essayist" in the older sense of the word; does what he can to convey the impression that he is on a holiday-excursion into a comparatively unmapped and little traveled land. He has seen many delightful things, he has formed many traveler's impressions; and he reports these sights and these impressions to enlist the interest of the general public and to stimulate scholarly investigation. Both these purposes his treatment of the subject was admirably calculated to serve. It related what was then a neglected and extremely obscure channel of European life to the central political, religious, social and literary interests of the day; and it thus engaged the attention of thousands of cultivated people who had thitherto no notion that the literature of the ancient Celts had any bearing on their concerns. Full of striking generalizations, it made conspicuous, if it did not settle, innumerable fascinating linguistic, literary and ethnological problems; and it thus stimulated many young scholars to enter a field where the harvest was ripe and the reapers few. It helped to prepare the way, on the one hand, for the Anglo-Celtic Renaissance engineered by Mr. Yeats, and, on the other hand, for the foundation of schools of Irish learning and chairs of Celtic in the universities. With results like these, a critic who desires that what he writes may "lead to something" may feel reasonably well satisfied.

We have given what Arnold would have called an "historical estimate" of the importance of his rather light-hearted excursion among the Celts. If the essay has accomplished its immediate purpose, what value has it now? If there are to-day more experienced guides to the literature of the Celts, if interest in it is widely diffused, why should we turn any longer to this "popular" and "pioneer" discussion? One might give many reasons: the charm of its style, its incidental appreciations, its critical digressions, the fact that many of its guesses are as good as any one's guesses, its suggestive comparison of national traits and tendencies, its reprehension of national pride and arrogance, its various persuasions to the study of perfection. The chief reason, however, for still turning to the essay is suggested by its "historical" influence: it was and it is still a vigorous stimulus to *intellectual curiosity*. This virtue abides in it and distinguishes it just as the virtue of a stimulus to *esthetic sensibility* abides in and distinguishes the lectures on Homer. Intellectual curiosity was one of the "stops" which Arnold desired to pull out "in that powerful but at present somewhat narrow-minded organ, the modern Englishman." That he did not consider intellectual curiosity the supreme mark of a wise man is revealed in his criticism of Sainte-Beuve; but that he considered it the beginning of wisdom it is the effort of this essay to make manifest. His dealing with the Celts, unscientific as it may be in its method and results, is his most extended tribute in the field of literary criticism to the catholicism and the multiform energy of the scientific spirit. The bane of the modern English, he would say, and the bane of us all, we may add, is our lethargic disdain for what we do not understand, is our indolence and dulness in the presence of "alien" things and thoughts— like philology, ethnology, and the Irish! Taking Celtic literature, the most "alien" matter at hand, he makes his own brilliant intelligence play through it and all around it, illuminating it and its relationships, making it at least momentarily important, and thus initiating the reader into the function of curiosity. The reader who follows him will be invited in the end to make all sorts of moral and esthetic and social applications of what he has seen; but the primary invitation is to open the eyes of the mind on unfamiliar fields, to enliven ourselves by variegating our interests, to enlarge our sympathies by widening our knowledge.

The discourses on Homer and the Celts are not the most frequently applauded portions of Arnold's literary criticism. We have lingered over them here because so many persons who have written about Arnold have not lingered over them, but, fixing attention rather exclusively upon portions of his work in which moral stimulus is the predominant impulse, have not exhibited his critical effort "whole"—have failed properly to emphasize its essential, its characteristic, many-sidedness. Having now indicated extensive studies in which the esthetic stimulus and the intellectual stimulus are the predominant impulses, we may cordially recognize the grave and appealing beauty of his "spiritual portraits"—the two "Guérins," "Joubert," "Heine," "Spinoza," "Marcus Aurelius," "Obermann," "Amiel," "George Sand." In the presence of these portraits one rightly feels that one is becoming intimate with Arnold; for, here is a curious fact, every one of them is in a sense a "partial portrait" of him. It is not that he interposes himself between the observer and the canvas, blurring the delineation, so to speak, with personal comment. On the contrary his method is apparently self-repressive; he tends to confine comment to the task of connecting and elucidating passages in which the subject of study speaks for himself. The self-repression is, however, only apparent. Arnold is present, and is peculiarly revealed, in the selection and composition of the passages; for he aims not at a complete realistic presentment, but at an ideal portrait. He chooses and arranges what in human characters he has admired and loved and wishes others to love and admire. Consequently one could fashion an adequate spiritual portrait of Arnold himself by selecting and composing his appreciations of other men and his extracts from their works. In such a portrait would appear something of Maurice de Guérin's "profound and delicate sense of the life of Nature," something of his sister's spiritual "distinction," Joubert's passion for style and his penetrating intuitions, Heine's wit and his intellectual emancipation, Spinoza's de-

sire for "the love and knowledge of God," the resignation and austerity of Marcus Aurelius, the rich
melancholy of "Obermann," the critical acumen of
Amiel, the social passion of George Sand.

In the essay on Spinoza Arnold distinguishes the
Christian's love of God, which is primarily emotional, from Spinoza's love of God, which is primarily intellectual. One may say that the love
which Arnold exhibits for most of the objects of
his appreciative criticism is primarily of the intellectual quality. He writes criticisms customarily in a
"dry light," seldom permitting his more intimate personal emotion to reveal itself in the movement or diction of his prose—a usurpation, as he held it, of the
function of poetry. There are two especially noteworthy exceptions. One of them occurs at the close
of his "Marcus Aurelius." The wistful solitude of
the emperor in his high seriousness troubled the still
waters of Arnold's spiritual life. In the following
passage he illustrates well the difference between an
intellectual and an emotional love. Through the
penultimate paragraph he preserves the tone of a
judicious, admiring and dispassionate friend; but
deep calls unto deep in the valediction:

"In general, however, the action Marcus Aurelius
prescribes is action which every sound nature must
recognize as right, and the motives he assigns are
motives which every clear reason must recognize
as valid. And so he remains the especial friend

and comforter of all clear-headed and scrupulous, yet pure-hearted and upward-striving men, in those ages most especially that walk by sight, not by faith, but yet have no open vision. He cannot give such souls, perhaps, all they yearn for, but he gives them much; and what he gives them, they can receive.

"Yet no, it is not for what he thus gives them that such souls love him most! it is rather because of the emotion which lends to his voice so touching an accent, it is because he too yearns as they do for something unattained by him. What an affinity for Christianity had this persecutor of the Christians! The effusion of Christianity, its relieving tears, its happy self-sacrifice, were the very element, one feels, for which his soul longed; they were near him, they brushed him, he touched them, he passed them by. . . . Granted that he might have found, like the *Alogi* of modern times, in the most beautiful of the gospels, the Gospel which has leavened Christianity most powerfully, the Gospel of St. John, too much metaphysics, too much *gnosis;* granted that this Gospel might have looked too like what he knew already to be a total surprise to him: what, then, would he have said to the Sermon on the Mount, to the twenty-sixth chapter of St. Matthew? What would have become of the *exitiabilis superstitio,* of the 'obstinacy of the Christians'? Vain question! yet the greatest charm of Marcus Aurelius is that he makes us ask it. We see him wise, just, self-governed, tender, thankful, blameless; yet, with all this stretching out his arms for something beyond,—*tendentemque manus ripae ulterioris amore.*"

Because Arnold is speaking here about an experience identical with his own he speaks with an intense emotion of sympathy and he seems almost to be speaking about himself. Of a similar transparency and emotional candor is his essay on George Sand; one sees through it the moral lineaments of the author. "Nothing else!"—complain those who weary of his powerful application of ideas to life —"no handling of her novels as novels, no presentment of the French novelist as she really was!" How differently Mr. George Moore, for example, would have treated the theme! With what esthetic musings and malicious innuendo and scandalous anecdote would he have drawn out a portrait of the half-mannish, inky, smoky female Bohemian! Well, there are various ways to approach an author; and "George Sand" particularly well illustrates the merits and defects of Arnold's way, because, he tells us, he wrote it to please himself. George Sand had been one of the inspirations of his early manhood; in writing a commemorative notice of her he undertakes to define what she had meant to him: *"'Le sentiment de la vie idéale, qui n'est autre que la vie normale telle que nous sommes appelés à la connaître'*;—'the sentiment of the ideal life, which is none other than man's normal life as we shall some day know it,'—those words from one of her last publications give the ruling thought of George Sand, the ground-*motive,* as they say in music, of all her strain. It is as a personage inspired by this motive that she interests us."

With an exquisite recollection of his visit to the Château of Nohant thirty years before and with a passing reference to the novels "as novels," he remarks: "We do not know her unless we feel the spirit which goes through her work as a whole." This spirit he analyzes into three elements: "the cry of agony and revolt, the trust in nature and beauty, the aspiration towards a purged and renewed human society." He then proceeds to illustrate by carefully selected passages the presence of these elements in George Sand's work. In doing so, he is retracing his own spiritual development; he has lived through all that. Those cries of "agony and revolt," he had uttered them all in his lyrics, long years ago when he was a poet, long years ago when he found in the French woman's novels companionship to alleviate the bitter melancholy of his disillusion. The emotion recollected in tranquillity quickens the pulse of his prose: "George Sand speaks somewhere of her 'days of *Corinne*.' Days of *Valentine*, many of us may in like manner say,— days of *Valentine*, days of *Lélia*, days never to return! They are gone, we shall read the books no more, and yet how ineffaceable is their impression! How the sentences from George Sand's works of that period still linger in our memory and haunt the ear with their cadences! Grandiose and moving, they come, those cadences, like the sighing of the wind, through the forest, like the breaking of the waves on the seashore." Passing to the second element of her "spirit," Arnold asks, with the same unwonted poetic heightening of his style, "How should she faint and fail before her time, because of a world out of joint, because of the reign of stupidity, because of the passions of youth—she who could feel so well the power of those eternal consolers, nature and beauty? From the very first they introduce a note of suavity in her strain of grief and passion. Who can forget the lanes and meadows of *Valentine?*" One can turn to the bitter author of "Empedocles on Etna" and say: *Et tu in Arcadia*—who can forget the scholar-gipsy's "dark blue-bells drenched with dews of summer eves"? "In all this," Arnold continues, "we are passing from the second element in George Sand to the third,—her aspiration for a social new-birth, a *renaissance sociale*. It is eminently the ideal of France; it was hers. Her religion connected itself with this ideal." In developing this last topic the critic is discussing indirectly his own major effort. The weight of his entire experience is in his brief comment on a passage from the novelist's Journal: "All the later work of George Sand, however, all her hope of genuine social renovation, take the simple and serious ground so necessary. 'The cure for us is far more simple than we will believe. All the better natures among us see it and feel it. It is a good direction given by ourselves to our hearts and consciences;—*une bonne direction donnée par nous-mêmes à nos cœurs et à nos consciences.*' "

To give a good direction to our hearts and consciences:—that may appear to many readers in these progressive days a homely and old-fashioned function to be performed by literary criticism; but Arnold was unquestionably very greatly interested in giving that. His character adds weight and importance to his morality. His fine intelligence and pure elevated feeling invest his morality with a winsome beauty. So let a stimulus to the heart and conscience be reckoned with the stimulus to esthetic sensibility and the stimulus to intellectual curiosity as the three vital elements which the reader may expect to find in his essays on criticism.

CHAPTER V

EDUCATION

Comme au temps de Rabelais, c'est la méthode qui résoudra les difficultés.—*Notebooks,* 116.

La souveraine habileté consiste à bien connaitre le prix des choses.—*Notebooks,* 129.

ARNOLD'S writing on education, like his poetry, derives a good deal of interest from its close relation to the "main movement of mind" in his time. He was what we call nowadays an "educational expert," but one is inclined to say that he was that only incidentally and in a somewhat old-fashioned sense; for there is no smack in him of statistical method, child-psychology, or the deeper mysteries of pedagogy. He writes, to be sure, with extensive knowledge of schools and universities, but he writes like a man of broad general scholarship, like an accomplished man of letters, like an intelligent man of the world, like an alert student of society. In his attention to the means of education he never for an instant forgets the ends. If power had been conferred upon him, he might have been an educational statesman; for he steadily sees his

186

subject and handles it in full consciousness of its
political and social bearings. He has the statesman's
sense of the central inevitable drift of things, and
the statesman's passion for steering the drift.

What first reconciled him to his inspectorship of
schools was his perception that the education of the
people was to be one of the big tasks of his day.
At the very outset of his career he was tremen-
dously impressed by his conviction that the government of England was not much longer to remain
in the hands of a cultivated aristocracy. The extension of the franchise from 1832 onward meant
the coming into political power of first the middle
and then the lower classes. The political emergence
of the artisan, the shopkeeper, and the "common
laborer" made the educational question appear to
Arnold a remarkably "live issue." Since he regarded this emergence as irresistible, it seemed to
him imperative to prepare for it. It seemed to him,
for political reasons if for no other, imperative with
all possible speed to educate the democracy. Carlyle
told the governing class that in extending the suf-
frage to fools they were rushing straight to destruction—they were "shooting Niagara." Arnold,
equally anxious but more resourceful, said that if
intelligent people did not wish their political destinies dictated by the ignorant masses they must in
a thoroughgoing fashion regenerate and enlighten
the masses. He felt, furthermore, that the need for

regeneration and enlightenment was not confined to the masses.

To the solution of the grand problems of the educational statesman—what to do, and how to do it —he contributed in three distinct ways. In the first place, as inspector of schools he supplied to the Education Department careful reports on the existing system of elementary education in England—the training of teachers, the proficiency of pupils, the text-books and methods in vogue, the effect of government grants to local boards, and kindred matters; his nineteen General Reports were collected and published in 1889. In the second place, he prepared for the Education Commissioners and for the public elaborate reports on Continental systems of education: *The Popular Education of France with Notices of That in Holland and Switzerland,* 1861; *A French Eton; or Middle Class Education and the State,* 1864; *Schools and Universities on the Continent,* 1868; *Higher Schools and Universities in Germany,* 1874; and a *Special Report on . . . Elementary Education in Germany, Switzerland, and France,* 1888. In the third place, he set forth, in these reports and elsewhere in his works, his own ideas of educational administration and organization, and the choice of studies. The special student will find all these writings full of matter and suggestiveness. The descriptive portions, however, have now mainly an historical interest, and we shall accordingly limit ourselves to a brief consideration of his leading ideas.

In his survey of English education he became conscious that its deficiencies were due largely to the fact that like Topsy it had "just growed." It had "muddled along" voluntarily, parochially, privately, under denominational control, without standards, wise supervision, or definitely conceived ends. Its presiding spirit had been the too much extolled "English love of liberty," which meant in this case liberty to be as little educated or as badly educated as one pleased. In his survey of Continental systems, on the other hand, he was everywhere impressed by the fact that educational statesmanship had been at work. In Germany, Frederick the Great and Humboldt, in France Napoleon and Guizot, grasping the immense potentialities of the imperfect instrument at hand, had nationalized education, and had brought the highest order of intelligence to its administration and organization. Arnold repeatedly declared that public instruction would never be on the right footing in England till there was a man like Guizot or Humboldt responsibly at the head of it. Meanwhile, taking his cue from the Continent, he urged certain reforms in elementary, secondary and higher education.

The first step, he held, toward social regeneration and enlightenment was to make elementary education sound and uniform, public and universal. If it was to be sound and uniform, it must be wisely supervised and effectively controlled. If it was to be public and universal, it must be accessible to all and compulsory for all. The second step was to multiply in the interest of the middle classes good public secondary schools such as at Eton and Rugby and Harrow already existed yet were enjoyed mainly by the wealthy and aristocratic classes. The third step was to add to Oxford, Cambridge, and London universities ten or a dozen institutions for higher learning in the "provinces"; and to make these institutions universities in the Continental sense of the word, that is to say, centers of productive scholarship and scientific research. Here in rough outline is Arnold's program for improving the educational *machinery* of a young and backward democracy, rather heavily encumbered by its inheritance of fixed ideas and habits from an older régime. In such circumstances, to propose the program was the least of his tasks. To overcome the innate English antipathy to compulsion and supervision; to rouse the middle class from its conceit and self-satisfaction; to make people feel their need for new ideas and fresh information—these were the real labors and difficulties. In these tasks Arnold's literary talent comes into play.

His most delightful development of the implications of compulsion in education is to be found in the sixth and seventh letters of *Friendship's Gar-*

land, which constitute a good-tempered yet biting satire on educational conditions in all classes of English society. In this brilliant series of skits Arnold ironically assumes the position of the jealous defender of British institutions against the brutally caustic criticism of his friend, the young Prussian *savant,* Arminius ("he was christened Herman, but I call him Arminius, because it is more in the grand style"). Arnold here represents himself as seizing the occasion of a magistrates' day for sitting in a certain country town "to show off our local self-government to a bureaucracy-ridden Prussian like Arminius." The prisoner, Zephaniah Diggs—"an old fellow in a smock-frock, with a white head, a low forehead, a red nose, and a foxy expression of countenance"—is up for snaring a hare. "The worst of the story, to my mind," says Arnold slyly, "was that the old rogue had a heap of young children by a second wife whom he had married late in life, and that not one of these children would he send to school, but persisted in letting them run wild, and grow up in utter barbarism. . . . Do you know, Arminius, I begin to think, that the time has almost come for taking a leaf out of your Prussian book, and applying, in the education of children of this class, what the great Kant calls the categorical imperative. The gap between them and our educated classes is really too frightful. 'Your educated and intelligent classes!' sneered Arminius, in his very most offensive manner; 'where are they? I should like to see them.' "

In reply Arnold exhibits the magistrates, declaring that they "embody our whole national life;—the land, religion, commerce are all represented by them. Lord Lumpington is a peer of old family and great estate; Esau Hittall is a clergyman; Mr. Bottles is one of our self-made middle-class men. Their politics are not all of one color, and that color the government's. Lumpington is a Constitutional Whig; Hittall is a benighted old Tory. As for Mr. Bottles, he is a radical of the purest water; quite one of the Manchester school." " 'That is all very well as to their politics,' said Arminius, but I want to hear about their education and intelligence.' " Lumpington, Arnold explains, was at Eton; Hittall was the last of six nephews nominated to the Charterhouse by his uncle, a distinguished prelate, "who had thoroughly learnt the divine lesson that charity begins at home." Arminius insists on inquiring what they learnt at Eton and at the Charterhouse, and whether their minds were much braced by the mental gymnastics of "the grand old, fortifying, classical curriculum." "Well," returns Arnold, "during their three years at Oxford they were so much occupied with Bullingdon and hunting that there was no great opportunity to judge. But for my part I have always thought their both getting their degree at last with flying colours, after three weeks of a famous coach for fast men, four nights without going to bed, and an incredible consumption of wet towels, strong cigars, and brandy-and-water, was one of the most astonishing feats I ever heard of." As for Mr. Bottles, he was educated in the Lycurgus House Academy by Archimedes Silverpump, Ph. D., a man of modern views, thus summarized by his pupil: "Original man, Silverpump! fine mind! fine system! None of your antiquated rubbish—all practical work —latest discoveries in science—mind constantly kept excited—lots of interesting experiments—lights of all colours—fizz! fizz! bang! bang! That's what I call forming a man."

So much for English *laissez-faire* in education. Arnold's destructive and constructive criticism of what Lumpington, Hittall, and Bottles represent he appropriately expresses through his Prussian friend.

" 'But,' continued Arminius, 'you were talking of compulsory education, and your common people's want of it. Now, my dear friend, I want you to understand what this principle of compulsory education really means. It means that to ensure, as far as you can, every man's being fit for his business in life, you put education as a bar, or condition, between him and what he aims at. The principle is just as good for one class as another, and it is only by applying it impartially that you save its application from being insolent and invidious. Our Prussian peasant stands our compelling him to instruct himself before he may go about his calling, because he sees we believe in instruction, and compel our own class, too, in a way to make it really feel the pressure, to instruct itself before it may go about its calling. Now, you propose to make old Diggs's boys instruct themselves before they may go bird-scaring or sheep-tending. I want to know what you do to make those three worthies in that justice-room instruct themselves before they may go acting as magistrates and judges.' 'Do?' said I; 'why, just look what they have done all of themselves. Lumpington and Hittall have had a public-school and university education; Bottles has had Dr. Silverpump's, and the practical training of business. What on earth would you have us make them do more?' 'Qualify themselves for administrative or judicial functions, if they exercise them,' said Arminius. 'That is what really answers, in their case, to the compulsion you propose to apply to Diggs's boys. Sending Lord Lumpington and Mr. Hittall to school is nothing; the natural course of things takes them there. Don't suppose that, by doing this, you are applying the principle of compulsory education fairly, and as you apply it to Diggs's boys. You are not interposing, for the rich, education as a bar or condition between them and that which they aim at. But interpose it, as we do, between the rich and things they aim at, and I will say something to you. I should like to know what has made Lord Lumpington a magistrate?' 'Made Lord Lumpington a magistrate?' said I; 'why, the Lumpington estate, to be sure.' 'And the Reverend Esau Hittall?' continued Arminius. 'Why, the Lumpington living, of course,' said I. 'And that man Bottles?' he went on. 'His English energy and self-reliance,' I answered very stiffly, for Arminius's incessant carping began to put me in a huff; 'those same incomparable and truly British qualities which have just triumphed over every obstacle and given us the Atlantic telegraph! —and let me tell you, Von T., in my opinion it will be a long time before the "Geist" of any pedant of a Prussian professor gives us anything half so valuable as that.' 'Pshaw!' replied Arminius, contemptuously: 'that great rope, with a Philistine at each end of it talking inutilities!

" 'But in my country,' he went on, 'we should have begun to put a pressure on these future magistrates at school. Before we allowed Lord Lumpington and Mr. Hittall to go to the university at all, we should have examined them, and we should not have trusted the keepers of that absurd cockpit you took me down to see, to examine them as they choose, and send them jogging comfortably off to the university on their lame longs and shorts. No; there would have been some Mr. Grote as School Board Commissioner, pitching into them questions about history, and some Mr. Lowe, as Crown Patronage Commissary, pitching into them questions about English literature; and these young men would have been kept from the university, as Diggs's boys are kept from their bird-scaring, till they instructed themselves. Then, if, after three years of their university, they wanted to be magistrates, another pressure!—a great Civil Service examination before a board of experts, an examination in English law, Roman law, English history, history of jurisprudence. . . . ' 'A most abominable liberty to take with Lumpington and Hittall!' exclaimed I. 'Then your compulsory education is a most abom-

inable liberty to take with Diggs's boys,' retorted
Arminius. 'But, good gracious! my dear Arminius,'
expostulated I, 'do you really mean to maintain that
a man can't put old Diggs in quod for snaring a
hare without all this elaborate apparatus of Roman
law and history of jurisprudence?' 'And do you
really mean to maintain,' returned Arminius, 'that
a man can't go bird-scaring or sheep-tending without all this elaborate apparatus of a compulsory
school?' 'Oh, but,' I answered, 'to live at all, even at
the lowest stage of human life, a man needs instruction.' 'Well,' returned Arminius, 'and to administer
at all, even at the lowest stage of public administration, a man needs instruction.' 'We have never
found it so,' said I."

The principle of compulsion illustrated by the
case of the magistrates bears upon the educational
inefficiency which is due to indolence. The principle of supervision in which Arnold is equally interested, bears upon the inefficiency which is due to
misdirected effort. He agrees with the stoutest
champions of liberty that nothing should be done by
the state to discourage individual initiative and local,
denominational, and class enterprise in educational
matters. But he feels very strongly that most individuals, most localities, most denominations, and
most classes stand in need, in the long run, of a
power outside themselves to help them to realize
their best selves, and to hold them up to the level of
their highest possibilities. That power, he believes,

may best be lodged in the state, and exercised practically through state supervision, examination, and pecuniary aid. On the Continent he finds the government conscientiously and intelligently leading and directing educational effort. In England, on the contrary, the habit of governors, when they let their countenances shine upon the people, is to flatter them in their misdirection. In the third chapter of *Culture and Anarchy* he illustrates, with a somewhat Socratic air, this distressing difference between the English and the Germans:

"The Liscensed Victuallers or the Commercial Travellers propose to make a school for their children; and I suppose, in the matter of schools, one may call the Licensed Victuallers or the Commercial Travellers ordinary men, with their natural taste for the bathos still strong; and a Sovereign with the advice of men like Wilhelm von Humboldt or Schleiermacher may, in this matter, be a better judge, and nearer to right reason. And it will be allowed, probably, that right reason would suggest that, to have a sheer school of Licensed Victuallers' children, or a sheer school of Commercial Travellers' children, and to bring them all up, not only at home but at school too, in a kind of odour of licensed victualism or bagmanism, is not a wise training to give to these children. And in Germany, I have said, the action of the national guides or governors is to suggest and provide a better. But, in England, the action of the national guides or governors is, for a Royal Prince or a great Minister to go down to the opening of the Licensed Victuallers' or of the Commercial Travellers' school, to take the chair to extol the energy and self-reliance of the Licensed Victuallers or the Commercial Travellers, to be all of their way of thinking, to predict full success to their schools, and never so much as to hint to them that they are probably doing a very foolish thing, and that the right way to go to work with their children's education is quite different. And it is the same in almost every department of affairs. While, on the Continent, the idea prevails that it is the business of the heads and representatives of the nation, by virtue of their superior means, power, and information, to set an example and to provide suggestions of right reason, among us the idea is that the business of the heads and representatives of the nation is to do nothing of the kind, but to applaud the natural taste for the bathos showing itself vigorously in any part of the community, and to encourage its works."

To education no less than to literature Arnold applied Goethe's maxim, *Alles Grandioses ist bildend* —everything in the grand style is formative. A school for Licensed Victuallers or for Seventh Day Baptists could not but impress him as inadequately and even viciously conceived—as the institutional equivalent of an inferior and vulgar poetry. There were, he said in *A French Eton,* "numberless endowed schools and 'educational homes'—some of them good, many of them middling, most of them bad; but none of them invested with much consideration or dignity." What he desired for the children of the middle class was an institution which should give them "largeness of soul," lifting them out of the middle class into the life of the nation— the educational equivalent of epic poetry. The readiest way to introduce the element of grandeur where it was so much needed was by the public establishment of schools for the middle class on something like the scale established in France. Let us quote from *The Popular Education of France* a passage which well illustrates his sense of the moral and social ends to be attained by such establishments:

"The aristocratic classes in England may, perhaps, be well content to rest satisfied with their Eton and Harrow; the State is not likely to do better for them; nay, the superior confidence, spirit, and style, engendered by a training in the great public schools, constitute for these classes a real privilege, a real engine of command, which they might, if they were selfish, be sorry to lose by the establishment of schools great enough to beget a like spirit in the classes below them. But the middle classes in England have every reason not to remain content with their private schools; the State can do a great deal better for them; by giving to schools for these classes a public character, it can bring the instruction in them under a criticism which the knowledge of these classes is not in itself at present able to supply; by giving to them a national character, it can confer on them a greatness and a noble spirit, which the tone of these classes is not in itself at present adequate to impart. Such schools would soon prove notable competitors with the existing public schools: they would do these a great service by stimulating them, and making them look into their own weak points more closely: economical, because with charges uniform and under severe supervision, they would do a great service to that large body of persons, who, at present, seeing that on the whole the best secondary instruction to be found is that of the existing public schools, obtain it for their children from a sense of duty, although they can ill afford it, and although its cost is certainly exorbitant. Thus the middle classes might, by the aid of the State, better their instruction, while still keeping its cost moderate. This in itself would be a gain; but this gain would be nothing in comparison with that of acquiring the sense of belonging to great and honourable seats of learning, and of breathing in their youth the air of the best culture of their nation. This sense would be an educational influence for them of the highest value; it would really augment their self-respect and moral force; it would truly fuse them with the class above, and tend to bring about for them the Equality which they desire."

The English governing class in Arnold's time was vastly more concerned about elementary and secondary than about higher education. In his *Higher Schools and Universities in Germany* he emphatically indicates the course that England must take to bring her most venerated institutions of learning "up to date." He dwells, according to his custom, upon the characteristic excellencies of the German

institutions, remarking, however, that the English
deficiency is not in *Lehrfreiheit* and *Lernfreiheit*
—academic freedom—but in *Wissenschaft,* which he
glosses as "knowledge systematically pursued and
prized in and for itself." "Our university system,"
he continues, "is a routine, indeed, but it is our
want of science, not our want of liberty, which
makes it a routine. It is science that we have most
need to borrow from the German universities. The
French university has no liberty, and the English
universities have no science; the German universities
have both." The dawn of genuine university instruction in the United States is marked for us by
the foundation of the Johns Hopkins University in
1867; but the distinction between the function of
the old-fashioned college and the function of the
modern university is none too firmly established
among us, even in these days. It is to Arnold's
credit that he made the distinction sharp and *pointed*
it as early as 1874:

"The want of the idea of science, of systematic
knowledge, is, as I have said again and again, the
capital want of English education and of English
life; it is the university, or the superior school,
which ought to foster this idea. The university or
superior school ought to provide facilities, after the
general education is finished, for the young man to
go on in the line where his special aptitudes lead him,
be it that of languages and literature, of mathematics, of the natural sciences, of the application of

these sciences, or any other line, and follow the studies of this line systematically under first-rate teaching. Our great universities, Oxford and Cambridge, do next to nothing towards this end. They are, as Signor Matteuci called them, *hauts lycées;* and though valuable in their way as places where the youth of the upper classes prolong to a very great age, and under some very admirable influences, their school education, and though in this respect to be envied by the youth of the upper class abroad, and, if possible, instituted for their benefit, yet, with their college and tutor system, nay, with their examination and degree system, they are still, in fact, *schools,* and do not carry education beyond the stage of general and school education. The examination for the degree of bachelor of arts, which we place at the end of our three years' university course, is merely the *Abiturientenexamen* of Germany, the *épreuve du baccalauréat* of France, placed in both of these countries at the entrance to university studies instead of, as with us, at their close. Scientific instruction, university instruction, really begins when the degree of bachelor (*bas chevalier,* knight of low degree) is taken, and the preparation for mastership in any line of study, or for doctorship (fitness to teach it), commences. But for mastership or doctorship, Oxford and Cambridge have, as is well known, either no examination at all, or an examination which is a mere form; they have consequently no instruction directed to these grades; no real university-instruction, therefore, at all."

The age of private endowment, Arnold expressly declared, was over. It would be pleasant to record that, ignoring institutions like Harvard and Yale and Andover and Exeter, ignoring also the countless poverty-stricken and badly manned and ignorantly directed, privately endowed institutions in the United States, he found in our high schools and in our state universities models for the public establishment of secondary and higher education in England. If he had been inclined to the utterance of comforting prophecy, if he had been disposed to flatter the "American cousins," he might at least have told us that we had drawn the plans and laid the foundations for a grand system. What he actually said—in a letter to Charles Eliot Norton, August 27, 1886—was this: "I am doubtful about your petty academies, just as I am doubtful about your pullulating colleges and universities. *Das Gemeine* is the American danger, and a few and good secondary schools and universities, setting a high standard, are what you seem to me to want, rather than a multitude of institutions which their promoters delude themselves by taking seriously, but which no serious person can so take."

We have been discussing up to this point Arnold's program for the improvement of educational machinery. We may now remark that if he had not been officially concerned with educational machinery he would probably have given little attention to the need for administrative centralization, organization, coordination, extension, efficiency, and the similar abstractions with which the tongue of the educational "engineer" has made us familiar. Called to the task, he develops, with a constant desire to steer and control the "liberty" of a growing democracy, his ideas of an adequate, modern, educational instrument. His personal, as distinguished from his official, interest was, however, not in the machine but in its product. He is nearer home when he discusses the choice of studies than when he discusses the coordination of schools. He has more closely at heart what education can do for the individual than what an educational system can do for the state.

Now the choice of studies was made in the third quarter of the nineteenth century a particularly "live issue" by the new claims put forth in behalf of the natural sciences. The immediate effect in the field of education produced by the immense scientific activity of the century was an inquiry whether the traditional educational disciplines were not antiquated. It was of course to be expected that as soon as a large body of new scientific knowledge was available its discoverers and popularizers would demand a place for it in the curricula of schools and colleges. The discoverers and popularizers were not slow nor excessively modest in presenting their case. They demanded for modern science not merely a place but the predominant place in a reformed educational program. Pointing to the rich fruits of recent scientific effort, they challenged the "classicists" to exhibit an equivalent. They brought about a new battle of the ancients and the moderns, a head-on collision of the "sciences" and the "humanities," with the echoes of which the educational world still rings.

With relation to this great clash of opinion Arnold sets forth in "Literature and Science" his doctrine on the choice of studies. Incidentally he takes up—we must not say the cudgels—he draws his rapier in behalf of the humanists, and exchanges a few courteous thrusts with Darwin's brilliant expositor, Thomas Huxley. The *cudgels* had been employed, some years earlier, by Herbert Spencer, the quasi-official philosopher of evolution; and, though explicit reference is not made to him in Arnold's lecture, he must certainly have been in Arnold's mind as the very Goliath among the men of science. With Huxley, who asked large concessions from the humanists, Arnold could come to an understanding, if not to a perfect agreement. But with Spencer, who wished to destroy the humanists, he could hardly have found any common ground. In philosophical circles Spencer seems to have dwindled from a star of the first magnitude to a rather contemned candle, guttering and smoking toward extinction. In departments of Pedagogy, however, his *Education*—published in 1861, two years after the *Origin of Species*—is still studied as a classic; and in college faculties it is still quoted as a gospel by the men of science who acquired their leading ideas when Spencer was a name to conjure with. The temper, training and writings of Spencer as educator give us just the right foil for the exhibition of Arnold in the same capacity.

Spencer was brought up in a religious environment of a Quaker and Methodist complexion. Educationally a "self-made man," he knew nothing at first hand of the influence of the traditional humanistic disciplines at Oxford or Cambridge. He followed unchecked his natural bent, which inclined him strongly toward the natural sciences, mathematics, and abstract reasoning. He began his career as a civil engineer on the Birmingham railway; served for a time as sub-editor on an economic periodical; and then passed to reading and writing in the fields of the natural sciences, psychology, sociology and philosophy. All his thinking was pervaded by an optimistic faith in progress, which was his first philosophical deduction from the scientific theory of evolution. He cheerfully accepted the theory of the descent of man from the anthropoid apes; and one may say that his central conception of man was derived from the study of biology and physiology. He thought steadily of man as an animal who owed his place in nature to the skill with which he had adapted himself to his environment; and, as his *Autobiography* reveals, he thought steadily of himself as the most illustrious example of "adaptation."

Spencer's educational theory develops out of his elementary conception of man as an animal, and out of his elementary conception of adaptation to environment. His entire treatise has a twang of zoology and anthropology. Considering the matter as a convinced naturalist, he can not see that the study of Greek and Latin is of any appreciable service to the modern animal in the powers of adaptation. He has read a good deal in the history of savage tribes, and, with a display of his elephantine humor, he opens his argument by comparing the function of the classics among civilized people to that of finery among barbarians: "We are guilty of something like a platitude when we say that throughout his after career a boy, in nine cases out of ten, applies his Latin and Greek to no practical purpose. The remark is trite that in his shop, or his office, in managing his estate or his family, in playing his part as director of a bank or a railway, he is very little aided by this knowledge he took so many years to acquire. If we enquire what is the real motive for giving boys a classical education, we find it to be simply conformity to public opinion. . . . As the Oronoco Indian puts on his paint before leaving his hut, not with a view to any direct benefit, but because he would be ashamed to be seen without it, so a boy's drilling in Latin and Greek is insisted on, not because of their intrinsic value, but that he may not be disgraced by being found ignorant of them."

After these preliminary flings, Spencer tells us that we need to revise our ideas and set up a new and real standard of educational values. Whereupon, dividing the subject into five parts, he sets up the following standard: "That education which prepares for direct self-preservation; that which prepares for indirect self-preservation; that which prepares for parenthood; that which prepares for citizenship; that which prepares for the miscellaneous refinements of life." This enumeration, in the order of the relative importance of the parts, we shall compare in a moment with Arnold's division of the subject. But let us notice now its significant features: three out of five parts of education are to deal with the preservation and propagation of the physical species to which man belongs; one part is to prepare for civic responsibility; the fifth, for the "miscellaneous refinements"—the beads and gewgaws, so to speak.

Spencer contemplates the education of an industrious democracy: "Leaving out some very small classes, what are all men employed in? They are employed in the production, preparation and distribution of commodities. And on what does efficiency in the production, preparation and distribution of commodities depend? It depends on the use of methods fitted to the respective natures of these commodities; it depends on an adequate knowledge of their physical, chemical, or vital properties, as the

case may be; that is, it depends on science. This
order of knowledge, which is in great part ignored
in our school courses, is the order of knowledge underlying the right performance of all those processes
by which civilized life is made possible." In this passage "science" obviously means physics (including
mathematics), chemistry, biology, and their
branches. The passage may also mean that civilized life consists mainly in the "production, preparation, and distribution of commodities"; but that is
not quite so clear. Proceeding with his argument,
Spencer shows in great detail how science enters into
our business if not into our bosoms; how essential
mathematics is to the carpenter; how physics with
mathematics builds the steam engine and operates in
the kitchen; how chemistry serves the dyer, the gas
maker, the soap boiler; how biology concerns the
sheep raiser; how physiology opens the door for the
dietitian; how important psychology and physiology
are in the rearing of children; and finally how fundamental the various sciences are even to the interpretation of history, the creation of art, etc., etc.,
etc. This searching inquiry he concludes with a
triumphant summary, calculated to make the classicists ask themselves what reason they had for
longer encumbering the earth:

"For direct self-preservation, or the maintenance
of life and health, the all-important knowledge is—
Science.

"For that indirect self-preservation which we call gaining a livelihood, the knowledge of greatest value is—Science.

"For the due discharge of parental functions, the proper guidance is to be found only in—Science.

"For the interpretation of national life, past and present, without which the citizen cannot regulate his conduct, the indispensable key is—Science.

"And for the purposes of discipline—intellectual, moral, religious—the most efficient study is, once more, Science."

At the conclusion of his chapter on "What Knowledge is of Most Worth," he speaks of science as up to that time a household drudge kept in the background "that her haughty sisters might flaunt their fripperies in the eyes of the world." But thenceforth, he says, their positions will be changed, "and while these haughty sisters sink into merited neglect, Science, proclaimed as highest alike in worth and beauty, will reign supreme." We are to believe, the immense immediate influence of Spencer constrains us to believe, that by this sort of thing men in the 'sixties and 'seventies were stirred as with the sound of a trumpet.

Arnold's lecture on "Literature and Science," delivered in America in 1883, was addressed to a people mainly employed, like those for whom Spencer legislated, in the "production, preparation and distribution of commodities." But when we turn from Spencer's *Education* to this lecture we are in the presence of a quite different order of ideas. The difference is not felt merely in the fact that we have turned from a self-educated man to a man who has undergone the best traditional disciplines, from an advocate of the natural sciences to an advocate of humane letters, from an educational theorist to an educational expert intimately in touch for thirty years with educational practise in England and on the Continent. No: the difference is felt primarily in the opposition of two unlike conceptions of man and his destiny on the planet. To Spencer, man is an animal, who by natural cunning has managed to get his head a little higher than the apes and to live more comfortably than they, and who by the scientific extension of his cunning may expect to live still more comfortably. To Arnold, who waives the question of man's ultimate origin, man is now *essentially* a moral being, who by certain discipline has fortified his instinct for righteousness, wisdom and beauty, and who by the continued use of these disciplines may expect to make progress in perfecting his essence. Between the lines of scientific cunning along which an animal achieves comfort and the lines of discipline along which a moral being perfects his essence there are many points of contact and coincidence. But the ends are not the same. Between the ultimate ideals there is an irreconcilable conflict which it is idle to slur over or to attempt to disguise. The special service of Arnold's light-

handed but firm critical meditation is in showing
how far literature and the natural sciences go together, and where they part.

"Practical people," he begins, "talk with a smile
of Plato and of his absolute ideas; and it is impossible to deny that Plato's ideas do often seem unprac-
tical and impracticable, and especially when one
views them in connexion with the life of a great
work-a-day world like the United States. The necessary staple of such a world Plato regards with
disdain; handicraft and trade and the working
professions he regards with disdain; but what becomes of the life of an industrial modern community if you take handicraft and trade and the
working professions out of it? . . . Now education, many people go on to say, is still mainly governed by the ideas of a man like Plato, who lived
when the warrior caste and the priestly or philosophical class were alone in honour, and the really
useful part of the community were slaves. . . .
And how absurd it is, people end by saying, to
inflict this education upon an industrious modern
community, where very few indeed are persons of
leisure, and the mass to be considered has not leisure, but is bound, for its own great good, and for
the great good of the world at large, to plain labour
and to industrial pursuits, and the education in question tends necessarily to make men dissatisfied with
these pursuits and unfitted for them!"

Arnold admits that much in Plato is obsolete,
"that his scorn of trade and handicraft is fantastic,"

but he makes a distinction: "So far I must defend Plato, as to plead that his view of education and studies is in the general, as it seems to me, sound enough, and fitted for all sorts and conditions of men, whatever their pursuits may be. 'An intelligent man,' says Plato, 'will prize those studies which result in his soul getting soberness, righteousness, and wisdom, and will less value the others.' I cannot consider that a bad description of the aim of education, and of the motives which should govern us, whether we are preparing for a hereditary seat in the English House of Lords or for the pork trade in Chicago." Here we may contrast the central conceptions of the educational function held by a man of science with that held by a humanist. By all odds the most important function of education as Spencer describes it relates to the care of the body and to the perpetuation of the physical life of the race. Arnold, following Plato, begins almost at the point where Spencer leaves off: without a word about self-preservation, "direct" or "indirect," he begins with the moral being and the desires which it is entitled to satisfy. For him obviously the primary consideration is the perpetuation of the moral life of the race. A significant difference in emphasis is unquestionable.

Spencer, anticipating a flanking movement against his position, had, it will be remembered, prepared his defense in advance when he said: "For the purposes of discipline—intellectual, moral, religious—the most efficient study is, once more, Science." Arnold's attack is in that "sector." "The moral education in the past," he says, "has been mainly literary. The question is whether the studies which were long supposed to be the best for all of us are practically the best now; whether others are not better. The tyranny of the past, many think, weighs on us injuriously in the predominance given to letters in education. . . . The design of abasing what is called 'mere literary instruction and education,' and of exalting what is called 'sound, extensive, and practical scientific knowledge,' is, in this intensely modern world of the United States, even more perhaps than in Europe, a very popular design. I am going to ask . . . whether this brisk and flourishing movement ought to prevail, and whether it is likely to prevail."

First, however, Arnold clears away an important misunderstanding—a misunderstanding, unfortunately, which the humanist has usually still to remove when he disputes with a man from the left wing of science. In defending humane letters Arnold explains that he is not advocating a belletristic program of an ornamental character from which scientific knowledge is excluded. On the contrary, the program which he defends will provide for scientific knowledge of the natural world, and will reform the study of the classics and of belles-lettres in general by introducing into it something of the systematic and thoroughgoing spirit which animates workers in the natural sciences:

"But as I do not mean, by knowing ancient Rome, knowing merely more or less of Latin *belles lettres,* and taking no account of Rome's military, and political, and legal, and administrative work in the world; and as, by knowing Greece, I understand knowing her as the giver of Greek art, and the guide to a free and right use of reason and to scientific method, and the founder of our mathematics and physics and astronomy and biology—I understand knowing her as all this, and not merely knowing certain Greek poems, and histories, and treatises, and speeches,—so as to the knowledge of modern nations also. By knowing modern nations, I mean not merely knowing their belles lettres, but knowing also what has been done by such men as Copernicus, Galileo, Newton, Darwin. . . .   There is, therefore, really no question between Professor Huxley and me as to whether knowing the great results of the modern scientific study of nature is not required as a part of our culture, as well as knowing the products of literature and art."

"But," he says—returning to the attack, "to follow the processes by which these results are reached, ought, say the friends of physical science, to be made the staple of education for the bulk of mankind. And here there does arise a question between those whom Professor Huxley calls with playful sarcasm 'the Levites of culture,' and those whom the poor humanist is sometimes apt to regard as its Nebuchadnezzars. . . .   All knowledge is interesting to a wise man, and the knowledge of nature is interesting to all men. It is very interesting to know, that, from the albuminous white of the egg, the chick in the egg gets the materials for its flesh, bones, blood, and feathers. . . . It is less interesting, perhaps, but still it is interesting to know that when a taper burns, the wax is converted into carbonic acid and water. . . . We must all admit that in natural science the habit gained of dealing with facts is a most valuable discipline, and that everyone should have some experience of it. More than this, however, is demanded by the reformers. It is proposed to make the training in natural science the main part of education, for the great majority of mankind at any rate. And here, I confess, I part company with the friends of physical science, with whom up to this point I have been agreeing."

Why? Well, says Arnold, "at present it seems to me, that those who are for giving to natural knowledge, as they call it, the chief place in the education of the majority of mankind, leave one important thing out of their account: the constitution of human nature." Let us recall here once more Spencer's fivefold division of the powers of education: education for (1) self-preservation, (2) indirect self-preservation, (3) parenthood, (4) civic responsibility, and (5) "miscellaneous refinements." Arnold makes a fourfold division, "not pretending to scientific exactness," with moral, intellectual, esthetic, and social branches. The powers which

go to the building up of human life, he says,
are: "The power of conduct, the power of intellect
and knowledge, the power of beauty, and the power
of social life and manners. . . . Human nature
is built up by these powers; we have need for all of
them. When we have rightly met and adjusted the
claims of them all, we shall then be in a fair way for
getting soberness and righteousness, with wisdom.
This is evident enough, and the friends of science
would admit it." The argument which Arnold con-
structs upon this conception of human nature does
not proceed to demonstrate the superiority of letters
over science in every sphere. It makes a distinction:
in the sphere of "intellect and knowledge," the study
of the natural sciences is of very great service; in the
spheres of "conduct," "beauty," and "social life
and manners" it is, for the mass of mankind, of
negligible service, certainly of far less service than
the study of letters. With this conclusion all good
humanists will agree. The agreement of men of
science will depend upon their various notions of the
constituent elements in a satisfactory civilization;
will depend upon the presence in them of a non-
scientific sense—the sense for human values. In
reaching it Arnold enters into some interesting and
amusing developments.

"We experience, as we go on learning and knowing,—the vast majority of us experience,—the need
of relating what we have learnt and known to the

sense which we have in us for conduct, to the sense which we have in us for beauty. . . . But, no doubt, some kinds of knowledge cannot be made to directly serve the instinct in question, cannot be related to the sense for beauty, to the sense for conduct. These are instrument-knowledges; they lead on to other knowledges, which can. A man who passes his life in instrument-knowledges is a specialist. They may be invaluable as instruments to something beyond, for those who have the gift thus to employ them; and they may be disciplines in themselves wherein it is useful for every one to have some schooling. But it is inconceivable that the generality of men should pass all their mental life with Greek accents or with formal logic. . . . In the very Senate House and heart of our English Cambridge I once ventured, though not without an apology for my profaneness, to hazard the opinion that for the majority of mankind a little of mathematics, even, goes a long way. . . .

"The natural sciences do not, however, stand on the same footing with the instrument-knowledges. . . . And one piece of natural knowledge is added to another, and others are added to that, and at last we come to propositions so interesting as Mr. Darwin's famous proposition that 'our ancestor was a hairy quadruped furnished with a tail and pointed ears, probably arboreal in his habits.' Or we come to propositions of such reach and magnitude as Professor Huxley delivers, when he says that the notions of our forefathers about the beginning and the end of the world were all wrong, and that nature is the expression of a definite order with which nothing interferes.

"Interesting, indeed, these results of science are, important they are, and we should all of us be acquainted with them. But what I now wish you to mark is, that we are still, when they are propounded to us and we receive them, we are still in the sphere of intellect and knowledge. And for the generality of men there will be found, I say, to arise, when they have duly taken in the proposition that their ancestor was 'a hairy quadruped furnished with a tail and pointed ears, probably arboreal in his habits,' there will be found to arise an invincible desire to relate this proposition to the sense in us for conduct, and to the sense in us for beauty. But this the men of science will not do for us, and will hardly even profess to do."

"The success of modern science in extirpating what it calls 'mediæval thinking' " has not diminished the demands of man's emotional nature, though it has destroyed for many men one of the chief means of satisfying them. An individual here and there will be found—Darwin, for example —who does not suffer from the loss of the old religious consolations. But, as the work of science progresses, most men will more and more feel the need of a substitute for the forms of emotional satisfaction which science has discredited. At this point Arnold develops his idea that humane letters—especially poetry—are the available equivalent to religion.

"First, have poetry and eloquence the power of

calling out the emotions? The appeal is to experience. Experience shows us that for the vast majority of men, for mankind in general, they have
the power. Next, do they exercise it? They do.
But then, *how* do they exercise it so as to affect
man's sense for conduct, his sense for beauty? And
this is perhaps a case for applying the Preacher's
words: 'Though a man labour to seek it out, yet he
shall not find it; yea, farther, though a wise man
think to know it, yet shall he not be able to find it.'
Why should it be one thing, in its effect upon the
emotions to say, 'Patience is a virtue,' and quite another thing, in its effect upon the emotions, to say
with Homer,

Πλητὸν γὰρ Μοῖραι θυμὸν θέσαν ἀνθρώποισιν—

'for an enduring heart have the destinies appointed
to the children of men'? Why should it be one thing,
in its effect upon the emotions to say with the philosopher Spinoza, *Felicitas in eo consistit quod homo
summ esse conservare potest*—'Man's happiness consists in his being able to preserve his own essence'?
and quite another thing, in its effect upon the emotions, to say with the Gospel, 'What is a man advan-
taged, if he gain the whole world, and lose himself,
forfeit himself?' How does this difference of effect
arise? I cannot tell, and I am not much concerned to
know; the important thing is that it does arise, and
that we can profit by it. But how, finally, are poetry
and eloquence to exercise the power of relating the
modern results of natural science to man's instinct
for conduct, his instinct for beauty. And here again
I answer that I do not know how they will exercise

it, but that they can and will exercise it I am sure.
. . . I mean that we shall find that the art and
poetry and eloquence of men who lived, perhaps,
long ago, who had the most limited natural knowledge, who had the most erroneous conceptions about
many important matters, we shall find that this art,
and poetry, and eloquence, have in fact not only the
power of refreshing and delighting us, they have
also the power,—such is the strength and worth, in
essentials, of their author's criticism of life,—they
have a fortifying, and elevating, and quickening,
and suggestive power, capable of wonderfully help-
ing us to relate the results of modern science to our
need for conduct, our need for beauty. Homer's
conceptions of the physical universe were, I imagine, grotesque; but really, under the shock of hearing from modern science that 'the world is not subordinated to man's use, and that man is not the
cynosure of things terrestrial,' I could, for my own
part, desire no better comfort than Homer's line
which I quoted just now,

Πλητὸν γὰρ Μοῖραι θυμὸν θέσαν ἀνθρώποισιν—

'for an enduring heart have the destinies appointed
to the children of men.' "

There is here a playful touch in the expression of
Arnold's thought, which should not obscure for us
its essential and really profound seriousness. If he
had said outright that the study of letters helps us
to *bear* the grand results of science, he would not
have been guilty of a superficial epigram; he would

have spoken from the depths of his experience. We
are now at the very heart of his humanistic convictions. Truth about the natural world is not to be
denied or resisted. Much of it man can turn at once
to his own material advantage. Yet some of the
leading discoveries and ideas of science have griev-
ously wounded and desolated the human spirit. The
idea that the earth is but a grain of sand in the universe, the idea that civilization is but a moment in
the history of that grain of sand, the idea of the
"hairy quadruped furnished with a tail"—these
ideas, pressed upon our attention by the explorers
in the natural sciences, have no very tonic or bracing effect upon our self-respect. Dwelling on our
relative insignificance in time and space, and on our
community with the beasts of the fields has, on the
contrary, a powerful tendency to unbalance us men-
tally and to unstring us morally with an excessive
and hopeless contempt of ourselves and of our destiny. What is needed in the presence of such ideas
is another scale of values altogether. Man can not
hold himself much higher than the apes so long as
he measures his worth in terms of time and space.
But let him withdraw, so to speak, from the visible
world into the world without spatial or temporal
dimensions, the world which he has been building
since he lost his tail and became a man, the world
of his moral and esthetic ideas—and he will find
there a scale of values infinite, like time and space,

but, unlike them, commensurable with the reaches of his own soul. In the presence of this scale of values he regains his self-respect, his mental equilibrium, his moral tension. To set up this scale of values and to live by it, to measure one's self by it, is at least a partial deliverance from the fear of bodily calamity and the extinction of death; it is in short to be a man. The great poets of the world are men who have dwelt habitually in this world of human values, and have felt profoundly and expressed powerfully its magnificence. When Homer says that the destinies have appointed to the children of men an enduring heart, he expresses an aspect of this magnificence; he sets the children of men illustriously off from the hairy quadrupeds with tails, and inspires them to go about their human business —including, perhaps, the study of Greek.

The study of humane letters advanced on these grounds is on solid grounds; and there we may leave it, adding only, by way of contrast to the blare of Spencer's victorious trumpet, Arnold's assurance that the humanist can afford to wait quietly through the "period of unsettlement and confusion" till experience brings the children of men around to him again: "Letters will not in the end lose their leading place. If they lose it for a time, they will get it back again. We shall be brought back to them by our wants and aspirations. And a poor humanist may possess his soul in patience, neither strive nor cry, admit the energy and brilliancy of the partisans of physical science, and their present favour with the public, to be far greater than his own, and still have a happy faith that the nature of things works silently on behalf of the studies which he loves, and that while we shall all have to acquaint ourselves with the great results reached by modern science, and to give ourselves as much training in its disciplines as we can conveniently carry, yet the majority of men will always require humane letters; and so much the more, as they have the more and the greater results of science to relate to the need in man for conduct, and to the need in him for beauty."

CHAPTER VI

POLITICS AND SOCIETY

This treatment of politics with one's thought, or with one's imagination, or with one's soul, in place of the common treatment of them with one's Philistinism and with one's passions, is the only thing that can reconcile, it seems to me, any serious person to politics, with their inevitable wear, waste, and sore trial to all that is best in one.—*Letters,* I, 249.

ARNOLD'S political and his social thought are indetachably related. He always treated politics as an instrument for the renovation of society. It was the renovation of society, however,—not the instrument for the renovation,—which really excited his "thought," his "imagination," his "soul." This he declared to the Ipswich Working Men's College in the address called "Ecce, Convertimur Ad Gentes" (*Mixed Essays*): "I am no politician. . . . Indeed, I have no very ardent interest,—if you will allow me to speak for a moment of myself and of what interests me,—in politics in their present state in this country. What interests me is English civilization; and our politics in their present state do not seem to me to have much bearing upon that. English civilization,—the humanising, the bring-

225

ing into one harmonious and truly humane life, of the whole body of English society,—that is what interests me. I try to be a disinterested observer of all which really helps and hinders that."

But though Arnold was not a politician, he was that thorn in the flesh of "practical" politicians—an independent political critic. A stalwart partisan he could not be. A political critic in his sense of the word—a man bent upon knowing the best and striving to make it prevail—can not tie himself to any set of politicians or to any fixed body of party principles. He must keep himself free to expose energetically the errors of all parties, and to second effort in the right direction, wherever it is initiated. His tendency is just the opposite of that of the practical politician. The practical politician apparently strives to emphasize and widen the gulf between his party and the opposition by a wholly uncritical denunciation of the opposition and a wholly uncritical laudation of his own party; his passion for prevailing predominates over his desire to know the best. The political critic, whose passion for knowing the best predominates over his desire to prevail, tends to meditate between the parties, and to draw them ever more closely together by condemning the characteristic excesses of both, and by commending the characteristic virtues of each to the other. Much as practical politicians despise and fear the independent critic, he holds the whip of political progress.   In a democracy, that party remains in power longest which follows his hint and invites his vote by quietly assimilating as much as it can of the virtues of the opposition.

Arnold's political independence is the result of his internal equilibrium.   If one asks, not what were his political ideas, but what was his political temper, the answer may be given with assurance: He was of the conservative temper.   Everything that was instinctive in him inclined him toward the anciently established aristocratic order of things in England. His early education and his social connections tended to strengthen his conservative instincts.   Yet as a matter of fact he was neither a reactionary nor a "standpatter"; he declared that he would never vote for a Tory.   He could not settle back in an easy chair and praise the existing order, nor express the irresponsible hope that it would last out his time. By taking thought he had become ardently progressive.   He supplemented and controlled his temperament with ideas and with the intellectual passion which they begot.   To the instinct for preserving what was good in the past he added an eager vision and a desire of something better in the future.   He wanted the "something better" in the future to be much more widely distributed than "what was good" in the past.   He could not be happy in a small cultivated class surrounded by a great multitude of Philistines.   He aimed at something like the democracy of Athens—without the slaves. He aspired toward a society "in the grand style" for everybody —a society as free and equal and fraternal as that expected by Robespierre, but intellectually fine and esthetically finished, like that enjoyed by Pericles. He was, in short, so passionately aristocratic that he wanted to make all men aristocratic. That remote ideal he had in mind when he called himself "a Liberal of the future."

Toward that good he could not see that either the Conservatives or the Liberals of his own day were making much progress. To the Tory element he devotes relatively little attention. His criticism of them is in general directed at their mental inflexibility and at their indisposition to do anything important. A Tory at the best is a man of sense and some grounding in the eternal verities; but he is disposed to be sluggish, averse to change, hostile to new ideas; he wishes to preserve things as they are; he is content to "muddle along." He is respectable in that he is not the dupe of theorizers; he keeps in touch with realities. What he lacks is vision, generosity, passion for improvement. Many more and much harsher criticisms than these, Arnold utters against the contemporary Whigs or Liberals—not that he loved them less, but that he expected more of them. The liberal movement, in an age of triumphing democracy, was the movement which most needed and most invited critical direction. His criticism of the Liberals, including the radical Left, is directed mainly at their insistence upon abstract rights, their *laissez-faire* theories, their worship of machinery, their materialistic ideals, their strident individualism, their tendency toward anarchy.

As a man of letters turning to politics in the third quarter of the nineteenth century,—turning to politics with conservative temper and progressive ideas, —Arnold was probably more interested in Thomas Carlyle and John Stuart Mill than in Disraeli and Gladstone. "Heckling" the leading statesman was the task of the "politicians." His task as a man of letters was to draw, with reference to his own ideal, the right line between the political tendency represented by Carlyle, which was essentially aristocratic, and the political tendency represented by Mill, which was essentially democratic. When he published his *Culture and Anarchy* in 1869, the main work of his two great literary predecessors in the field was already completed. His work was built upon theirs. He was deeply indebted to both of them; and he entertained for both of them quite as much respect as most of us feel for those whose efforts have enabled us to leave them behind. He valued Mill's mental receptivity, his zeal for progress, his passion for social solidarity. He valued Carlyle's insight into the eternal verities: "The scope and upshot of his teaching," he says in his essay on Emerson, "are true." But he thought them both incomplete. Carlyle had a soundly conservative temper, but he was deficient in progressive ideas, and he had pushed the virtue of his tendency to excess, becoming by the middle of the century a violent reactionary, thanking God when men called him a Tory. There was much, too, in Carlyle's literary manners that Arnold disapproved: his overstrained earnestness, his heat and fury, his eccentricities of expression. Mill, on the other hand, had progressive ideas, but he lacked the stability and soundness of the conservative temper; he pushed the virtue of his tendency to excess, becoming thin and unrealistic in his radicalism; he speculated and dogmatized about government, liberty, natural rights too much like a political geometrician of the eighteenth century—in the void. Arnold's problem was to shun the excesses of both, and to complement the virtues of one with the virtues of the other; for in politics, as in everything else, he sought not mediocrity but the genuine golden mean of Aristotle. Carlyle was right in his regard for a wise and energetic government; the excess of his virtue was his contempt for the governed. Mill was right in his regard for the individual interests of the many; the excess of his virtue was his desire to emasculate government. What the "Liberal of the future" looked forward to was a wise and energetic government by true representatives of a wise and energetic people.

It is interesting to see how he laces the thought of

Carlyle and the thought of Mill together in the essay called "Numbers," which was delivered to an American audience: "It may be better, it is better, that the body of the people, with all its faults, should act for itself, and control its own affairs, than that it should be set aside as ignorant and incapable, and have its affairs managed for it by a so-called superior class, possessing property and intelligence. Property and intelligence cannot be trusted to show a sound majority themselves; the exercise of power by the people tends to educate the people."   So far the passage is exactly in the spirit of Mill.   The following sentences are exactly in the spirit of Carlyle: "But still, the world being what it is, we must surely expect the aims and doings of the great majority of men to be at present very faulty, and this in a numerous community no less than in a small one.   So much we must certainly, I think, concede to the sages and to the saints."

A similar interlacing of conservative and radical thought appears in his important essay on "Equality," in which he discusses the "sacred" institution of property for the benefit of the Royal Institution. "It cannot be too often repeated: peasants and workmen have no natural rights, not one.   Only we ought instantly to add, that kings and nobles have none either.   If it is the sound English doctrine that all rights are created by law and are based on expediency, and are alterable as the public advantage may require, certainly that orthodox doctrine is mine." That is pretty nearly in the spirit of Burke; it is Carlyle shorn of his transcendental doctrine of "divine right." But now hear Arnold's radicalism, or rather his progressivism, speaking: "Our present organization has been an appointed stage in our growth; it has been of good use, and has enabled us to do great things. But the use is at an end, and the stage is over. Ask yourselves if you do not sometimes feel in yourselves a sense, that in spite of the strenuous efforts for good of so many excellent persons among us, we begin somehow to flounder and to beat the air; that we seem to be finding ourselves stopped on this line of advance and on that, and to be threatened with a sort of standstill. It is that we are trying to live with a social organization of which the day is over. Certainly equality will never of itself alone give us a perfect civilization. But, with such inequality as ours, a perfect civilization is impossible." This is pretty nearly in the spirit of Mill; it is Mill shorn of his abstract Revolutionary theory that equality is the normal state of human beings. Arnold is friendly to certain measures for the division of the great estates of the aristocracy, not because every man has an equal right to land, but because he considers an aristocratic monopoly of land a hindrance to the civilization of all three classes of society by augmenting the natural pride and indolence of the upper class and discouraging the other two. The political vivacity and intelligence of the French people as a whole are in considerable measure the consequence, he repeatedly reminds his readers, of the Revolutionary land reforms which enabled a relatively large proportion of the peasant class to enjoy the self-respect derivable from the possession of property.

The most important of Arnold's more purely political essays is that on "Democracy." And here, once more, the central motive is to be as authoritative as Carlyle and as progressive as Mill—to preserve the real virtue of aristocratic government in democratic institutions. "It is the chief virtue of a healthy and uncorrupted aristocracy," he says, "that it is in the grand style. That elevation of character, that noble way of thinking and behaving, which is an eminent gift of nature to some individuals, is also often generated in whole classes of men (at least when these come of a strong and good race) by the possession of power, by the importance and responsibility of high station, by habitual dealing with great things, by being placed above the necessity of constantly struggling for the little things. And it is the source of great virtues. It may go along with a not very quick or open intelligence; but it cannot well go along with a conduct vulgar and ignoble. A governing class imbued with it may not be capable of intelligently leading the masses of a people to the highest pitch of welfare for them; but it sets them an invaluable example of qualities without which no really high welfare can exist. This has been done for their nation by the best aristocracies." All this is exactly in line with Burke; such considerations made Carlyle turn in his later years toward the existing aristocracy to save England from the masses. Arnold says, "The time has arrived, however, when it is becoming impossible for the aristocracy of England to conduct and wield the English nation any longer." This is of course in line with Mill.

This problem then arises for the lover of the grand style in politics, as in all things: What is to be done to preserve us from the natural vulgarity and ignobility of popular government? "On what action may we rely to replace, for some time at any rate, that action of the aristocracy upon the people of this country, which we have seen exercise an influence in many respects elevating and beneficial, but which is rapidly, and from inevitable causes, ceasing? In other words, and to use a short and significant modern expression which every one understands, what influence may help us to prevent the English from becoming, with the growth of democracy, *Americanised?* I confess I am disposed to answer: On the action of the State. . . . The question is, whether, retaining all its powers of control over a government which should abuse its trust, the nation may not now find advantage in voluntarily allowing to it purposes somewhat ampler, and limits somewhat wider within which to execute them, than formerly; whether the nation may not thus acquire in the State an ideal of high reason and right feeling, representing its best self, commanding general respect, and forming a rallying-point for the intelligence and for the worthiest instincts of the community, which will herein find a true bond of union."

Arnold proposes this solution with his eye on France and on Germany. "The power of France in Europe is at this day," he says, "mainly owing to the completeness with which she has organised democratic institutions." The power of Germany, as he points out in his educational writings, is in the completeness with which she has organized her public instruction. France politically and Germany educationally are the most enlightened nations of Europe. State action in both these countries is excessive. If Arnold were preaching to the French, he would make English localism and liberty his text. His lack of reverence for the Prussian spirit in politics is rather roughly brought out in the following passage from *Friendship's Garland:* "I know German constitutionalism pretty well. It comes up to the throne, 'With fullest heart-devotion we approach Prussia's king, reverently beseeching him to turn away his unconstitutional ministers.' Prussia's gracious king gives a grunt, and administers a sound kick to his petitioner's behind, who then departs, singing in fervent tones: '*Hoch* for King and fatherland!'" But State action, Arnold believes, may immensely extend and develop its control over property, education, religion and so forth, without danger of abasing and degrading a people like the English, cradled and nourished in the passion for liberty. His immediate political demand, then, is for an intelligent and efficient State, working strenuously through all its institutions. When the State had accomplished its social business the "Liberal of the future" might begin to talk again about liberty.

In considering Arnold's ideas of education we remarked that his sense of the importance of the subject was due to the arrival of the middle class in politics and to the necessity of educating the middle class before allowing them to assume control. In his essay on "The Future of Liberalism" *(Mixed Essays)* he defines his leading *political* idea, also with reference to the emergence in the political arena of the middle class: "The master-thought by which my politics are governed is rather this— the thought of the bad civilization of the English middle class." In "Ecce, Convertimur Ad Gentes" he says: "The middle class cannot assume rule as they are at present—it is impossible. And yet in the rule of this immense class, this class with so many correspondences, communications, and openings into the lower class, lies our future." In another passage in "The Future of Liberalism" he gives his "master-thought" its full scope: "Now of man in society the capital need is, that the whole body of society should come to live with a life worthy to be called *human,* and corresponding to man's true aspirations and powers. This, the humanisation of man in society, is civilisation. The aim for us all is to promote it, and to promote it is above all the aim of the true politician."

What Arnold means by civilization he explains most fully in the first chapter of *Culture and Anarchy*. Civilization, as the Prussians of our day tell us, is *Kultur*. Arnold calls it Culture, and his definition and description of the thing have fixed the meaning of the word for English-speaking people. It is one of his grand general ideas. Culture, he tells us, implies a knowledge of the best that is known and thought in the world. But culture originates in the love of perfection. "It moves by the force, not merely or primarily of the scientific passion for pure knowledge, but also of the moral and social passion for doing good. As, in the first view of it, we took for its worthy motto Montesquieu's words: 'To render an intelligent being yet more intelligent!' so, in the second view of it, there is no better motto which it can have than these words of Bishop Wilson: 'To make reason and the will of God prevail!'" Culture, furthermore, is patient:

"Knowing that no action or institution can be salutary and stable which is not based on reason and the will of God, it is not so bent on acting and instituting, even with the great aim of diminishing human error and misery ever before its thoughts, but that it can remember that acting and instituting are of little use, unless we know how and what we ought to act and institute."   Culture is like religion in its inwardness: "Religion says, *The kingdom of God is within you;* and culture, in like manner, places human perfection in an *internal* condition, in the growth and predominance of our humanity proper, as distinguished from our animality.   It places it in the ever-increasing efficacy and in the general harmonious expansion of those gifts of thought and feeling, which make the peculiar dignity, wealth, and happiness of human nature."   Culture, finally, is not an affair for the individual alone: it is a social enterprise: "Because men are all members of one great whole, and the sympathy which is in human nature will not allow one member to be indifferent to the rest or to have a perfect welfare independent of the rest, the expansion of our humanity to suit the idea of perfection which culture forms, must be a *general* expansion. . . . The individual is required, under pain of being stunted and enfeebled in his own development if he disobeys, to carry others along with him in his march towards perfection, to be continually doing all he can to enlarge and increase the volume of the human stream sweeping thitherward." A people, then, possess "civilization" in Arnold's sense of the word, when the best available knowledge is widely diffused among them, when they are animated by a passion for the harmonious perfection of their faculties, when they have a true sense of human values, when their social sympathy is quick. This is to possess "sweetness and light."

To present and labor for ideals like these, is not to work on a political platform; it is to preach a social gospel. And that is exactly what Arnold most earnestly sets himself to do: to preach the gospel of "culture," first to the English, and then to all nations. What he does, one will observe, is to seize upon the *object* of the "true politician," and to proclaim that object as the "one thing needful." Here is the essence of Arnold's aristocratic equalitarianism: "Plenty of people," he says, "will try to give the masses, as they call them, an intellectual food prepared and adapted in the way they think proper for the real condition of the masses. The ordinary popular literature is an example of this way of working on the masses. Plenty of people will try to indoctrinate the masses with the set of ideas and judgments constituting the creed of their own profession or party. Our religious and political organisations give an example of this way of working on the masses. I condemn neither; but culture works differently. . . . The men of culture are the true apostles of equality. The great men of culture are those who have had a passion for diffusing, for making prevail, for carrying from one end of society to the other, the best knowledge, the best ideas of their time; who have labored to divest knowledge of all that was harsh, uncouth, difficult, abstract, professional, exclusive; to humanise it, to make it efficient outside the clique of the cultivated and learned, yet still remaining the *best* knowledge and thought of the time, and a true source, therefore, of sweetness and light."

Some powerful tendency, Arnold asserts, opposes all the important teachings of culture: "The idea of perfection as an *inward* condition of the mind and spirit is all at variance with the mechanical and material civilization in esteem with us. The idea of perfection as a *general* expansion of the human family is at variance with our strong individualism, our hatred of all limits to the unrestrained swing of the individual's personality, our maxim of 'every man for himself.' Above all, the idea of perfection as a *harmonious* expansion of human nature is at variance with our want of flexibility, with our inaptitude for seeing more than one side of a thing, with our intense energetic absorption in the particular pursuit we happen to be following. So culture has a rough task to achieve in this country. . . ."

When Arnold writes against a "mechanical and material civilization" he is continuing the work of Carlyle. The following passage is but a translation into his own quieter style of the gospel of *Sartor* and the stormy denunciations of *Past and Present:*

"Faith in machinery is, I said, our besetting danger; often in machinery most absurdly disproportioned to the end which this machinery, if it is to do any good at all, is to serve; but always in machinery, as if it had a value in and for itself. What is freedom but machinery? what is population but machinery? what is coal but machinery? what are railroads but machinery? what is wealth but machinery? what are, even, religious organisations but machinery? Now almost every voice in England is accustomed to speak of these things as if they were precious ends in themselves, and therefore had some of the characters of perfection indisputably joined to them. I have before now noticed Mr. Roebuck's stock argument for proving the greatness and happiness of England as she is, and for quite stopping the mouths of all gainsayers. Mr. Roebuck is never weary of reiterating this argument of his, so I do not know why I should be weary of noticing it. 'May not every man in England say what he likes?'—Mr. Roebuck perpetually asks, and that, he thinks, is quite sufficient, and when every man may say what he likes, our aspirations ought to be satisfied. But the aspirations of culture, which is the study of perfection, are not satisfied, unless what men say, when they may say what they like, is worth saying—has good in it, and more good than bad. In the same way the *Times,* replying to some foreign strictures on the dress, looks, and behaviour of the English abroad, urges that the English ideal is that every one should be free to do and to look just as he likes. But culture indefatigably tries, not to make what each raw person may like the rule by which he fashions himself; but to draw ever nearer to a sense of what is indeed beautiful, graceful, and becoming, and to get the raw person to like that."

Of these things which are classified as "machinery," the most important in relation to the liberal movement was "freedom." Belief in liberty as a good in itself, irrespective of the end for which it was used, was an ancient English superstition, which had acquired an air of respectability in the Revolutionary Era, and had become a talismanic catch-word of the Liberal politicians. To the criticism of liberty as a good in itself Arnold devotes an entire chapter of *Culture and Anarchy.* He cleverly deprives the talisman of half its power by entitling the chapter "Doing As One Likes"; the phrase is an equivalent, yet it lacks historical glamour! Though he aims his attack directly at contemporary popular orators and demagogues, he strikes through them at the "Philosophic Radicalism" of the Utilitarians. Mill's *Liberty* he had read when it came out, in 1859, and had written of it to his sister on July ninth of that year: "Have you seen Mill's book on Liberty. It is worth reading attentively, being one of the few books that inculcate tolerance in an unalarming and inoffensive way." "Doing As One Likes," published ten years later, gives us his reflections upon the practical consequences of carrying out Mill's central doctrine.

This doctrine was thus announced by its author: "The object of this essay is to assert one very simple principle as entitled to govern absolutely the dealings of society with the individual in the way of compulsion and control, whether the means used be physical force, or the moral coercion of public opinion. That principle is, that the sole end for which mankind are warranted, individually or collectively, in interfering with the liberty of action of any of their members is self-protection." According to Mill's theory, which was also the theory of eighteenth-century thinkers like Godwin and Paine, government is at best but a "necessary evil"; therefore it followed, as the night the day, that the less one had of it the better.

What, practically, has been, Arnold asks, the result of this popular doctrine?

"This and that man, and this and that body of men, all over the country, are beginning to assert and put in practice an Englishman's right to do what he likes; his right to march where he likes, meet where he likes, enter where he likes, hoot as he likes, threaten as he likes, smash as he likes. All this, I say, tends to anarchy; and though a number of excellent people, and particularly my friends of the Liberal or progressive party, as they call themselves, are kind enough to reassure us by saying that these are trifles, that a few transient outbreaks of rowdyism signify nothing, that our system of liberty is one which itself cures all the evils which it works, that the educated and intelligent classes stand in overwhelming strength and majestic repose, ready, like our military force in riots, to act at a moment's notice—yet one finds that one's Liberal friends generally say this because they have such faith in themselves and their nostrums, when they shall return, as the public welfare requires, to place and power. But this faith of theirs one cannot exactly share, when one has so long had them and their nostrums at work, and sees that they have not prevented our coming to our present embarrassed condition. . . .

"Mr. Murphy lectures at Birmingham, and showers on the population of that town 'words,' says the Home Secretary, 'only fit to be addressed to thieves or murderers.' . . . 'I will carry out my lectures (says Mr. Murphy) if they walk over my body as a dead corpse, and I say to the Mayor of Birmingham that he is my servant while I am in Birmingham, and as my servant he must do his duty and protect me.' Touching and beautiful words, which find a sympathetic chord in every British bosom! The moment it is plainly put before us that a man is asserting his personal liberty, we are half disarmed; because we are believers in freedom, and not in some dream of a right reason to which the assertion of our freedom is to be subordinated. Accordingly, the Secretary of State had to say that although the lecturer's language was 'only fit to be addressed to thieves or murderers,' yet, 'I do not think he is to be deprived, I do not think that anything I have said could justify the inference that he is to be deprived, of the right of protection in a place built by him for the purpose of these lectures; because the language was not language which afforded grounds for a criminal prosecution.' No, nor to be silenced by Mayor, or Home Secretary, or any administrative authority on earth, simply on their notion of what is discreet and reasonable! This is in perfect consonance with our public opinion, and with our national love for the assertion of personal liberty."

Arnold opposed this practise and the theory underlying it on the ground taken in the eighteenth century by Burke, who, in his *Reflection on the Revolution in France,* had said: "Men have no right to what is not reasonable, and what is not for their benefit." Carlyle had taken up this intellectual proposition, and had saturated it with moral feeling in his *Sartor:* "Obedience is our universal duty and destiny; wherein whoso will not bend must break: too early and too thoroughly we cannot be trained to know that Would, in this world of ours, is a mere zero to Should, and for most part as the smallest of fractions to Shall." Arnold says expressly that men have no natural rights, independent of their social duties and responsibilities. He declares that an attempt to assert such rights leads straight to anarchy. He reiterates indefatigably that liberty is only a means to a good and not a good in itself. He enlarges on the idea that true good comes to the individual, not through the unchecked expansion of his impulse to do as he likes, but through his efforts to conform to a standard of right reason outside himself and unaffected by the fitful impressions of the hour. He insists that this standard is to be found by criticism disinterestedly studying the best that is known and thought in the world. Finally, he believes that this standard can best be maintained and made to prevail by the action of the State. In thus magnifying immensely the function of government, Arnold is quite at one with Carlyle and quite at odds with Mill.

Now rises the question, a very vital question, What does Arnold mean by the State? Who is going to enforce the standards of right reason upon the people? It is at this point that Arnold parts company with Carlyle, with whom he has hitherto found so much in common. Carlyle would have the power in the hands of an "aristocracy of talent"; but in his later years he turned more and more toward the actually existing aristocracy, which he had upbraided as the "do-nothing aristocracy," to furnish the talent, to continue to bear the burdens of government. To Arnold this was not a satisfactory solution of the problem. He thought that the age of aristocratic government in the interest of the aristocratic class was over; and, on the other hand, he thought that one class ought not to attempt to legislate for the other classes, because it would not know what the other classes wanted, that is to say, what they needed. In this respect, no class was fit to bear the rule; a shift of power from the aristocracy to the middle class or from the middle class to the lower class would modify the complexion of government, would change the seat of pain; but it would not essentially alter the character of class government, which is inevitably a compromise of jealousies, a truce in an eternal conflict. He himself was bent upon more or less abolishing all classes by permeating all grades of society with culture, so that the State, which Burke had defined as "the nation in its collective and corporate character," should be thoroughly "the representative acting-power of the nation."

It is to show the unfitness of each class for rule, and to demonstrate the need for a national integration and regeneration by culture, that Arnold makes, in the third chapter of *Culture and Anarchy,* his famous analysis of the existing classes of society. Here again—though he coins a new set of catchwords and nicknames, and though his emphasis is slightly different—his general outlook is very much like that of Carlyle.

The upper class, which Carlyle had scornfully denominated the Do-Nothing Aristocracy, the Double-barreled Game-Preservers, and the Dilettantes, Arnold calls, with allusion to their somewhat remote ancestors, the Barbarians. In his delicate ironical description of their merits there is a certain smiling gentleness, quite foreign to Carlyle, which one may attribute to Arnold's personal fondness for their manners and for their recreations:

"The Barbarians, to whom we all owe so much, and who reinvigorated and renewed our worn-out Europe, had, as is well known, eminent merits. . . . The Barbarians brought with them that staunch individualism, as the modern phrase is, and that passion for doing as one likes, for the assertion of personal liberty, which appears to Mr. Bright the central idea of English life, and of which we have, at any rate, a very rich supply. The stronghold and natural seat of this passion was in the nobles of whom our aristocratic class are the inheritors; and this class, accordingly, have signally manifested it, and have done much by their example to recommend it to the body of the nation, who already, indeed, had it in their blood. The Barbarians, again, had the passion for field-sports; and they have handed it on to our aristocratic class, who of this passion too, as of the passion for asserting one's personal liberty, are the great natural stronghold. The care of the Barbarians for the body, and for all manly exercises; the vigour, good looks, and fine complexion which they acquired and perpetuated in their families by these means—all this may be observed still in our aristocratic class. The chivalry of the Barbarians, with its characteristics of high spirit, choice manners, and distinguished bearing,—what is this but the attractive commencement of the politeness of our aristocratic class? In some Barbarian noble, no doubt, one would have admired, if one could have been then alive to see it, the rudiments of our politest peer. Only, all this culture (to call it by that name) of the Barbarians was an exterior culture mainly. It consisted principally in outward gifts and graces, in looks, manners, accomplishments, prowess. The chief inward gifts which had part in it were the most exterior, so to speak, of inward gifts, those which come nearest to outward ones; they were courage, a high spirit, self-confidence. Far within, and unawakened, lay a whole range of powers of thought and feeling, to which these interesting productions of nature had, from the circumstances of their life, no access. Making allowances for the difference of the times, surely we can observe precisely the same thing now in our aristocratic class. In general its culture is exterior chiefly; all the exterior graces and accomplishments, and the more external of the inward virtues, seem to be principally its portion. It now, of course, cannot but be often in contact with those studies by which, from the world of thought and feeling, true culture teaches us to fetch sweetness and light; but its hold upon these very studies appears remarkably external, and unable to exert any deep power upon its spirit. Therefore the one insufficiency which we noted in the perfect mean of this class was an insufficiency of light. And owing to the same causes, does not a subtle criticism lead us to make, even on the good looks and politeness of our aristocratic class, and of even the most fascinating half of that class, the feminine half, the one qualifying remark, that in these charming gifts there should perhaps be, for ideal perfection, a shade more *soul?"*

Let us add to this description of the Barbarian this delicious morsel out of *Friendship's Garland:*

"Everybody knows Lord Elcho's appearance, and how admirably he looks the part of our governing classes; to my mind, indeed, *the mere cock of his lordship's hat is one of the finest and most aristocratic things we have.* So of course I pointed Lord Elcho out to Arminius. Arminius eyed him with a jacobinical sort of a smile, and then: 'Cedar of Lebanon which God has not yet broken!' sneered he. I was pleased at Arminius knowing his St. Augustine, for the Prussians are in general thought to be much tainted with irreligion; but I felt at the time, and I feel still, that this was not by any means the proper way of speaking of a dashing nobleman like Lord Elcho."

The middle classes, Carlyle's Giant-working Mammonism, Arnold, alluding to the enemies of the Biblical Children of Light, called the Philistines. It is in his account of these classes that one feels the most pronounced difference of emphasis as between him and "the prophet of Cheyne Row." Toward the "captains of industry" Carlyle had manifested an immense admiration; he looked upon them as the real heroes of modern times—not the most exalted type, to be sure, yet assuredly heroes and

therefore greatly to be praised.   Toward industrial
heroes Arnold manifests, in his most conciliatory
passages, a qualified respect which may be illustrated by this from "On the Study of Celtic Literature":

"All tendencies of human nature are in themselves vital and profitable; when they are blamed,
they are only to be blamed relatively, not absolutely.
.   .   .   Out of the already humdrum habit of the
creeping Saxon, as the Celt calls him—out of his
way of going near the ground—has come, no doubt,
Philistinism, that plant of essentially Germanic
growth, flourishing with its genuine marks only
in the German Fatherland, Great Britain and her
colonies, and the United States of America; but
what a soul of goodness there is in Philistinism itself!   And this soul of goodness I, who am often
supposed to be Philistinism's mortal enemy merely
because I do not wish it to have things all its own
way, cherish as much as anybody.   This steady-going
habit leads at last, as I have said, up to science, up to
the comprehension and interpretation of the world.
With us in Great Britain, it is true, it does not
seem to lead so far as that; it is in Germany, where
the habit is more unmixed, that it can lead to science.
Here with us it seems at a certain point to meet with
a conflicting force, which checks it and prevents its
pushing on to science; but before reaching this point
what conquests has it not won! and all the more,
perhaps, for stopping short at this point, for spend-
ing its exertions within a bounded field, the field of
plain sense, of direct practical utility.   How it has

augmented the comforts and conveniences of life for us! Doors that open, windows that shut, locks that turn, razors that shave, coats that wear, watches that go, and a thousand more such good things, are the invention of the Philistines."

It was not by words like these that Arnold became known as "Philistinism's mortal enemy." His general habit was to leave the task of extolling "the soul of goodness there is in Philistinism" to Philistinism's own orators, and then to make game of the orators and their orations. It is more in his characteristic vein to write of the upper part of the working class that it "looks forward to the happy day when it will sit on thrones with commercial members of Parliament and other middle-class potentates, to survey as Mr. Bright beautifully says, 'the cities it has built, the railroads it has made, the manufactures it has produced, the cargoes which freight the ships of the greatest mercantile navy the world has ever seen.'" It is more in his vein to say of the lower working class, "which gives all its energies to organising itself, through trades unions and other means, so as to constitute, first a great working-class power independent of the middle and aristocratic classes, and then, by dint of members, give the law to them and itself reign absolutely"—it is more in his vein to say that the lower working class must go with the Philistines, "because it is its class and its class instinct which it seeks to affirm—its ordinary self, not its best self; and it is machinery, an industrial machinery, and power and pre-eminence and other external goods, which fill its thoughts, and not an inward perfection. It is wholly occupied, according to Plato's subtle expression, with the things of itself and not its real self, with the things of the State and not the real State."

Of the narrowness and self-satisfaction of the middle classes he was particularly ashamed because these classes, constituting the bulk of the population, were mainly responsible for the impression England made upon other countries. Americans who are irritated by his distasteful comment upon American life may find some consolation in knowing that he took great pains to bring unfavorable comment upon English life to the attention of his fellow countrymen. In his essay on Heine he speaks with malicious pleasure of the poet's detestation for England as the land of Philistines. The English, Arnold explains, have "become, in a sense, of all people the most inaccessible to ideas and the most impatient of them; inaccessible to them, because of their want of familiarity with them; and impatient of them because they have got on so well without them, that they despise those who, not having got on as well as themselves, still make a fuss for what they themselves have done so well without. But there has followed from hence, in this country, somewhat of a general depression of pure intelligence: Philistia has come to be thought by us the true Land of Promise, and it is anything but that; the born lover of ideas, the born hater of commonplaces, must feel in this country, that the sky over his head is of brass and iron." There is a passage well designed to keep the middle classes from the self-satisfaction which is vulgarizing and degrading!

The lower class Carlyle had designated, rather in compassion than in contempt, the White Negroes or the Poor-Slaves. His compassion for them, it is to be noted, was unmixed with any desire for their political enfranchisement or with any very lively interest in their intellectual welfare. What he desired was to regiment them and put them in charge of governmental drill-sergeants of labor. Considering this class politically, as a potential element of the State, Arnold says: "That vast portion, lastly, of the working class which, raw and undeveloped, has long lain half-hidden amidst its poverty and squalor, and is now issuing from its hiding-place to assert an Englishman's heaven-born privilege of doing as he likes, and is beginning to perplex us by marching where it likes, meeting where it likes, bawling what it likes, breaking what it likes,—to this vast residuum we may with great propriety give the name of *Populace*."

A writer who expatiates upon class distinctions

is on dangerous ground. He runs the risk of rousing in members of each class a Pharasaical gratitude for their exemption from the faults of the other classes. To guard against this peril, to stimulate each of his readers to earnest self-examination, Arnold reminds us that there is a "common basis of human nature" underlying all the classes, and that there are latent in every one of us "the same tendencies and passions which have made our fellow-citizens of other classes what they are." With altogether charming sweetness and light he takes himself for an illustration:

"I myself am properly speaking a Philistine,—Mr. Swinburne would add, the son of a Philistine. And although, through circumstances which will perhaps one day be known if ever the affecting history of my conversion comes to be written, I have for the most part, broken with the ideas and the tea-meetings of my own class, yet I have not, on that account, been brought much the nearer to the ideas and works of the Barbarians or of the Populace. Nevertheless, I never take a gun or a fishing-rod in my hands without feeling that I have in the ground of my nature the self-same seeds which, fostered by circumstances, do so much to make the Barbarian; and that, with the Barbarian's advantages, I might have rivalled him. Place me in one of his fortified posts, with these seeds of a love for field sports sown in my nature, with all the means of developing them, with all the pleasures at my command, with most whom I met deferring to me, every one I met smiling on me, and with every appearance of permanence and security before me and behind me, —then I too might have grown, I feel, into a very passable child of the established fact, of commendable spirit and politeness, and, at the same time, a little inaccessible to ideas and light; not, of course, with either the eminent fine spirit of our type of aristocratic perfection, or the eminent turn for resistance of our type of aristocratic excess, but, according to the measure of the common run of mankind, something between the two. And as to the Populace, who, whether he be Barbarian or Philistine, can look at them without sympathy, when he remembers how often,—every time that we snatch up a vehement opinion in ignorance and passion, every time that we long to crush an adversary by sheer violence, every time that we are envious, every time that we are brutal, every time that we adore mere power or success, every time that we add our voice to swell a blind clamour against some unpopular personage, every time that we trample savagely on the fallen,—he has found in his own bosom the eternal spirit of the Populace, and that there needs only a little help from circumstances to make it triumph in him untamably."

Since the instinctive self of all of us participates in the faults of Barbarians, Philistines and Populace, our salvation is not to follow our instincts but to discipline and subdue them, and to rise above class feeling. Those who thus master their native impulses constitute what Arnold calls "the saving remnant." That saving remnant is the hopeful nu-

cleus of regeneration and the inspiring model for
the homogeneous society of the future, in which an
aristocrat can be whole-heartedly a Liberal.

"In each class there are born a certain number of
natures with a curiosity about their best self, with a
bent for seeing things as they are, for disentangling
themselves from machinery, for simply concerning
themselves with reason and the will of God, and doing their best to make these prevail;—for the pursuit, in a word, of perfection.   To certain manifestations of this love for perfection mankind have
accustomed themselves to give the name of genius;
implying, by this name, something original and
heaven-bestowed in the passion.   But the passion is
to be found far beyond those manifestations of
it to which the world usually gives the name of
genius and in which there is, for the most part, a
talent of some kind or other, a special and striking
execution, informed by the heaven-bestowed ardour,
or genius.   It is to be found in many manifestations
beside these, and may best be called, as we have
called it, the love and pursuit of perfection; culture
being the true nurse of the pursuing love, and sweetness and light the true character of the pursued perfection.   Natures with this bent emerge in all
classes,—among the Barbarians, among the Philistines, among the Populace.   And this bent always
tends to take them out of their class, and to make
their distinguishing characteristic not their Barba-
rianism or their Philistinism, but their *humanity*.
They have, in general, a rough time of it in their
lives; but they are sown more abundantly than one
might think, they appear where and when one least

expects it, they set up a fire which enfilades, so to speak, the class with which they are ranked; and, in general, by the extrication of their best self as the self to develop, and by the simplicity of the ends fixed by them as paramount, they hinder the unchecked predominance of that class-life which is the affirmation of our ordinary self, and seasonably disconcert mankind in their worship of machinery."

Arnold's "saving remnant" bears some resemblance to Carlyle's "aristocracy of talent." But it is differently constituted and its functions are different. The distinctive function of the "aristocracy of talent" was immediately to govern England; the distinctive function of the "saving remnant" is gradually to regenerate society. The distinctive characteristic of Carlyle's choice few was precisely heaven-given *talent*—the divine and unpurchasable power of genius. Arnold perhaps regards genius as too rare a phenomenon to wait for and to depend upon from year to year and from generation to generation. There seem to be considerable periods in the life of every nation when there are no first-rate geniuses in sight! There never are in the world geniuses enough to "go around." Furthermore, those upon whom heaven's fire has descended are liable to be a little scorched on one side. The distinctive characteristic of Arnold's choice few is their symmetrically rounded *humanity*. The wisdom of setting up *humanity* and not *talent* as the mark to be aimed at is this: a symmetrically rounded humanity *is,* in a sense, purchasable; it can in some measure be attained by an effort of the will and the understanding. It is a high but a soundly democratic ideal; it is open to everybody to strive toward it. To strive toward talent or genius is an absurdity. To set up genius as the mark is to exclude ninety-nine per cent. of the marksmen. It is to establish hero-worship. Hero-worship calls forth some admirable emotions; it appeals to reverence; it inspires fidelity and obedience; but it does not challenge the will to self-dependent effort nor the intellectual powers to a general opening.

The check that Arnold imposed upon his instinctive "transcendentalism" is indicated in a peculiarly interesting passage of a letter to his mother, March 3, 1865: "No one has a stronger and more abiding sense than I have of the dæmonic element—as Goethe called it—which underlies and encompasses our life; but I think, as Goethe thought, that the right thing is, while conscious of this element, and of all there is inexplicable around one, to keep pushing on one's posts into the darkness, and to establish no post that is not perfectly in light and firm."

This passage marks the point at which Arnold very respectfully shook hands with Carlyle, and moved toward the intellectual position of Mill. "Whoso," says Carlyle in *Sartor Resartus,* "whoso recognizes the unfathomable, all-pervading domain of Mystery, which is everywhere under our feet and among our hands; to whom the Universe is an Oracle and Temple, as well as a Kitchen and Cattle Stall,—he shall be a delirious Mystic." Mill, on the other hand, made it the work of his life to destroy mysticism in England; the "intuitive philosophy" he considered the inner citadel of the enemies of social progress. Delirious wonder in the presence of the universe he held to be caused by the vastness of the universe and due to the lack of moral cultivation in the beholder. Arnold steered midway between the two positions; he respected the mystic but not the delirium! Something might come to man from the encompassing dæmonic element; but that emphatically was not the element for man's will and understanding to work in or even habitually to dwell upon. Mill said in his essay on Nature: "Allowing everything to be an instinct which anybody has ever asserted to be one, it remains true that nearly every respectable attribute of humanity is the result not of instinct, but of a victory over instinct, and there is hardly anything valuable in the natural man except capabilities—a whole world of possibilities, all of them dependent upon eminently artificial discipline for being realized." That passage marks the point at which Arnold clasps hands with Mill.

And so Arnold brings his light artillery to bear upon the image of the inaffable, heavy-witted, instinctive John Bull—"stupid in speech and wise in action"—which Carlyle had set up for admiration, and which Mr. G. K. Chesterton in our time has tried to refurbish. The national characteristic of the English, Arnold says, is "energy with honesty": the deepest current of John Bull's being sets that way. Yet Carlyle, in the voice of the Hebrew prophets, had constantly exhorted this honest energetic creature to fear God and to work while it was yet day. To Arnold these injunctions seemed relatively superfluous; and Carlyle's endless insistence upon them impresses him as a misdirected effort of criticism. The timely critic does not shout for what is abundantly present; he seeks to foster and bring out the undeveloped elements in individual and national character. A month after the elder prophet's death in 1881, Arnold, forgetting his debts and the admiration of his youth, wrote to a French correspondent: "I never much liked Carlyle. He seemed to me to be 'carrying coals to Newcastle,' as our proverb says; preaching earnestness to a nation which had plenty of it by nature, but was less abundantly supplied with several other useful things."

Among the "other useful things" Arnold had chiefly in mind sweetness of disposition and manner and the light of a well-nourished intelligence. In neither of these qualities did the honest energetic John Bull abound; and Carlyle had not been greatly disquieted by their absence—had, indeed, said much to encourage the multitude of fools to acquiesce in their own folly, to abandon the attempt to play the wise men, and to submit with docility to their heaven-sent leaders. For fools the specific was morality strongly flavored with obedience. Mill had gone to the other extreme in assuming in his ethical and political discussion that the multitude is mainly composed of quite rational beings. Arnold aims to correct the errors of both Mill and Carlyle by fostering and bringing out the latent intelligence of the multitude. The distinction which he drew between the special character of his own effort and that of Renan holds in a general way as between his own effort and that of Carlyle: "The difference is, perhaps, that he tends to inculcate *morality* in a high sense of the word, upon the French nation as what they most want, while I tend to inculcate *intelligence,* also in a high sense of the word, upon the English nation as what they most want."

In countries like England and the United States, where an ideal of spiritual perfection, and an inadequate ideal of spiritual perfection, has been established by the English Puritans, nothing could be more timely, more salutary, than Arnold's respectful yet vigorous exposure of the inadequacy of that ideal. Mark Twain's "Be good and you will be lonesome" is a humorous hint at a defect in the traditional American conception of perfection. The completed goodness which Arnold envisages is not "lonesome," for it is affable, engaging, winsome.

Let us put beside Mark Twain's aphorism the Englishman's humorous hint at the defect of the incomplete kind: "Notwithstanding the mighty results of the Pilgrim Fathers' voyage, they and their standard of perfection are rightly judged when we figure to ourselves Shakespeare or Virgil,—souls in whom sweetness and light, and all that in human nature is most humane, were eminent,—accompanying them on their voyage, and think what intolerable company Shakespeare and Virgil would have found them! In the same way let us judge the religious organisations which are all around us."

Arnold did not relish lonesomeness; worse than that he hated being "bored"; the great fault which he found with the society dominated by Puritan "spirituality" in England and America was that it was so uninteresting and so unintelligent. He expressed his dissatisfaction in a tone of such deep conviction that he awakened concern about the subject:

"Nothing is more common than for people to confound the inward peace and satisfaction which follows the subduing of the obvious faults of our animality with what I may call absolute inward peace and satisfaction,—the peace and satisfaction which are reached as we draw near to complete spiritual perfection, and not merely to moral perfection, or rather to relative moral perfection. No people in the world have done more and struggled more to attain this relative moral perfection than our English race has. For no people in the world has the command to *resist the devil,* to *overcome the wicked one,* in the nearest and most obvious sense of those words, had such a pressing force and reality. And we have had our reward, not only in the great worldly prosperity which our obedience to this command has brought us, but also, and far more, in great inward peace and satisfaction. But to me few things are more pathetic than to see people, on the strength of the inward peace and satisfaction which their rudimentary efforts towards perfection have brought them, employ, concerning their incomplete perfection and the religious organisations within which they have found it, language which properly applies only to complete perfection, and is a far-off echo of the human soul's prophecy of it."

To distinguish sharply intelligence from righteousness, and to accentuate the importance of intelligence without seeming to undervalue righteousness are the difficult tasks performed in the fourth chapter of *Culture and Anarchy,* called "Hebraism and Hellenism." The entire chapter one may consider as a carefully qualified protest against the excessive Hebraizing tendency of Carlyle:

"Let me go back for a moment to Bishop Wilson, who says: 'First, never go against the best light you have; secondly, take care that your light be not darkness.' We show, as a nation, laudable energy and persistence in walking according to the best light we have, but are not quite careful enough, perhaps, to see that our light be not darkness. This is only another version of the old story that energy is our strong point and favorable characteristic, rather than intelligence. But we may give to this idea a more general form still, in which it will have a yet larger range of application. We may regard this energy driving at practice, this paramount sense of the obligation of duty, self-control, and work, this earnestness in going manfully with the best light we have, as one force. And we may regard the intelligence driving at those ideas which are, after all, the basis of right practice, the ardent sense for all the new and changing combinations of them which man's development brings with it, the indomitable impulse to know and adjust them perfectly, as another force. And these two forces we may regard as in some sense rivals,—rivals not by the necessity of their own nature, but as exhibited in man and his history,—and rivals dividing the empire of the world between them. And to give these forces names from the two races of men who have supplied the most signal and splendid manifestations of them, we may call them respectively the forces of Hebraism and Hellenism. Hebraism and Hellenism,—between these two points of influence moves our world. At one time it feels more powerfully the attraction of one of them, at another time of the other; and it ought to be, though it never is, evenly and happily balanced between them.

"The final aim of both Hellenism and Hebraism, as of all great spiritual disciplines, is no doubt the same: man's perfection or salvation. The very langauge which they both of them use in schooling us to reach this aim is often identical. Even when their language indicates by variation,—sometimes a broad variation, often a but slight and subtle variation,—the different courses of thought which are uppermost in each discipline, even then the unity of the final end and aim is still apparent. To employ the actual words of that discipline with which we ourselves are all of us most familiar, and the words of which, therefore, come most home to us, that final end and aim is 'that we might be partakers of the divine nature.' These are the words of a Hebrew apostle, but of Hellenism and Hebraism alike this is, I say, the aim.   .   .   .

"Still they pursue this aim by very different courses. The uppermost idea with Hellenism is to see things as they really are; the uppermost idea with Hebraism is conduct and obedience. Nothing can do away with this ineffaceable difference. The Greek quarrel with the body and its desires is, that they hinder right thinking; the Hebrew quarrel with them is, that they hinder right acting. 'He that keepeth the law, happy is he;' 'Blessed is the man that feareth the Eternal, that delighteth greatly in his commandments;'—that is the Hebrew notion of felicity; and, pursued with passion and tenacity, this notion would not let the Hebrew rest till, as is well known, he had at last got out of the law a network of prescriptions to enwrap his whole life, to govern every moment of it, every impulse, every action. The Greek notion of felicity, on the other hand, is perfectly conveyed in these words of a great French moralist: *'C'est le bonheur des hommes,'*—when? when they abhor that which is evil?—no; when they exercise themselves in the law of the Lord day and night?—no;

when they die daily?—no; when they walk about
the New Jerusalem with palms in their hands?—no;
but when they think aright, when their thought hits;
'quand ils pensent juste.' At the bottom of both the
Greek and the Hebrew notion is the desire, native in
man, for reason and the will of God, the feeling
after the universal order,—in a word, the love of
God. But, while Hebraism seizes upon certain plain,
capital intimations of the universal order, and rivets
itself, one may say, with unequalled grandeur of
earnestness and intensity on the study and observ-
ance of them, the bent of Hellenism is to follow,
with flexible activity, the whole play of the universal
order, to be apprehensive of missing any part of it,
of sacrificing one part to another, to slip away from
resting in this or that intimation of it, however
capital. An unclouded clearness of mind, an unim-
peded play of thought, is what this bent drives at.
The governing idea of Hellenism is *spontaneity of
consciousness;* that of Hebraism, *strictness of conscience.*

"Christianity changed nothing in this essential
bent of Hebraism to set doing above knowing. Self-
conquest, self-devotion, the following not our own
individual will, but the will of God, *obedience,* is the
fundamental idea of this form, also, of the discipline to which we have attached the general name of
Hebraism."

The essence of traditional Christianity in other
words is a devout hero-worship—an infinitely salutary exercise for the will, for the conscience, for the
emotions, but not directly strengthening or en-

lightening to those faculties of man which operate in the sphere of science.

"The real *unum necessarium* for us is to come to our best at all points. Instead of our 'one thing needful,' justifying in us vulgarity, hideousness, ignorance, violence,—our vulgarity, hideousness, ignorance, violence, are really so many touchstones which try our one thing needful, and which prove that in the state, at any rate, in which we ourselves have it, it is not all we want. And as the force which encourages us to stand staunch and fast by the rule and ground we have is Hebraism, so the force which encourages us to go back upon this rule, and to try the very ground on which we appear to stand, is Hellenism,—a turn for giving our consciousness free play and enlarging its range. And what I say is, not that Hellenism is always for everybody more wanted than Hebraism, but that for Mr. Murphy at this particular moment, and for the great majority of us his fellow-countrymen, it is more wanted."

We are now in a position to bring together Arnold's leading political and social ideals as they were together in his own mind. The modern politician must work in a democracy. The final object of the true politician is to create a society characterized by sweetness and light. The potentially most powerful instrument for accomplishing that end is the State. In order that it may do its work properly and speedily the State must be rendered efficient by a thoroughly scientific organization and administration of all its functions through all its institutions. The ideal State by this attention is not, in the words of St. Paul, "puffed up"; for, like charity, she seeketh not her own, but the intellectual, esthetic and moral perfection of her children. Their culture—whenever she slips into the temptation to behave herself unseemly, to glorify herself and her admirable machinery—their culture and their criticism keep her from the self-satisfaction which is vulgarizing and degrading, and send her back to her task, the humanization of man in society.

CHAPTER VII

RELIGION

"I write to convince the lover of religion that by following habits of intellectual seriousness he need not, so far as religion is concerned, lose anything."—Preface to *God and the Bible*.

" 'This is an aspect of the truth which was lost almost as soon as it was found; and yet it has to be recovered by everyone for himself who would pass the limits of proverbial and popular philosophy. The moral and intellectual are always dividing, yet they must be reunited, and in the highest conception of them are inseparable.' "—Jowett, quoted in Preface to *Last Essays on Church and Religion*.

IT is quite incontrovertible that Arnold was a friend to religion and to its public establishment. He was, however, a steadily critical friend. In the field of religion, where sensibilities are, on the whole, much more "delicate" than in the field of politics, one suspects that the majority of men prefer the deceitful kisses of an enemy to the faithful wounds of a friend. Certainly none of Arnold's other activities excited so much opposition among his contemporaries as did his writing on theology, religion, and the church. Mr. Herbert Paul quotes Gladstone as saying, "He combined a sincere devotion to the Christian religion with a faculty for presenting it in such a form as to be recognisable neither by friend or foe." Mr. R. H. Hutton remarks in his *Contemporary Thought and Thinkers,* "Mr. Matthew Arnold returns to his curiously hopeless task of convincing people that the Bible can be read, understood, enjoyed, and turned to the most fruitful moral account, without according any credence to the supernatural experience and belief of its writers." In the *Posthumous Essays* of John Churton Collins, published so recently as 1912, one finds a disposition to dismiss Arnold's "theology" with an epigram: "Perhaps the best criticism of it would be what Doctor Cuffe said of Bacon's Novum Organum, that 'a foolish man could not, and a wise man would not, have written it.'" Professor Saintsbury, whose works fill all the world, has striven to convey the impression that in handling the church and the Bible Arnold was attempting to decide a case beyond his jurisdiction, and that his decisions are of little interest or consequence.

Now, since Arnold's books were designed to carry persuasion to the hearts of such men as Gladstone, Hutton, Collins and Professor Saintsbury, one is constrained to admit that they did not invariably perform their errand! Having made this concession, one should hasten to add that to many men who were reluctantly drifting from their religious moorings Arnold showed a practical anchorage for the spirit;

and that such refuge as he provided more than forty years ago has lost little of its security by the lapse of time. Furthermore, one can not see Arnold whole unless one knows well *St. Paul and Protestantism, Literature and Dogma,* and *God and the Bible;* to neglect these books is to miss some of his best writing, some of his most penetrating and permanently valuable literary criticism, some of the central aspects of his character, and an integral part of his effort to civilize the world.

It is important to understand just why he entered the field of theology and religion. At first thought the attention which he devoted to these subjects appears inconsistent with his frequent assertion that they had received too much of the attention of Englishmen. A letter of March 25, 1881, written four years after the publication of his *Last Essays on Church and Religion,* indicates no wavering in his conviction that England's mind and thought stood in more need of critical direction than her heart and morals.

"The force which is shaping the future," he says, "is not with any of the orthodox religions, or with any of the neo-religious developments which propose to themselves to supersede them. Both the one and the other give to what they call religion, and to religious ideas and discussions, too large and absorbing a place in human life; man feels himself to be a more various and richly-endowed animal than the old religious theory of human life allowed, and he is endeavouring to give satisfaction to the long-suppressed and still imperfectly-understood instincts of this varied nature. I think this revolution is happening everywhere; it is certainly happening in England, where the somberness and narrowness of the religious world, and the rigid hold it long had upon us, have done so much to provoke it. I think it is, like all inevitable revolutions, a salutary one, but it greatly requires watching and guiding. The growing desire, throughout the community, for amusement and pleasure; the wonderful relaxation, in the middle class, of the old strictness as to theatres, dancing, and such things, are features which alarm many people; but they have their good side. They belong to this revolution of which I speak. The awakening demand for beauty, a demand so little made in this country for the last century and more, is another sign of the revolution, and a clearly favorable sign of it. . . . The moral is that whoever treats religion, religious discussions, questions of churches and sects, as absorbing, is not in vital sympathy with the movement of men's minds at present."

This passage partly explains why Arnold came to the discussion of religion comparatively late in life and with genuine reluctance: he wished to give the greater part of his attention to "the force which is shaping the future," and that force, he was convinced, was not in the churches. In passing, let us mark here with special emphasis his observation that all inevitable revolutions are "salutary." A clever but superficial writer in *The Unpopular Review*[1] expresses the current superficial notion that Arnold was quite out of sympathy with his times, in these words: "Think, for instance, of Matthew Arnold, and how easily he set a nation by the ears just by his inability to accept its favorite thinker without limiting the sphere of his appeal; and how by his uncompromising opposition to all the social, literary, and religious tastes of his time, he held his own countrymen off at arms' length, and lectured them into a fine indifference to him. And then recall the remark of a friend on hearing of his death: 'Poor Arnold! He won't like God.'" Now "uncompromising opposition" describes fairly well the later temper of Carlyle; Arnold's temper it does not describe. Arnold is a believer, a chastened believer, in progress. That belief is central and continuous in him; it underlies all his efforts. He accepts modern science, he accepts modern democracy, and he seeks to work with these forces toward the accomplishment of inevitable and, on the whole, salutary revolutions. In his discourse on Emerson he sets Emerson above Carlyle by virtue of his profound hopefulness and his sympathetic relationship with the master tendencies of his age; and he singles out for admiration Emerson's famous injunc-

---

[1] "Popularity, Impopularity, Unpopularity," in October-December issue, 1916.

tion against getting into uncompromising opposition: "Accept the place the Divine Providence has found for you, the society of your contemporaries, the connexion of events. Great men have always done so, *and confided themselves childlike to the genius of their age;* betraying their perception that the Eternal was stirring at their heart, working through their hands, predominating in all their being."

Still the great man who is also a wise man always participates in a revolution with a certain measure of reluctance. He wishes to assure himself first that the revolution is indeed "inevitable," and that it is indeed the Eternal who is stirring the hands of men against the foundations of the existing order. There is something, he knows, uncontrollable and contagious in an attack upon established institutions. The philosopher, the critic, the reformer advance and undermine, perhaps, with circumspection and preconsidered purpose and reconstructive passion and plan. But greed and jealousy and ignorance flock to the scene of every assault; and "the man in the crowd," seized by a blind fury, catches up a brick and hurls it without aim or intention. This fact of "mob psychology" tends to make a person of truly conservative temper cautious about the general publication of certain of his radically progressive ideas, even when he is quite certain that they are perfectly sound ideas. He is apprehensive lest the moment the crowd gets hold of them they may receive the little warp, the little twist, to which new and imperfectly understood ideas are subject; and so become false and dangerous. Thus Arnold, in his preface to *Literature and Dogma,* quotes Goethe to this effect: "I keep silence at many things for I would not mislead men, and am well content if others can find satisfaction in what gives me offence."

This seems to have represented for a considerable period Arnold's attitude with regard to the deeper religious questions of the day. In an age of ebbing faith he questioned the expediency of accelerating the ebb. Holding as he did that conduct is three-fourths of life, he might easily have concluded that it was better for men to go morally right on an unsound religious basis than to go morally wrong on the soundest intellectual foundation. So long as a belief in what were for him unbelievable things seemed for the majority of men the most trustworthy and efficacious insurance of conduct, he was loath to propose a substitute. "There is no surer proof," he says, "of a narrow and ill-conditioned mind, than to think and uphold that what a man takes to be the truth on religious matters is always to be proclaimed." So long as the traditional interpretation of the Bible was accepted by the masses, he was not anxious to popularize for them the interpretation of it by modern historical criticism, the upshot of which he had himself accepted.

But by 1870 Arnold was convinced that the gradual revolution of modern thought against religious authority and traditional beliefs had ruined the foundations of the old religious order. The signs were many. Newman had attempted a medievalizing revival within the Church of England, but, going over to Rome, had "adopted," says Arnold in his "Emerson," "for the doubts and difficulties which beset men's minds to-day, a solution which, to speak frankly, is impossible." Carlyle had treated the churches and creeds as Hebrew "old clothes," had found the teachings of Jesus unpalatable except in German translations, and had preached Goethe as the new Messiah. Mill had declared traditional Christian morality reactionary, negative, selfish, and pusillanimous;[2] and had offered in his *Utilitarianism* a new gospel. Frederic Harrison and other English Positivists were looking to Auguste Comte as their savior. Leading men of science and "scientific philosophers" like Darwin and Herbert Spencer were indifferent or absolutely hostile to Christianity. The various sects of Dissenters were uniting politically with the various groups of radical free-thinkers to disestablish the Church of England.

---

[2] See his chapter, "Of the Liberty of Thought and Discussion," in *Liberty*.

The emancipative ideas of the leaders of thought were rapidly reaching and unsettling the masses. The drift was toward a secularized State, a discredited Bible, religious individualism, and irreligion, with a loosening of the moral bonds which hold society together. A part of this "liberal" movement Arnold regarded as inevitable and salutary; but he thought there was grave danger that the revolution would go too far, and sweep away things precious and indispensable.

The Church of England as it existed in his day he considered inadequate to its task; it needed thoroughgoing reconstruction. But of the idea of a national church he would cry, *Esto perpetua*. His attitude toward the State establishment of religion is absolutely in accord with his attitude toward the State establishment of education and with his attitude toward the State establishment of an Academy. That is to say, he held that great and abiding interests of society like religion, education, and literature should be publicly and splendidly recognized, should be instituted and maintained in the grand style, should have the dignity and power and preeminence belonging to central organs of the national life. While others proposed disestablishment, he, like his father before him, proposed the comprehension and union of the other churches within the national church.

Speaking before the London clergy at Sion College he says:

"I regard the Church of England as, in fact, a great national society for the promotion of what is commonly called *goodness,* and for promoting it through the most effectual means possible, the only means which are really and truly effectual for the object: through the means of the Christian religion and of the Bible. This plain practical object is undeniably the object of the Church of England and of the clergy. But surely, the moment we consider religion and Christianity in a large way as goodness, and a Church as a society for the promotion of goodness, all that is said about having such a society before men's eyes as a city set upon a hill, all that is said about making the Gospel more and more a witness to mankind, applies in favour of the State adopting some form of religion or other,—that which seems best suited to the majority,—even though it may not be perfect; and putting that forward as the national form of religion. Force the Church of England has certainly some; perhaps a good deal. But its true strength is in relying, not on its powers of force, but on its powers of attractiveness. And by opening itself to the glow of the old and true ideal of the Christian Gospel, by fidelity to reason, by placing the stress of its religion on goodness, by cultivating grace and peace, it will inspire attachment, to which the attachment which it inspires now, deep though that is, will be as nothing; it will last, be sure, as long as this nation." ("The Church of England" in *Last Essays on Church and Religion.*)

But though Arnold regards a national catholic church as eminently desirable, he declares that the question whether the church shall be connected with the nation in its collective and corporate character or no is, *at the present juncture,* "absolutely unimportant." The important thing is, he says in his preface to *Literature and Dogma,*

". . . to recast religion. If this is done, the new religion will be the national one; if it is not done, separating the nation in its collective and corporate character from religion will not do it. It is as if men's minds were much unsettled about mineralogy, and the teachers of it were at variance, and no teacher was convincing, and many people, therefore, were disposed to throw the study of mineralogy overboard altogether. What would naturally be the business for every friend of the study? Surely to establish on sure grounds the value of the study, and to put its claim in a new light where they could no longer be denied. But if he acted as our Dissenters act in religion, what would he do? Give himself, heart and soul, to a furious crusade against keeping the Government School of Mines.

"But meanwhile there is now an end to all fear of doing harm by gainsaying the received theology of the churches and sects. For this theology is itself now a hindrance to the Bible rather than a help; nay, to abandon it, to put some other construction on the Bible than this theology puts, to find some other basis for the Bible than this theology finds, is indispensable, if we would have the Bible reach

the people. . . . Here, then, is the problem: to
find for the Bible a basis in something that can be
verified, instead of in something which has to be assumed. So true and prophetic are Vinet's words:
'We must,' he said, 'make it our business to bring
forward the rational side of Christianity, and to
show that for thinkers, too, it has a right to be an
authority.' Yes, and the problem we have stated
must be the first stage of the business; with this unsolved, all other religious discussion is idle trifling."

Before we consider Arnold's Bible criticism in detail, let us clear away a possible misconception. Arnold had of course studied theological doctrines; but
he was not a theologian, for he did not acknowledge
any *science* of God. He approaches the Bible as a
literary critic, dissatisfied with the way in which
theologians have interpreted what is for him a
grand literary work—the Scriptures of the He-
brews. He denies to the authors of the Bible any
special revelation different in kind from that vouch-
safed to, let us say, Dante or Milton. He looks
upon the Bible as the splendid record of a race endowed with an exceptional instinct for righteousness and spirituality. Interpreted as literature, as
poetry, as human experience, he considers this record of inestimable value—a great repository of
truth about the moral nature of man, a great source
of inspiration to a higher life. Such portions of it
as appear to him mythical or fabulous he treats exactly as if he had found them in Herodotus or

Homer. And exactly as he treats in his *Essays in Criticism* the character and message of Aurelius and Spinoza and Joubert, so he treats the character and message of Jesus and John and Paul. His final object is to show that when everything contrary to reason and experience has been rejected, nothing is lost which is important for religion.

The God whose existence is proved by miracles he rejects tenderly but firmly as an altogether human creation of a superstitious age, as no longer credible, because quite unverifiable. His discussion of this subject may be found in the fifth chapter of *Literature and Dogma,* entitled "The Proof from Miracles," and in the first chapter of *God and the Bible,* entitled "The God of Miracles." "The God of Israel, for popular religion," he says in *Literature and Dogma,* "is a magnified and non-natural man who has really worked stupendous miracles, whereas the Gods of the heathen were vainly imagined to be able to work them, but could not, and had therefore no real existence. Of this God, Jesus for popular religion is the Son. He came to appease God's wrath against sinful men by the sacrifice of himself; and he proved his Sonship by a course of stupendous miracles, and by the wonderful accomplishment in him of the supernatural Messianic predictions of prophecy. . . . Learned religion elucidates and develops the relationship of the Son to the Father by a copious exhibition of metaphysics; but for popular religion the relationship, and the authority of Jesus which derives from it, is altogether by *miracle.*"

It is entirely clear to Arnold that a religion of which the authority is derived from miracles can not go into the future prosperously. In modern times miracles do not attach serious minds to Christianity but rather repel them from it. He deems it therefore a genuine service to religion to show that the value of Christianity is not in the least dependent upon the miraculous. Many of his readers to-day will probably feel that in arguing against Christian miracles he was unnecessarily striking at a falling edifice; but those who recall the critical tumult excited by his niece's *Robert Elsmere* will understand why he thought it expedient to hasten the dissolving touch of time. Let us have a brief illustration of his method in "destructive" criticism:

"Roman Catholics fancy that Bible miracles and the miracles of their Church form a class by themselves; Protestants fancy that Bible miracles, alone, form a class by themselves. This was eminently the posture of mind of the late Archbishop Whately:— to hold that all other miracles would turn out to be impostures, or capable of a natural explanation, but that Bible miracles would stand sifting by a London special jury or by a committee of scientific men. No acuteness can save such notions, as our knowledge widens, from being seen to be mere extravagances, and the Protestant notion is doomed to an earlier ruin than the Catholic. For the Catholic notion admits miracles in the mass; the Protestant notion invites to a criticism by which it must finally itself perish. When Stephen was martyred, he looked up into heaven and saw the glory of God, and Jesus standing on the right hand of God. That, says the Protestant, is solid fact. At the martyrdom of St. Fructuosus, Babylas and Mygdone, the Christian servants of the Roman governor, saw the heavens open, and the saint and his deacon Eulogius carried up on high with crowns on their heads. That is, says the Protestant, imposture or else illusion. St. Paul hears on his way to Damascus the voice of Jesus say to him: 'Saul, Saul, why persecutest thou me?' That, again, is solid fact. The companion of St. Thomas Aquinas hears a voice from the crucifix say to the praying saint: 'Thou hast written well of me, Thomas; what recompense dost thou desire?' That, again, is imposture or else illusion. Why? It is impossible to find any criterion by which one of these incidents may establish its claim to a solidity which we refuse to the others.

"One of two things must be made out in order to place either the Bible miracles alone, or the Bible miracles and the miracles of the Catholic Church with them, in a class by themselves. Either they must be shown to have arisen in a time eminently unfavorable to such a process as Shakespeare describes, to amplification and the production of legend; or they must be shown to be recorded in documents of an eminently historical mode of birth and publication. But surely it is manifest that the Bible miracles fulfil neither of these conditions."

Having compared Protestant and Catholic miracles, Arnold proceeds to compare Christian and Pagan miracles: for example, the alleged miraculous passage of Alexander the Great through the Pamphylian Sea with the passage through the Red Sea of the Children of Israel. In the first case, we readily accept any natural explanation that science offers; in the second case we cling to the miracle.

"Yet," says Arnold, "the time and circumstances of the flight from Egypt were a thousand times more favourable to the rise of some natural incident into a miracle, than the age of Alexander. . . . Experience of the history of the human mind, and of men's habits of seeing, sifting, and relating, convinces us that the miraculous stories of Herodotus or Plutarch do grow out of the process described by Shakespeare. But we shall find ourselves inevitably led, sooner or later, to extend the same rule to all miraculous stories; nay, the considerations which apply in other cases apply, we shall most surely discover, with even greater force in the case of Bible miracles."

The God whose existence is proved by metaphysics Arnold rejects as firmly as "the God of Miracles," and perhaps rather less tenderly. His discussion of this subject may be found in the ninth chapter of *Literature and Dogma,* entitled "Aberglaube Reinvading," and in the second chapter of *God and the Bible,* entitled "The God of Metaphysics." The "learned" theology elaborated in the Middle Ages by the application of formal logic to the texts of the Bible and to the dogmas of the church was, in the Middle Ages, eminently respectable, because it was the best account of the relations between God and man that medieval culture and criticism could produce. But it was founded upon unverifiable assumptions; its rigorously systematic deductions were derived from major premises which modern criticism must regard as myth and symbol and poetry. As poetry and symbol and myth Arnold himself can accept the idea of a "Triune God" and the doctrine of Justification. What he refuses to believe is that these conceptions have any scientific validity. Writing mainly for Protestants, his line of attack is to show that the principle of criticism by which they condemn Catholic doctrines as "degrading superstitions" condemns equally their own doctrines. But, he insists, neither Catholic nor Protestant doctrine is degrading provided it is rightly interpreted—interpreted, that is, not as science, but as poetry of high seriousness. In the following passage, from *Literature and Dogma,* he seems to prefer the Catholic doctrine of the Mass to the Protestant doctrine of Justification as better poetry, as morally more efficacious:

"The fourth book of the 'Imitation,' which treats of *The Sacrament of the Altar,* is of later date and lesser merit than the three books which precede it;

but it is worth while to quote from this book a few words, for the sake of the testimony they bear to the practical operation, in many cases at any rate, of this belief. 'To us in our weakness thou hast given, for the refreshment of mind and body, thy sacred Body. The devout communicant thou, my God, raisest from the depth of his own dejection to the hope of thy protection, and with a hitherto unknown grace renewest him and enlightenest him within; so that they who at first, before this Communion, had felt themselves distressed and affectionless, after the refreshment of this meat and drink from heaven find themselves changed to a new and better man. For this most high and worthy Sacrament is the saving health of soul and body, the medicine of all spiritual languor; *by it my vices are cured, my passions bridled, temptations are conquered or diminished, a larger grace is infused, the beginnings of virtue are made to grow, faith is confirmed, hope strengthened, and charity takes fire and dilates into flame.*' So little is the doctrine of the Mass to be called a 'degrading superstition,' either in its character or in its working.

"But it is *false!* sternly breaks in the Evangelical Protestant. O Evangelical Protestant, is thine own doctrine, then, so true? As the Romish doctrine of the mass, the Real Presence, is a rude and blind criticism of: *He that eateth me shall live by me;* so the Protestant tenet of Justification, 'pleading the Blood of the Covenant,' is a rude and blind criticism of: *The Son of Man came to give his life a ransom for many;*—it is a taking of the words of Scripture literally and unintelligently. And our friends, the philosophical Liberals, are not slow to call this, too, a degrading superstition, just as Protestants call the doctrine of the Mass a degrading superstition. We say, on the contrary, that a degrading superstition neither the one nor the other is. In imagining a sort of infinitely magnified and improved Lord Shaftesbury, with a race of vile offenders to deal with, whom his natural goodness would incline him to let off, only his sense of justice will not allow it, then a younger Lord Shaftesbury, on the scale of his father and very dear to him, who might live in grandeur and splendor if he liked, but who prefers to leave his home, to go and live among the race of offenders, and to be put to an ignominious death, on condition that his merits shall be counted against their demerits, and that his father's goodness shall be restrained no longer from taking effect, but any offender shall be admitted to the benefit of it on simply pleading the satisfaction made by the son; and then, finally, a third Lord Shaftesbury, still on the same high scale, who keeps very much in the background, and works in a very occult manner, but very efficaciously nevertheless, and who is busy in applying everywhere the benefits of the son's satisfaction and the father's goodness;—in an imagination, I say, such as this, there is nothing degrading, and this is precisely the Protestant story of *Justification.* And how awe of the first Lord Shaftesbury, gratitude and love towards the second, and earnest co-operation with the third, may fill and rule men's hearts so as to transform their conduct, we need not go about to show, for we have all seen it with our eyes. Therefore in the practical working of this tenet there is nothing degrading; any more than there is anything degrading in this tenet as an imaginative conception. And looking to the infinite importance of getting right conduct—three fourths of human life—established, and to the inevitable anthropomorphism and extra-belief of men in dealing with ideas, one might well hesitate to attack an anthropomorphism or an extra-belief by which men helped themselves in conduct merely because an anthropomorphism or an extra-belief it is, so long as it served its purpose, so long as it was firmly and undoubtingly held, and almost universally prevailing.

"But, after all, the question sooner or later arises in respect to a matter taken for granted, like the Catholic doctrine of the Mass or the Protestant doctrine of Justification: Is it *sure?* can what is here assumed be *verified?* And this is the real objection both to the Catholic and Protestant doctrine as a basis for conduct; not that it is a degrading superstition, but that it is *not sure,* that it assumes what cannot be *verified.*"

Having disposed of the "God of miracles" set up by "popular theology," and having disposed of the "God of metaphysics" set up by "learned theology," Arnold endeavors to show that the God of the Bible is a God whose existence has been proved in the past and may be proved to-day by *experience.* This subject is discussed in the first and third chapters of *Literature and Dogma,* entitled respectively "Religion Given" and "Religion New-Given," and in the third chapter of *God and the Bible,* entitled "The God of Experience." Arnold's *theology,* strictly speaking, consists of a very brief definition of God. "For science," he says, "God is simply the stream of tendency by which all things fulfil the law of their being." This definition, Arnold argues, has the great advantage of being verifiable. It requires some elucidation. "That all things seem to us to have what we call a law of their being, and to tend to fulfil it, is certain and admitted; though whether we call this *God* or not is a matter of choice. Suppose, however, we call it *God,* we then give the name of *God* to a certain and admitted reality; this, at least, is an advantage. And the notion does, in fact, enter into the term God, in men's common use of it. To please God, to serve God, to obey God's will, does mean to follow a law of things which is found in conscience, and which is an indication, irrespective of our arbitrary wish and fancy, of what we ought to do. There *is,* then, a real power which makes for righteousness; and it is the greatest of realities for us." The clearest and simplest form of his definition is this: God is "the not ourselves which makes for righteousness." A deep inalterable conviction that human nature and the universe are so framed that man can not permanently prosper except in the ways of righteousness is the rock bottom of Arnold's theology, tested and proved, he believes, by the history of the race and the experience of every serious individual.

This matter may perhaps be clarified by reference

to what we may call Arnold's "psychology."
Throughout his work one will find the persistent
presence of the doctrine of the two selves in man.
(See,[3] for examples, page XIX of the Preface to
St. Paul and Protestantism; also pages 39-40 of the
same; page 166 of the Preface to *Last Essays on
Church and Religion;* and pages 281-282 in "Bishop
Butler and the Zeit-Geist." The doctrine is notably
applied in *Culture and Anarchy,* especially in the
chapter "Barbarians, Philistines, and Populace.")
Let us take a passage from the Preface to the *Last
Essays on Church and Religion:* "It will generally
be admitted, too, that all experience as to conduct
brings us at last to the fact of two selves, or instincts,
or forces,—name them how we will, and how-
ever we may suppose them to have arisen,—contending for the mastery in man : one, a movement of first
impulse and more involuntary, leading us to gratify
any inclination that may solicit us, and called generally a movement of man's ordinary or passing
self, of sense, appetite, desire; the other, a movement of reflection and more voluntary, leading us
to submit inclination to some rule, and called generally a movement of man's higher or enduring self,
of reason, spirit, will. The thing is described in different words by different nations and men relating

---

[3] *St. Paul and Protestantism,* with an Essay on Puritanism
and the Church of England and *Last Essays on Church and
Religion,* N. Y., 1908.

their experience of it, but as to the thing itself they all, or all the most serious and important among them, agree. This, I think, will be admitted. Nor will it be denied that they all come to the conclusion that for a man to obey the higher self, or reason, or whatever it is to be called, is happiness and life for him; to obey the lower is death and misery." Here, then, is a fact of universal experience: the presence in man of a higher and a lower self. Here, then, is another fact of universal experience: man attains his being's end and aim, happiness, by obeying his higher self. Now, the "not ourself," call it what you like, which ordained that man should attain happiness by obeying his higher self Arnold calls God—the verifiable "God of experience." That, we say, is the sum of his theology.

Religion, as he understands the term, is a quite different matter from theology.

"Religion," he says in *Literature and Dogma,* "means simply either a binding to righteousness, or else a serious attending to righteousness and dwelling upon it; which of these two it most nearly means, depends upon the view we take of the word's derivation; but it means one of them, and they are really much the same. And so, when we are asked, What is the object of religion? let us reply, *Conduct.* And when we are asked further, What is conduct? let us answer, *Three-fourths of life.* If conduct is the object of religion, what is religion itself? Religion, if we follow the intention of human

thought and human language in the use of the word,
is ethics heightened, enkindled, lit up by feeling; the
passage from morality to religion is made, when to
morality is applied emotion.   And the true meaning
of religion is thus not simply *morality*, but *morality
touched by emotion.*   And this new elevation and inspiration of morality is well marked by the word
'righteousness.'   Conduct is the word of common
life, morality is the word of philosophical disquisition, righteousness is the word religion.   .   .   .

"And if some one now asks, But what is this application of emotion to morality, and by what marks
may we know it?—we can quite easily satisfy him;
not, indeed, by any disquisition of our own, but in a
much better way, by examples. 'By the dispensation
of Providence to mankind,' says Quintilian, 'goodness gives men most pleasure.'   That is morality.
'The path of the just is as a shining light which
shineth more and more unto the perfect day.'   That
is morality touched with emotion or religion.   'Hold
off from sensuality,' says Cicero; 'for, if you have
given yourself up to it, you will find yourself unable
to think of anything else.'   That is morality.
'Blessed are the pure in heart,' says Jesus; 'for they
shall see God.'   That is religion.   'We all want to
live honestly, but cannot,' says the Greek maxim-
maker.   That is morality.   'O wretched man that I
am, who shall deliver me from the body of this
death!' says St. Paul.   That is religion.   'Would
thou wert of as good conversation in deed as in
word!' is morality.   'Not every one that saith to me,
Lord, Lord, shall enter into the kingdom of Heaven,
but he that doeth the will of my Father which is in
Heaven!' is religion.   'Live as you were meant to

live!' is morality. 'Lay hold on eternal life!' is religion."

Now the abiding value of the Old Testament, Arnold declares, resides precisely in its powerful application of emotion to morality—resides in its verifiable religious message that "righteousness preserveth a nation."

"The Old Testament," he says, "I suppose nobody will deny, is filled with the word and thought of righteousness. 'In the way of righteousness is life, and in the pathway thereof is no death'; 'Righteousness tendeth to life'; 'The wicked man troubleth his own flesh'; 'The way of transgressors is hard';—nobody will deny that those texts may stand for the fundamental and ever-recurring idea of the Old Testament. No people ever felt so strongly as the people of the Old Testament, the Hebrew people, that conduct is three fourths of our life and its largest concern; no people ever felt so strongly that succeeding, going right, hitting the mark in this great concern, was *the way of peace,* the highest possible satisfaction. 'He that keepeth the law, happy is he; its ways are ways of pleasantness, and all its paths are peace; if thou hadst walked in its ways, thou shouldst have dwelt in peace forever!' Jeshurun, one of the ideal names of their race, is the *upright;* Israel, the other and greater, is the *wrestler with God,* he who has known the contention and strain it costs to stand upright. That mysterious personage, by whom their history first touches the hill of Sion, is Melchisedek, the *right-*

eous king; their holy city, Jerusalem, is the foundation, or vision, or inheritance, of that which righteousness achieves,—*peace*. The law of righteousness was such an object of attention to them, that its words were to 'be in their heart, and thou shalt teach them diligently unto thy children, and shalt talk of them when thou sittest in thine house, and when thou walkest by the way, and when thou liest down, and when thou risest up.' To keep them ever in mind, they wore them, went about with them, made talismans of them: 'Bind them upon thy fingers, bind them about thy neck; write them upon the table of thine heart!' 'Take fast hold of her,' they said of the doctrine of conduct, or righteousness, 'let her not go! keep her, for *she is thy life!*'

"People who thus spoke of righteousness could not but have had their minds long and deeply engaged with it; much more than the generality of mankind, who have nevertheless, as we saw, got as far as the notion of morals or conduct. And, if they were so deeply attentive to it, one thing could not fail to strike them. It is this: the very great part in righteousness which belongs, we may say, to *not ourselves*. In the first place, we did not make ourselves, or our nature, or *conduct* as the object of three fourths of that nature; we did not provide that happiness should follow conduct, as it undeniably does; that the sense of succeeding, going right, hitting the mark, in conduct, should give satisfaction, and a very high satisfaction, just as really as the sense of doing well in his work gives pleasure to a poet or painter, or accomplishing what he tries gives pleasure to a man who is learning to ride or shoot;

or as satisfying his hunger, also, gives pleasure to a man who is hungry. . . .

"All this we did not make; and, in the next place, our dealing with it at all, when it is made, is not wholly, or even nearly wholly, in our power. Our conduct is capable, irrespective of what we can ourselves certainly answer for, of almost infinitely different degrees of force and energy in the performance of it, of lucidity and vividness in the perception of it, of fulness in the satisfaction from it; and these degrees may vary from day to day, and quite incalculably. Facilities and felicities, whence do they come? suggestions and stimulations, where do they tend? hardly a day passes but we have some experience of them. And so Henry More was led to say 'that there was something about us that knew better, often, what we would be at than we ourselves.' "   ("Religion Given" in *Literature and Dogma.*)

The strength and the weakness of the Old Testament is that its morality is national and social rather than personal. It tends to reduce righteousness to a minute and exacting code: it externalizes righteousness. By the time of Christ Israel had lost the profound emotion which had accompanied its early intuition of the Eternal—had lost, that is to say, the religious power which had energized its morality. As Arnold says in the chapter "Religion New-Given,"

". . . the glad and immediate sense of being in the right way, in the way of peace, was gone; the sense of being wrong and astray, of sin, and of helplessness under sin, was oppressive. The thing was, by giving a fuller idea of righteousness to reapply *emotion* to it, and by reapplying emotion, to disperse the feeling of being amiss and helpless, to give the sense of being right and effective; to restore, in short, to righteousness the sanction of *happiness*.

"But this should only be done by attending to that inward world of feelings and dispositions which Judaism had too much neglected. The first need, therefore, for Israel at that time, was to make religion cease to be mainly a national and social matter. 'Thou blind Pharisee, cleanse first the *inside* of the cup, that the outside may be clean also!'—this was the very ground-principle of Christ's teaching. Instead of attending so much to your outward acts, attend, he said, first of all to your inward thoughts, to the state of your heart and feelings. This doctrine has perhaps been overstrained and misapplied by certain people since; but it was the lesson which at that time was above all needed. It is a great progress beyond even that advanced maxim of pious Jews: 'To do justice and judgment is more acceptable than sacrifice.' For to do justice and judgment is still, as we have remarked, something external, and may leave the feelings untouched, uncleared, and dead; what was wanted was to plough up, clear, and quicken the feelings themselves. And that is what Christ did. . . .

" 'My son, *give me thy heart!*' says the teacher of righteousness in the golden age of Israel. And when Israel had *the Eternal* revealed to him, and founded our religion, he *gave his heart*. But the time came when this direct vision ceased, and Israel's religion was a mere affair of tradition, and of doctrines and rules received from without. Then it might be truly said of this professed servant of the Eternal: 'This people honor me with their lips, but have removed their heart far from me, and their fear toward me is taught by the precept of men.' With little or no power of distinguishing between what was rule of ceremonial and what was rule of conduct, they followed the prescriptions of their religion with a servile and sullen mind, 'precept upon precept, line upon line, here a little and there a little,' and no end to it all. What a change since the days when it was *joy to the just to do judgment!* The prophets saw clearly enough the evil, nay, they even could point to the springs which must be touched in order to work a cure; but they could not press these springs steadily enough or skilfully enough to work the cure themselves.

"Christ's new and different way of putting things was the secret of his succeeding where the prophets could not. And this new way he had of putting things is what is indicated by the expression *epieikeia,* best rendered, as we have elsewhere said, by these two words—'sweet reasonableness.' For that which is *epieikes* is that which has an air of truth and likelihood; and that which has an air of truth and likelihood is prepossessing. Now, never were utterances concerning conduct and righteousness—Israel's master-concern, and the master-topic of the New Testament as well as of the Old—which so carried with them an air of consummate truth and likelihood as Christ's did; and never, therefore, were any utterances so irresistibly prepossessing. He put things in such a way that his hearer was led to take each rule or fact of conduct by its inward side, its effect on the heart and character; then the reason of the thing, the meaning of what had been mere matter of blind rule, flashed upon him. He could distinguish between what was only ceremony, and what was *conduct;* and the hardest rule of conduct came to appear to him infinitely reasonable and natural, and therefore infinitely prepossessing. *To find his own soul,* his true and permanent self, became set up in man's view as his chief concern, as the secret of happiness; and so it really is.

"Self-examination, self-renouncement, and mildness were, therefore, the great means by which Christ renewed righteousness and religion. All these means are indicated in the Old Testament: *God requireth truth in the inward parts; Not doing thine own ways, nor finding thine own pleasure; Before honor is humility.* But how far more strongly are they forced upon the attention in the New Testament, and set up clearly as the central mark for our endeavors! *Thou blind Pharisee, cleanse first the inside of the cup that the outside may be clean also! Whoever will come after me, let him renounce himself and take up his cross daily and follow me! Learn of me that I am mild and lowly in heart, and ye shall find rest unto your souls;* So that, although personal religion is clearly present in the Old Testament, nevertheless these injunctions of the New Testament effect so much more for the extrication and establishment of personal religion than the general exhortations in the Old to *offer the sacrifice of righteousness,* to *do judgment,* that, comparatively with the Old, the New Testament may be said to have really founded inward and personal religion. While the Old Testament says, *Attend to conduct!*

the New Testament says, *Attend to the feelings and dispositions whence conduct proceeds!* And as attending to conduct had very much degenerated into deadness and formality, attending to the *springs* of conduct was a revelation, a revival of intuitive and fresh perceptions, a touching of morals with emotion, a discovering of religion, similar to that which had been effected when Israel, struck with the abiding power, not of man's causing, which makes for righteousness, and filled with joy and awe by it, had, in the old days, named God *the Eternal*. Man came under a new dispensation and made with God a second covenant."

We need not examine in any detail Arnold's discussion of prophecy and miracle with reference to Christ. His argument in brief is this: The "divinity" of Christ is not in the least proved by prophecy or miracle; it is proved by the *experience* of those who have followed him and have done his will. That basis of Christianity is quite unshaken by the work of the "higher criticism" and the free-thinking of the nineteenth century. The "divinity" of Christ is proved by his marvelously direct insight into the means by which man may attain happiness and by the tremendous impulse which he gives to the will of man to adopt that means.

In the chapter of *Literature and Dogma* entitled "The Testimony of Jesus to Himself," Arnold insists that the power of Jesus is founded upon his penetrating understanding of human nature:

"His 'method' directed the disciple's eye inward and set his consciousness to work; and the first thing his consciousness told him was, that he had two selves pulling him different ways. Till we attend, till the *method* is set at work, it seems as if 'the wishes of the flesh and of current thoughts' were to be followed as a matter of course; as if an impulse to do a thing means that we should do it. But when we attend, we find that an impulse to do a thing is really in itself no reason at all why we should do it; because impulses proceed from two sources, quite different, and of quite different degrees of authority. . . . Jesus contrasts them as *life,* properly so named, and *life in this world.* And the moment we seriously attend to conscience, . . . we can see plainly enough from which source a suggestion comes, and that the suggestions from one source are to overrule those from the other. But this is a negative state of things, a reign of check and constraint, a reign, merely, of morality. Jesus changed it into what was positive and attractive, lighted it up, made it religion, by the idea of *two lives.* One of them, life properly so called, full of light, endurance, felicity, in connection with the higher and permanent self; and the other of them, life improperly so called, in connection with the lower and transient self. The first kind of life was already a cherished ideal with Israel . . .; and a man might be placed in it, Jesus said, by dying to the second. . . .

"Now, the value of this rule that one should die to one's apparent self, live to one's real self, depends upon whether it is true. And true it certainly is;— a profound truth of what our scientific friends, who have a systematic philosophy and a nomenclature to match, and who talk of *Egoism* and *Altruism,* would call, perhaps, psycho-physiology. And we may trace man's experience affirming and confirming it, from a very plain and level account of it to an account almost as high and solemn as that of Jesus. . . . Never, certainly, was the joy which in self-renouncement underlies the pain, so brought out, as when Jesus boldly called the suppression of our first impulses and current thoughts, *life, real life, eternal life.* So that Jesus not only *saw* this great necessary truth of their being, as Aristotle says, in human nature a part to rule and a part to be ruled; he saw it so *thoroughly,* that he saw through the suffering at its surface to the joy at its centre, filled it with promise and hope, and made it infinitely attractive."

Taking up Arnold's Biblical criticism in the order of the Scriptures, we have come last to the book which he wrote first, *St. Paul and Protestantism.* He himself was particularly pleased with the style of *God and the Bible;* "I seem to find some chapters in it," he wrote to Charles Eliot Norton on October 8, 1884, "to be the best prose I have ever succeeded in writing." In some respects, however, the *St. Paul* is a work of more abiding interest and value. Composed before he had provoked the critics to buzzing about his ears, it is less occupied than *God and the Bible* with the tasks of refutation and defense. It is more purely and serenely a piece of literary criticism and interpretation. It has, to be sure, a strong controversial purpose. It takes as its point of departure Renan's volume on St. Paul and his conclusion that "after having been for three hundred years, thanks to Protestantism, the Christian doctor *par excellence,* Paul is now coming to an end of his reign." Arnold would agree with Renan that Paul as interpreted by Protestant theologians has lost his hold upon the minds of modern men. But what Arnold proposes to do is to free St. Paul from the encumbrance of Protestant theology; to reinterpret his character and message in the light of modern scientific and literary culture; and so to preserve him as an acceptable hero and an inspiring force in contemporary religious life and thought. "His fundamental ideas," he said, "disengaged from the elaborate misconceptions with which Protestantism has overlaid them, will have an influence in the future greater than any which they have yet had,—an influence proportioned to their correspondence with a number of the deepest and most permanent facts of human nature itself."

Exactly as in his treatment of the Old Testament and exactly as in his treatment of the significance of Jesus, so in his treatment of St. Paul he insists that the rejection of the incredible, the metaphysical, the unverifiable, detracts nothing from the essential moral and religious worth of the "message"; and, indeed, that such a rejection is at the present time necessary if the message is to continue to receive the attention which it deserves, and exercise the power which is in it. "What essentially characterises a religious teacher," he says, "and gives him his permanent worth and vitality, is, after all, just the scientific value of his teaching, its correspondence with important facts, and the light it throws on them. Never was the truth of this so evident as now. The scientific sense in man never asserted its claim so strongly; the propensity of religion to neglect these claims, and the peril and loss to it from neglecting them, never were so manifest. The license of affirmation about God and his proceedings, in which the religious world indulge, is more and more met by the demand for verification. . . . Neither is it that the scientific sense in us refuses to admit willingly and reverently the name of God, as a point in which the religious and the scientific sense may meet, as the least inadequate name for that universal order which the intellect feels after as a law, and the heart feels after as a benefit."

Paul was in some ways a man after Arnold's own heart—a man like Arnold in his "high seriousness," in his love for the "will of God," in his passion for making the will of God "prevail," in his pursuit of perfection, and in his intellectualizing turn. Jesus and his simple-hearted disciples Arnold could divine and appreciate; Paul he was peculiarly fitted by a certain kinship of minds to understand. Paul's conscious taking of himself in hand, his deliberate and methodical and exacting introspection and self-discipline—all that side of the apostle's life Arnold could see into and discourse upon with the insight and relish of lifelong personal experience. "What is it sets Paul in motion?" he asks. "It is the impulse which we have elsewhere noted as the master-impulse of Hebraism—*the desire for righteousness.* 'I exercise myself,' he told Felix, *'to have a conscience void of offence towards God and men continually.'* "

In distinction from the theologians, who draw attention to the metaphysical portion of Paul's teaching and magnify it, Arnold urges us to consider Paul first of all as a great realistic moralist, and to observe how large a portion of his teaching is concerned with conduct—with the "three-fourths of life."

"St. Paul's piercing practical religious sense, joined to his strong intellectual power, enabled him to discern and follow the range of the commandment, both as to man's actions and as to his heart and thoughts, with extraordinary force and clearness. His religion had, so we shall see, a preponderantly mystical side, and nothing is so natural to the mystic as in rich single words, such as faith, light, love, to sum up and take for granted, without specially enumerating them, all good moral principles and habits; yet nothing is more remarkable in Paul than the frequent, nay, incessant lists, in the most particular detail, of moral habits to be pursued or avoided. Lists of this sort might in a less sincere and profound writer be formal and wearisome; but to no attentive reader of St. Paul will they be wearisome, for in making them he touched the solid ground which is the basis of his religion,—the solid ground of his hearty desire for righteousness and of his thorough conception of it,—and only on such a ground was so strong a superstructure possible. The more one studies these lists, the more does their significance come out. To illustrate this, let any one go through for himself the enumeration, too long to be quoted here, in the four last verses of the first chapter of the Epistle to the Romans, of 'things which are not convenient'; or let him merely consider with attention this catalogue towards the end of the fifth chapter of the Epistle to the Galatians, of the fruits of the spirit: 'love, joy, peace, long-suffering, kindness, goodness, faith, mildness, self-control.' The man who wrote with this searching minuteness knew accurately what he meant by sin and righteousness, and did not use these words at random. His diligent comprehensiveness in his plan of duties is only less admirable than his diligent sincerity. The sterner virtues and the gentler, his conscience will not let him rest till he has embraced them all. In his deep resolve 'to make out by actual trial what is that good and perfect and acceptable will of God,' he goes back upon himself again and again, he marks a duty at every point of our nature, and at points the most opposite, for fear he should by possibility be leaving behind him some weakness still indulged, some subtle prompting to evil not yet brought into captivity.

"It has not been enough remarked how this incomparable honesty and depth in Paul's love of righteousness is probably what chiefly explains his conversion. Most men have the defects, as the saying is, of their qualities. Because they are ardent and severe they have no sense for gentleness and sweetness; because they are sweet and gentle they have no sense for severity and ardor. A Puritan is a Puritan, and a man of feeling is a man of feeling. But with Paul the very same fulness of moral nature which made him an ardent Pharisee, 'as concerning zeal, persecuting the church, touching the righteousness which is in the law, blameless,' was so large that it carried him out of Pharisaism and beyond it, when once he found how much needed doing in him which Pharisaism could not do. . . . Never surely did such a controversialist, such a master of sarcasm and invective, commend, with such manifest sincerity and such persuasive emotion, the qualities of meekness and gentleness!"

Paul was, then, according to Arnold and in his fine phrase "an indefatigable explorer" of righteousness. A morality resting upon a profound acquaintance with human nature is the groundwork of his religion. "This man, whom Calvin and Luther and their followers have shut up into the two scholastic doctrines of election and justification, would have said, could we hear him, just what he said about circumcision and uncircumcision in his own day: 'Election is nothing, and justification is nothing, but the keeping of the commandments of God.' " All this part of Paul's religion is of scientific substance; it is in accord with the experience of mankind; it is verifiable. We are still, however, in the sphere of morals.

In the second chapter of the book Arnold passes to the discussion of Paul's religion in the stricter sense of the word—"that which binds us to the practice of righteousness." Here, again, Arnold insists, Paul came to his religion, not "theologically," but psychologically and experimentally, as he came to his morals. To put it briefly, he fell in love with the moral perfection of Christ; and the intense emotion of his love transfigured his righteousness and bound him to it. The working of emotion in this connection a little passes understanding; yet it is a fact of common human experience.

"Of such a mysterious power and its operation some clear notion may be got by anybody who has ever had any overpowering attachment, or has been, according to the common expression, in love. Every one knows how being in love changes for the time a man's spiritual atmosphere, and makes animation and buoyancy where before there was flatness and dulness. One may even say that this is the reason why being in love is so popular with the whole human race,—because it relieves in so irresistible and delightful a manner the tedium or depression of commonplace human life. And not only does it change the atmosphere of our spirits, making air, light, and movement where before there was stagnation and gloom, but it also sensibly and powerfully increases our faculties of action. It is matter of the commonest remark how a timid man who is in love will show courage, or an indolent man will show diligence. Nay, a timid man who would be only the more paralysed in a moment of danger by being told that it is his bounden duty as a man to show firmness, and that he must be ruined and disgraced for ever if he does not, will show firmness quite easily from being in love. An indolent man who shrinks back from vigorous effort only the more because he is told and knows that it is a man's business to show energy, and that it is shameful in him if he does not, will show energy quite easily from being in love. This, I say, we learn from the analogy of the most everyday experience; that a powerful attachment will give a man spirits and confidence which he could by no means call up or command of himself; and that in this mood he can do wonders which would not be possible to him without it."

One is tempted to dwell at some length upon this part of Arnold's exposition; for the great objection raised against his Christianity is that it is nothing but morality—that it leaves religion out. The criticism is unsound. Arnold's Christianity leaves theology out, the greater part of theology, theology considered as the science of God; but it unquestionably brings religion in, religion considered as the recognition, the emotional sense, and the use of the often mysterious power "not ourselves which makes for righteousness." To his mind the most tangible part of the "not ourselves which makes for righteousness" is precisely Jesus; and to Paul, also, with his constant mystical sense of living and moving and having his being in a divine "not ourselves," it is Jesus who is the most apprehensible and dynamic part of that power.

But, says Arnold, "we must here revert to what we have already said of the importance, for sound criticism of a man's ideas, of the order in which his ideas come. For us, who approach Christianity through a scholastic theology, it is Christ's divinity which establishes his being without sin. For Paul, who approached Christianity through his personal experience, it was Jesus Christ's being without sin which establishes his divinity. The large and complete conception of righteousness to which he himself had slowly and late, and only by Jesus Christ's help, awakened, in Jesus he seemed to see existing absolutely and naturally. The devotion to this conception which made it meat and drink to carry it into effect, a devotion of which he himself was strongly and deeply conscious, he saw in Jesus still stronger, by far, and deeper than in himself. But for attaining the righteousness of God, for reaching an absolute conformity with the moral order and with God's will, he saw no such impotence existing in Jesus Christ's case as in his own. For Jesus, the uncertain conflict between the law in our members and the law of the spirit did not appear to exist. Those eternal vicissitudes of victory and defeat, which drove Paul to despair, in Jesus were absent. Smoothly and inevitably he followed the real and eternal order, in preference to the momentary and apparent order. . . . He was led by the spirit of God; he was dead to sin, he lived to God; and in this life he persevered even to the bodily death of the cross. As many as are led by the spirit of God, says Paul, are the sons of God. If this be so even with us, who live to God so feebly and who render such an imperfect obedience, how much more is he who lives to God entirely and who renders an unalterable obedience, the unique and only son of God?

"If ever there was a case in which the wonder-

working power of attachment, in a man for whom
the moral sympathies and the desire of righteousness
were all-powerful, might employ itself and work its
wonders, it was here. Paul felt this power penetrate
him; and he felt, also, how by perfectly identifying
himself through it with Jesus, and in no other way,
could he ever get the confidence and the force to do
as Jesus did. He thus found a point in which the
mighty world outside man, and the weak world inside him, seemed to combine for his salvation. The
struggling stream of duty, which had not volume
enough to bear him to his goal, was suddenly rein-
forced by the immense tidal wave of sympathy and
emotion.

"To do this new and potent influence Paul gave
the name of *faith*. More fully he calls it: 'Faith
that worketh *through love.*' . . . Identifying
ourselves with Jesus Christ through this attachment
we become as he was. We live with his thoughts
and feelings, and we participate, therefore, in l.is
freedom from the ruinous law in our members, in
his obedience to the saving law of the spirit, in his
conformity to the eternal order, in the joy and peace
of his life to God. 'The law of the spirit of life in
Christ Jesus,' says Paul, 'freed me from the law of
sin and death.' This is what is done for us by
faith."

Faith, Arnold is concerned to show, does not
mean to Paul assent to theological doctrine. It
means a practical "holding fast to an unseen power
of goodness." It means dying, as Christ died, in the
lower self and living in the higher self. That, he

contends, is the spiritual and also the practical and verifiable meaning of "resurrection." Paul, he concedes, doubtless believed also in the literal resurrection of Christ; but the master idea in Paul's teaching is the new life, the risen and transfigured life, attainable by all men who are sufficiently in love with perfection to renounce utterly the promptings of the lower nature—"to die with Christ to the law of the flesh, to live with Christ to the law of the mind." To die so and to live so is to enter into the "eternal order"—into immortal life.

A more "personal" immortality than this Arnold probably craved in his earlier years. But as he grew older, he declared in his intimate correspondence that "to be less and less *personal* in one's desires and workings is the great matter." As he grew older he valued more and more the rest and peace of certitude. He found that peace and rest in the religious sphere by "laying hold of immortal life" in this real feasible moral sense of the words. He is so impressed with the soundness and present importance of the idea that he interrupts his exposition of Paul's teaching to urge upon his readers his own conviction of its practical worth. The object of his treatise, he says, "is not religious edification, but the true criticism of a great and misunderstood author. Yet it is impossible to be in the presence of this Pauline conception of faith without remarking on the incomparable power of edification which it contains. It is indeed a crowning evidence of that piercing practical religious sense which we have attributed to Paul. It is at once mystical and rational; and it enlists in its service the best forces of both worlds,—the world of reason and morals, and the world of sympathy and emotion. The world of reason and duty has an excellent clue to action, but wants motive power; the world of sympathy and influence has an irresistible force of motive-power, but wants a clue for directing its exertion. The danger of the one world is weariness in well-doing; the danger of the other is sterile raptures and immoral fanaticism. Paul takes from both worlds what can help him, and leaves what cannot."

We may well bring our study of Arnold's religion to a close on that note. In reviewing his Biblical criticism we have pretty completely ignored his discussions of the date and authorship of various books of the Scriptures. For this part of the work of a Biblical critic we are told that he was inadequately equipped; and very likely he was. From his point of view that part of the work was relatively unimportant; and it is relatively unimportant to us. His interest in the Bible, like his interest in Homer or Dante or Milton, was only secondarily in its historical evolution.

The Bible, like all other great works of literature, interested him primarily as a living force in contemporary life. He recognized it, as men in all ages have recognized it, as an incomparable source of moral wisdom and of religious emotion. To value its poetry and its morality he was eminently qualified. In an age when its hold upon both cultivated and ignorant minds was weakened by the general discrediting of the old theological interpretations, he performed a great service by uncompromisingly rejecting the theological interpretations as obsolete, and as, at the present day, absolutely unimportant to believers in sound morality and sound religion. Following in the spirit of his favorite apostle— "Prove all things; hold fast that which is good"— he firmly indicated those things in the Bible which to accept as science is incompatible with habits of intellectual seriousness. But when that work was done, he brought to the task of reconstructive interpretation the light of a wide secular culture, profound moral insight, an apprehension fresh and untrammeled by clerical cant, a passion for righteousness, and an instinct for religion. He gives to the reader for whom the great book has become dusty with neglect or staled by pulpit usage and thoughtless parroting new zest and new eyes for reading the Bible. More than that, he leaves one with strengthened conviction that Christianity has the key to "that universal order which the intellect feels after as a law, and the heart feels after as a benefit."

THE END

INDEX

INDEX

(Titles from Arnold's Works Are Indicated by Italics)